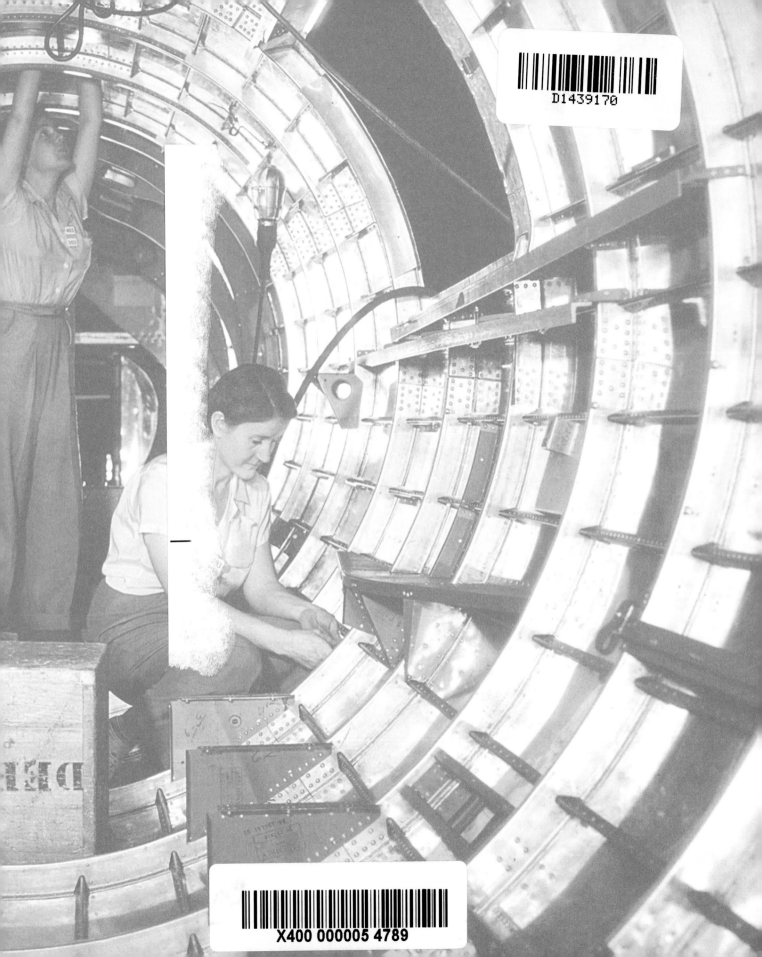

WOMEN
OUR HISTORY

Foreword Lucy Worsley

DK LONDON
Senior Editor Kathryn Hennessy
Senior Art Editor Gadi Farfour
Managing Editor Gareth Jones
Senior Managing Art Editor Lee Griffiths
Producer, Pre-Production Gillian Reid
Senior Producer Rachel Ng
Jacket Designer Surabhi Wadhwa
Design Development Manager Sophia M.T.T.
Associate Publishing Director Liz Wheeler
Art Director Karen Self
Publishing Director Jonathan Metcalf

DK DELHI
Senior Art Editor Chhaya Sajwan
Art Editors Jomin Johny, Anukriti Arora, Sourabh Challariya
Assistant Art Editor Simran Saini
Senior Editor Arani Sinha
Assistant Editors Devangana Ojha, Priyadarshini Gogoi
Managing Editor Soma B. Chowdhury
Senior Managing Art Editor Arunesh Talapatra
Senior Picture Researcher Surya Sankash Sarangi
Picture Research Manager Taiyaba Khatoon
Senior DTP Designers Neeraj Bhatia, Shanker Prasad, Vishal Bhatia
DTP Designers Syed Md Farhan, Vikram Singh
Production Manager Pankaj Sharma
Pre-production Manager Balwant Singh
Senior Jackets DTP Designer Harish Aggarwal
Jacket Designers Priyanka Bansal, Suhita Dharamjit
Jackets Editorial Coordinator Priyanka Sharma
Managing Jackets Editor Saloni Singh

Produced for DK by
TOUCAN BOOKS
Editorial Director Ellen Dupont
Senior Designer Leah Germann
Senior Editor Abigail Mitchell
Editors Carol King, Fiona Plowman, Dorothy Stannard
Editorial Assistants Ameera Patel, Isobel Rodol, Ella Whiddett
Proofreader Constance Novis
Indexer Marie Lorimer
Additional Picture Research Sharon Southren

First published in Great Britain in 2019 by
Dorling Kindersley Limited, 80 Strand, London, WC2R 0RL
Copyright © 2019 Dorling Kindersley Limited
A Penguin Random House Company
10 9 8 7 6 5 4 3 2 1
001-293637- Mar/2019

A CIP catalogue record for this book is available
from the British Library.
ISBN: 978-0-2413-5392-9
Printed and bound in Malaysia

All images © Dorling Kindersley Limited
For further information see: www.dkimages.com

A WORLD OF IDEAS:
SEE ALL THERE IS TO KNOW

www.dk.com

CONTENTS

1

The Birth of the Patriarchy

Up to 600CE

Dr Lucy Worsley is a historian, author, curator, and television presenter. She graduated with a first-class degree in Ancient and Modern History from Oxford University, before working at the Society for the Protection of Ancient Buildings and English Heritage. Today, she is Chief Curator at the independent charity Historic Royal Palaces and a BBC television historian. Lucy has written several non-fiction books, including a Sunday Times bestseller, and also writes historical fiction for younger readers. In 2018 she presented a special BBC One documentary about the Suffragettes for the centenary of the "Representation of the People" Act, and was awarded an OBE for her services to history and heritage.

CONSULTANTS

Dr Stephanie L. Budin is an independent scholar who earned her PhD from the University of Pennsylvania. Her research focuses on women, sexuality, and religion in the ancient eastern Mediterranean, focusing on Greece and the Levant. She has written six books and coedited two more.

Dr Holly Hurlburt is a professor in the Department of History at Southern Illinois University. Her research focuses on women, gender, and power in early modern Venice and the larger Mediterranean region.

Dr Julia Laite is a senior lecturer in history at Birkbeck, University of London. She is the author of *Common Prostitutes and Ordinary Citizens: Commercial Sex in London, 1885-1960*, and her research focuses the history of sex, gender, women, and migration in the modern world.

Dr Kelly Boyd is a senior research fellow at the Institute of Historical Research, University of London, where she co-convenes the Women's History Seminar. She has written on masculinity and the British boys' story paper, Victorian culture, and British culture in the face of Americanization.

CONTRIBUTORS

Georgie Carroll is a PhD candidate at SOAS University of London, working on eco-aesthetics in Indian literature. She is the author of *Mouse (Animal)* (2015) and a fiction writer.

Dr Jacob F. Field is a research associate at the University of Cambridge. His academic work focuses on the Great Fire of London and British social and economic history, and he has also written many titles for a popular audience.

Abigail Mitchell is an editor and historian with degrees from the University of Cambridge and University of Southern California. She contributed to DK's *The Vietnam War* and *The Feminism Book*, and developed and edited *Women: Our History*.

Additional contributors Melina Andreou, Alexandra Black, Nancy Dickmann, Helen Douglas-Cooper, Kathryn Gehred, Autumn Green, Dr John Haywood, Sheridan Humphreys, Liana Kirillova, Ann Kramer, Professor Lloyd Llewellyn-Jones, Dr Hannah McCann, Julie Peakman, Maria Sophia Quine, Christina Reitz, Raana Shah, Marian Smith-Holmes, Jo Stanley FRHistS, Shan Vahidy, Dr Shannon Weber

4

Knowledge and Power

1800–1914

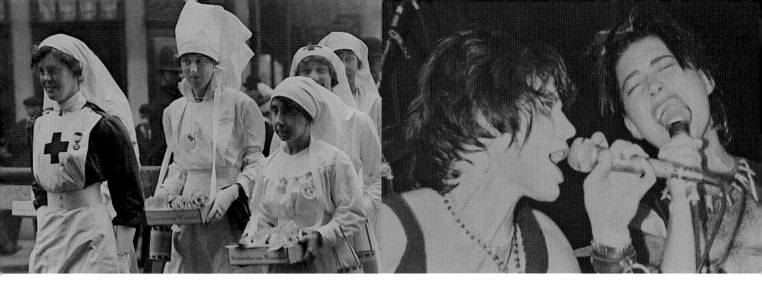

Foreword

Strange but true: a woman was once confined to a Georgian lunatic asylum for "excessive reading". No wonder, as books can be a danger to society. Reading can open the eyes, raise expectations, and make women dissatisfied with being treated as less than men. In this book, you can read a story that wasn't always told: the story of women across centuries and continents. And it deserves to be read "excessively", for retelling these stories will help reshape the world of today.

It's not all good. You'll find lots of suffering here – like poor 15th-century princess Joan of France, married at 12. Pity, too, any Vestal Virgin of ancient Rome who had the misfortune to be accused of adultery. She could not be executed, because it was forbidden to spill a Virgin's blood. Instead, her punishment was being buried alive. Then, we meet the Korean girls who were so unwelcome to their parents because of the cost of their dowries that they were known as "robber women", and the unfortunate Zeb-un-Nissa, who was imprisoned by an orthodox Mughal Emperor for the crime of daring to write poetry.

But there are also many women here to admire and to inspire: history's first recorded female physician, Merit-Ptah of ancient Egypt, and the self-made Catherine I of Russia, born a servant and raised to the position of Empress by her own efforts. There's the Mongol warrior Princess Khutulun, who amassed 10,000 horses by gambling against her would-be suitors. And I think that every book in the world needs a section, like this one has, entitled "notable women pirates".

The female pirates aren't the only fearsome-sounding characters you'll meet. Others include the Mesoamerican "jaguar goddess" Ix Chel, who had the power to raise storms and floods. There's Princess Anle of eighth-century China, who made a fortune by fraudulently ordaining 12,000 monks, and Lyudmila Pavlichenko, the top female Soviet sniper in World War II with 309 kills. And then there are the nattily-dressed women of the British Union of Fascists. The devil sometimes wears the best clothes, and it's important to remember that women aren't all victims or heroines. They are as good, bad, or indifferent as men.

One theme that runs throughout this book is the danger of making assumptions. We now realise that modern archaeologists studying the life of cave dwellers found evidence that the "gentle cave-wife" stayed "at home with the children" in part because this was the role of women they were familiar with from the 20th century. And maybe we've been jumping to the wrong conclusions about the horrific-looking iron device known as the "chastity belt". Not only was it used "against" women, but it was also worn by women in times of war as a form of protection against rape.

The vast scope of this book also makes it very clear that you would be foolish to assume that history moves in straight lines from "worse" towards "better". European colonists of New Zealand thought that the gender equality they encountered there among the Māori was backwards and "savage", and did their best to reverse it. Sometimes it's two steps forwards, one step back. Civil rights activist Rosa Parks became celebrated for refusing to give her seat to a white passenger on a bus in 1955, but such was the

misogyny of the National Association for the Advancement of Colored People, that they got her – the only woman present – to take the minutes at their meetings.

Some things get better over time; some get worse. The one sure thing you can take away from studying the past is the belief that change is possible. "The distance is great from belief to realization", said Queen Isabella of Castile. But learning about the women who created change gives you a starting point – that vital belief that women existed, they mattered, they can be emulated. No longer buried in the footnotes, it's time for history's women to step into the centre of the stage.

Lucy Worsley

Introduction

Women's impact on the world is a story that has slowly been coming to light over the past century. Through history, female warriors and queens have conquered foreign lands, female explorers have pushed back frontiers, and women artists, writers, and activists have changed prevailing attitudes and views. The problem is that in the patriarchal (male-ruled) societies that dominate the world, women's stories of the resistance they have faced and obstacles they have overcome have been marginalized, and have not always been told.

Women in history

It is thought that the sidelining of women by men began around 12,000 years ago. At the dawn of human history, during the Stone Age, early humans lived in hunter-gatherer societies, in which both men and women played a vital and complementary role. However, this changed with the Neolithic Revolution, when humans began to shift from nomadic to geographically-settled societies based on agriculture, which was controlled by men. As populations expanded, women's contributions to food production diminished and men began to place restrictions and controls on women, regulating their behaviour through institutions such as marriage, religion, and law.

In ancient civilizations such as those in China, Greece, Egypt, and Rome, the vast majority of women had far fewer freedoms than men. Despite this, women had status in the household and as mothers, and some became priestesses associated with goddesses in polytheistic religions. However, by the medieval era, when monotheism became dominant, particularly in the West and Near East, the spiritual role of women dwindled. Customs and laws created by men continued to limit the role of most medieval women.

Despite this, a number of queens and empresses across the world showed that women could be effective leaders.

The early modern era, from the 18th century, gave rise to western imperialism, which saw colonial powers impose their own concepts of gender roles on societies in the Americas, Africa, Asia, and Australasia, dislodging indigenous customs. At the same time, women participated in the waves of reformation and revolution that created the modern world. Over the course of the 19th century, as a result of the Industrial Revolution, the economic role of women shifted, and they entered the workplace in greater numbers. Working women, who contributed to the wealth of both their families and the wider society, demanded the same rights as men. Feminism began to emerge as a global movement, and women agitated for greater freedoms, including the right to vote.

Women made a major contribution to the world wars of the first half of the 20th century, which also boosted their place in society. By the second half of the century the role of women had been transformed – but there was still work to be done. The second and third waves of feminism, from the 1960s to the present day, have seen women campaign on a huge range of issues, including divorce and contraception, as well as LGBT rights, in the effort to break down traditional barriers and finally dislodge the patriarchy. At last, women's voices are being heard.

▶ **Wise woman**
This 6th-century mosaic in Ravenna, Italy, shows Empress Theodora, one of the most influential figures in the Eastern Roman Empire.

The Birth of the Patriarchy

up to 600CE

The role of women in prehistoric societies (before written records) is subject to debate, relying as it does on burial practices and excavated artefacts. However, evidence suggests that women played an important and active role in the prehistoric world. Pinpointing when patriarchies – in which men held all the power – began is a difficult task, but studies suggest that many ancient societies were early patriarchies. Ancient women faced a dichotomy: on the one hand, they could be revered as goddesses, mothers, objects of beauty, or the heads of households, yet on the other hand, they were rarely entitled to the same freedoms and rights as men.

THE WORLD'S
first women

> **The Neolithic woman's arm bones** were **stronger than** a modern-day **rower's** by up to
> # 16%

▲ **Venus of Willendorf**
Plump female figurines, once linked to fertility, may represent village elders, their size conveying status. This famous example was discovered in Austria and dates back to 28,000–25,000 BCE.

PREHISTORY TO THE BRONZE AGE

Early humans were nomadic hunter–gatherers who roamed the land and survived by hunting animals and gathering other foods, such as wild plants. For decades, many anthropologists assumed that men did the hunting and toolmaking, whereas women gathered berries and took care of the children. Yet, there is no firm archaeological evidence to support this division of labour. By analyzing bones and the fractures related to hunting large game at close range, scientists have concluded that among Neanderthals – humans' closest relatives – women and children also took part in the perilous task of hunting mammoth and other big game.

The stereotype of the caveman hunter wielding his club, and the gentle wife at home with the children is, modern scholars argue, the result of 20th-century ideas of gender roles influencing the interpretation of the physical evidence. The cave paintings that began appearing in Europe about 40,000 years ago were also assumed by many later historians to be the work of men. However, a recent study of the size and structure of hands in a sample of hand stencils revealed that many of the handprints discovered in caves were actually created by women.

Venus figurines

Women were the subject of another type of prehistoric artwork – the figurine. Between 35,000–40,000 years ago, humans started to make small sculptures from bone, ivory, soft stone, or fired clay. Some sculptures represented animals, but many took the shape of voluptuous women – dubbed "Venus figurines" by archaeologists. A number of these figurines, such as those found in the early 19th century in underground burial chambers on the island of Malta, exaggerated parts of the female body associated with

FROM CAVES TO PALACES

Prehistory is not just the story of early man. Women played a more active role than once thought – from hunting to creating art.

BEFORE 50,000 BCE

2.6 million years ago Human ancestors first begin to use stone tools.

300,000 years ago Modern humans (*Homo sapiens*) emerge as a distinct species.

50,000–15,000 BCE

40,800 Prehistoric peoples begin to create cave paintings in many locations, including France and Spain. Up to three-quarters of the handprint stencils are made by women.

40,000 Neanderthals, the closest relatives to modern humans, become extinct.

35,000–40,000 The Venus of Hohle Fels (the oldest representation of the human figure to be excavated) is sculpted from ivory.

29,000 The first ovens are made for cooking meat and other food.

28,000–25,000 An unknown artist sculpts the small limestone figurine known as the Venus of Willendorf.

18,000 The earliest pottery so far discovered is made in China.

15,000–1,000 BCE

13,000–8,000 Humans first begin to farm crops, sparking a revolution that leads to permanent settlements and civilizations.

5000 In some places, humans begin to smelt copper to make tools and weapons.

3500–2500 Burial temples called hypogea are built in Malta, containing figurines of women.

2100 Cretan hieroglyphs emerge in Greece as the Bronze Age Aegean period gets underway.

◄ **THE "LADIES IN BLUE" FRESCO** FEATURES THREE ELABORATELY ADORNED WOMEN FROM KNOSSOS, CRETE, C. 1525–1450 BCE.

»

sexuality and fertility, such as the breasts and hips. Some experts have suggested that these Venus figurines were fertility icons or goddess figures; others argue that the curvaceous bodies are not youthful and more likely represent older women, their size conveying prosperity and status in the community.

Over the years, experts have suggested that Neolithic societies were matriarchies, in which women served as head of the family and played a leadership role. Venus figurines were given as evidence to support this theory, which argued that Neolithic peoples worshipped a range of mother goddesses. However, other archaeological evidence in Malta and elsewhere does not support this theory; the true purpose of these Venus figurines – and indeed, their true creators – can perhaps never be proved. Meanwhile, at the Neolithic site of Çatalhüyük in modern-

▼ **Saffron gatherers**
This Minoan fresco shows young girls harvesting saffron, potentially as part of a coming-of-age ritual. In Minoan art, white was used to represent the pale skin of women, while red was used for men.

day Turkey, archaeologists have spent years sifting through the remains of hundreds of houses, built about 9,000 years ago. Analysis has shown that women and men had similar diets, and spent a similar amount of time indoors. After death, men and women's bodies were also buried in much the same way, so there is little evidence to suggest a significant division between men and women in terms of the tasks or roles they performed.

As the centuries passed, the hunter-gatherer lifestyle gradually gave way to a more settled existence. People began to occupy dwellings close to food and water sources, and grow crops instead of gathering wild plants. This change, called the Neolithic Revolution, had wide-reaching effects. For example, the rise of agriculture led to an increased reliance on grains as a dietary staple. Kernels were ground into flour to make them easier to eat, a process that required hard labour. Studies of female bones from the period, compared to those of modern students (some of them athletes) shows that many Neolithic women had stronger arms than the average contemporary woman, which could be the result of many hours spent grinding grain.

Historic women

The prehistoric period is characterized by its lack of written records. Early forms of writing began to be used in many cultures during what is called the Bronze Age. Writing emerged in Greece during the Aegean Bronze

Age (c. 3000–1000 BCE), but archaeologists have only managed to decipher one of the society's three scripts. If the Minoans wrote anything about women, scholars are yet to be able to read it. As in the prehistoric period, clues as to how women lived during this time are mostly found in art, artefacts, and burial sites. Minoan and Mycenaean women, for example, were frequently depicted in frescos engaged in a variety of activities – but notably pregnancy and childbirth are rarely shown. In Minoan Greece, women were painted seated on thrones more frequently than men, leading some scholars to infer that Minoan civilization was matriarchal.

▲ **Gold diadem**
Archaeologists previously used grave goods, like this gold, elliptical diadem from the "Grave of the Women" in Mycenae, to assume the gender of burials, but this method is now disputed (see pp. 204–205).

▶ **Shepperton woman**
This is a reconstruction of a 5,500-year-old Neolithic woman's head found in Shepperton, London. It gives a fairly accurate idea of how her face looked barring her eye and hair colour, and skin pigmentation.

"IT **WASN'T JUST** A BUNCH OF **GUYS** OUT THERE **CHASING BISON** AROUND."

DEAN SNOW, ARCHAEOLOGIST AND EXPERT ON CAVE ART

MANY CREATION MYTHS begin with a complementary male and female pair, such as an "earth mother" and "sky father". In Māori mythology, for example, this earth mother was Papatūānuku, and the sky father was Ranginui. A goddess who was also the land itself, Papatūānuku gave birth to every living thing. Such pairings of gods and goddesses, however, did not always put the two deities on an equal footing. In many myths, even goddesses were harassed and abused, reflecting the power human men exerted over women.

Most cultures had goddesses of birth, marriage, and love – domains shared with real women. Goddesses could also be bloodthirsty, powerful, and chaotic. From Kali, the Hindu and Buddhist goddess of destruction to Oya,

◀ **Lady of the moon**
According to Daoist mythology, Chang'e (depicted by Taiso Yoshitoshi in the 19th century) took an elixir to make her immortal, and ascended to the moon. Today, Daoists make and share moon cakes at the Mid-Autumn Moon Festival in her honour.

THROUGH THE AGES

Goddesses

In many societies, goddesses – great, terrible, benevolent, and volatile – had far more power than their human counterparts. Yet even goddesses, feared and adored by humans, were often subordinate to male deities, just as real women were to human men.

the Yoruba spirit of death and storms, these deities had powers that human women could only dream of. Even where real women had little access to education, there were nonetheless numerous goddesses of wisdom, such as Nisaba, a Mesopotamian goddess, or the Etruscan and Roman goddess Menvra, or Minerva. Goddess worship played an integral part in women's religious life in ancient societies – with priestesses often afforded freedoms that other women lacked – and many women also looked to the goddesses as models for their own behaviour.

HINDU GODDESS KALI, MURAL

Modern deities

Today, the majority of the world's major religions worship one god, usually believed to be male. The Hindu faith, however, is polytheistic, and their goddesses are worshiped by more than one billion people worldwide. In Nepal, since the 17th century, prepubescent girls from the Shakya caste have been chosen to be worshiped as "Kumari", living goddesses, as part of this religion. In Vietnam, people have worshipped a mother goddess since the 16th century, but *hau dong*, in which mediums enter a trance to commune with the goddess, was forbidden by the Communist government from the 1950s until 1987. In the West, second-wave feminism (see pp. 272–275) has also contributed to the growth of the Wiccan faith. This religion worships a mother goddess as its central figure, encapsulating the three stages of womanhood: maiden, mother, and crone.

▶ **Serpentine woman**
This figurine from c. 1600 BCE was found at a shrine at Knossos, Crete. Historians believe that it may depict an earth priestess wearing typical Minoan dress.

GLOBAL GODDESSES

Aset (Ancient Egypt) was a goddess of many attributes, including magic and healing. Often known by her Greek name, Isis, she originated in the Egyptian Age of the Pyramids, in the third millennium BCE, as the wife of Osiris. After her husband's death, she gathered his body parts together to make the first mummy, and brought him back to life to conceive their son, Horus.

Nüwa (Ancient China), a mother goddess, appears in the *Huainanzi*, a text dating to 139 BCE. Nüwa fixed the heavens after they fell by gathering coloured stones from the riverbed and cutting off the legs of a giant tortoise to make new pillars to support the sky. When the world was in chaos, Nüwa rescued it by killing a dragon, stopping a flood, and extinguishing fires.

The Morrígan (Celtic Ireland) appeared to warriors in battle as a harbinger of doom. She is featured in both the 1st-century CE *Ulster Cycle* and *Lebor Gabála Érenn* (The Book of Invasions), a mythological history of Ireland collected in the 11th century. The Morrígan was a member of a race called the Tuatha Dé Danann and a goddess of war and fate. In some tales, she was said to be three separate deities: Badb, or "crow," the war goddess; Macha, a sovereign goddess of land and kingship; and Nemain, who brought chaos and bloodlust.

Inanna (Ancient Sumeria) was a goddess from at least 4,000 BCE. One of her major myths concerns Inanna's descent to the underworld, where she was trapped before escaping and sending her husband down to take her place. After the rise of the Akkadian empire, Inanna was worshipped as Ishtar; she later became Astoreth in the Hebrew Bible, Astarte in Syria and Canaan, and Aphrodite in ancient Greece.

Sedna (Inuit people, North America) is a mermaid-like spirit with a human head and whale's body. As a human, she was tricked into marrying a man who was really a bird. Her father rescued her, but as they kayaked away, birds created a storm and her father threw her overboard to stop the kayak from filling with water. When she tried to hang on, he cut off her fingers, which became the creatures of the ocean. Sedna became an ocean spirit. Her myth has been passed down and told among the Inuit people for thousands of years.

QUEENS, SLAVES AND
pharaohs

ANCIENT EGYPT

The people of ancient Egypt had a deeprooted religious perspective on life. They believed in the concept of ma'at – meaning "order" or "balance" – which was embodied by the goddess of the same name. Ma'at maintained the masculine and feminine aspects of the universe in perfect balance. In Egyptian society, women were therefore seen as almost equal to men, even if they were not always treated as such.

Powerful goddesses

Egyptians worshipped many different gods and goddesses, each seen as being responsible for a different aspect of life. The variety of strong goddesses influenced the range of roles that women filled; people respected or feared their goddesses, and women aspired to have similar qualities. Hathor, often shown with a cow's head, was the goddess of fertility and love. Fierce, lion-headed Sekhmet was a goddess of war, and was at times regarded as another aspect of Hathor's nurturing character. Isis was a healer as well as an ideal wife and mother – the crucial roles for women at the time – and so served as a shining example for all women.

Women's rights

Egyptian women, particularly those in the upper classes, could own and pass on property, and own businesses, as well as initiate divorces or other legal proceedings, and serve as witnesses in court cases. The majority of women married and ran a household, often working the land as well; a married woman was called "mistress of the house." Some women performed roles outside the home, as priestesses, or as managers of textile workshops and breweries. In the clergy,

▶ **Status of slaves**
Egyptian slaves were given more than common peasants. They received security, housing, food, and did not pay taxes. This wall painting from the chapel of Nebamun, a wealthy scribe, shows slave girls entertaining guests at a feast.

▲ Golden sarcophagus
This outer coffin is ornately decorated - reflecting the status of its occupant. Henettawy was princess and priestess of the 21st Dynasty. She was also a singer - a woman of high status who served in the temple of the god Amun.

▶ Beauty and strength
Queen Nefertiti became an icon of beauty thanks to this bust. She played a key role in the cult of the sun god Aten, and may have ruled in her own right after her husband's death.

men and women had rather distinct functions. Especially in Egypt's New Kingdom (but not exclusively), women were far more likely to be entertainers for the deities, while men served more managerial roles. One of the most important priestesshoods was "God's Hand," which was usually reserved for women of royal rank. They "stimulated" the (male) creator deity Amun. Women were also "sealers" – a position with economic responsibility – using incised seals to mark the closures of rooms or containers and guard against theft.

Many women who worked were able to do so because they left the daily responsibilities of running a household to other family members, or to servants. Some homes even had slaves – usually captured in war – to do the work, although slavery was uncommon in ancient Egypt.

Female pharaohs

Well back into the Old Kingdom, it was common for powerful queens to serve as regents for their underaged sons. Hatshetsup, Egypt's longest-reigning female pharaoh, came to power this way around 1478 BCE, sharing the crown with two-year-old Thutmose III. One of ancient Egypt's most successful rulers, she adopted the full titles and regalia of a pharaoh – even the false beard that many wore. Queens could also wield some power as pharaohs' wives. Today, the most famous is Queen Nefertiti, who reigned alongside Akhenaten in the 14th century BCE, although she disappeared from the history books until the discovery of her bust renewed interest in her life. Her tomb has never been found.

"[He] pulled ... fabric off [her] body, but she **remained covered, her honour intact**."

TRANS. HIMANSHU AGARWAL, THE *MAHABHARATA*

INDIAN DIGNITY

The central female character in the Indian epic, the *Mahabharata* – which is thought to have reached its final form by the 4th century CE – is the heroine Draupadi. After Draupadi's husband inadvertently loses her to his wicked cousins in a game of dice, she is publicly dragged away by one of her enemies, who begins to tug at her sari in an attempt to disrobe her. As a pious and brave woman, Draupadi prays to Lord Krishna for protection, and he rescues her from humiliation by making her sari infinitely long so that she cannot be undressed. The *Mahabharata* reflects Indian society's patriarchal attitudes but Draupadi's actions in this scene – in which she boldly defends her honour – defy the Indian ideal of female submissiveness.

PRIESTESSES AND
courtesans

ANCIENT GREECE

The ancient Greek civilization emerged in the Bronze Age and declined with Rome's ascendancy five centuries later. Ancient Greek culture had a rich mythology, in which there were a number of powerful female figures, both immortal and mortal. These goddesses were idealized, worshipped, and valued just as highly as their male counterparts. However, ordinary Greek women were still considered inferior to men. Ancient Greece consisted of *poleis*, or city states, and the degree of independence experienced by women varied depending on their class and the city state they came from.

Women in the major city states of Athens and Sparta led very different lives. Spartan girls received public education (separate from Spartan boys) that included rigorous physical training. This ensured they would go on to produce strong and healthy babies, who would become great warriors. As Spartan men devoted their lives

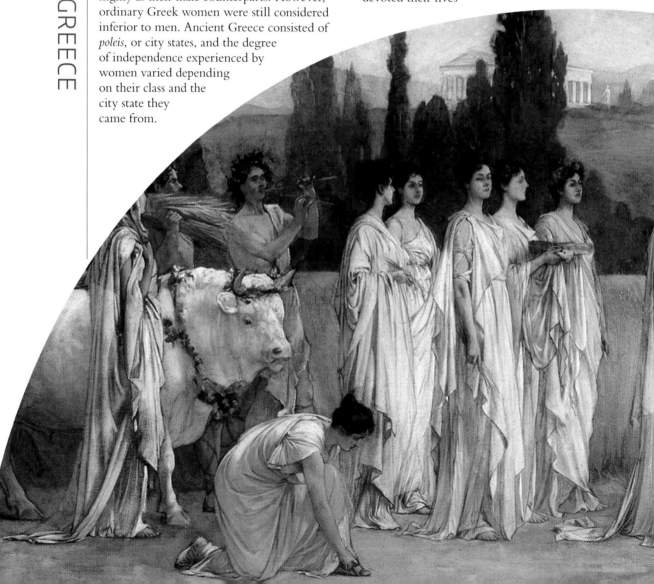

to the military, women wielded economic power; they had authority over the household, and could own, inherit, and transfer wealth.

Athenian women

Ancient Greece was famed for its democracy, but Athenian women did not have the same citizenship rights as their male counterparts. They were denied the opportunity to vote or participate in politics. Many women's daily lives were confined to running the household, spinning and weaving cloth, and producing children. They also had numerous religious functions, and many women had jobs outside the home. Women did not receive formal education, although wealthy women may have had the privilege of being taught how to read and write. The wealthy could also leave everyday tasks to slaves, brought to Greece as a

▲ **Funerary art**
This lekythos, or oil vessel, contained oil that would be applied to a woman's skin during funeral rites, if she died without marrying.

IN BRIEF
GREEK ANTIQUITY

There was no single universal experience for women across the city states of ancient Greece, but religion and warfare loomed large in many of their lives.

800 BCE

8th century The Delphic oracle is established.

776 The Heraean Games, the first official Panhellenic female athletic competition, is held in the stadium at Olympia.

700 BCE

c.630–612 Sappho of Lesbos, one of the earliest Greek lyric poets, is born; she dies c.570.

500 BCE

450 Athenian funerary monuments begin to depict women; the legal code of Gortyn, Crete, is inscribed on city walls, containing many laws pertaining to women – such as their right to some property in the case of divorce.

441 Sophocles premieres his play *Antigone* (about a young woman who stands up to the power of the state) at the City Dionysia festival.

430–420 The Adonia festival is celebrated annually by women to mourn the death of Adonis, the mortal lover of the goddess Aphrodite.

400 BCE

396 A Spartan princess, Cynisca, is the first woman to win at the Olympic Games, in the four-horse chariot race; previously, women were not allowed to attend the Games.

c.350 Praxiteles' Aphrodite of Knidos is the first life-size female nude sculpture.

330 A *hetaira* (companion) named Thaïs allegedly persuades Alexander the Great to burn down the Persian palace of Persepolis on his campaign in Asia Minor.

◀ *THESMOPHORIA* BY FRANCIS DAVIS MILLET (1897) ROMANTICIZED THE FESTIVAL AND INCORRECTLY DEPICTED MEN TAKING PART.

"spoil of war" or through the slave trade. Many slave women (and men) worked as domestic servants in wealthy households.

One unlikely group of women did have some freedom and access to education. Women known as *hetairai* (courtesans) served as companions for wealthy men in Athens. These women were often educated and able to live independently. They were hired for their company and friendship, and often attended aristocratic banquets known as symposia. A few women began as entertainers before becoming hetairai, and were therefore also skilled musicians and dancers.

Religious participation

Greek women played an active part in religious life and some festivals were celebrated only by women. The festival of Thesmophoria, held annually, was dedicated to the goddess Demeter and her daughter Persephone, and observed only by married women. Demeter was the goddess of the harvest and fertility and so this three-day celebration took place to promote agricultural fertility. It also referred to an episode from Greek mythology, commemorating Demeter's grief at the marriage of Persephone to Hades, god of the underworld. Under no circumstances were men allowed to participate in the festival, and preparations to exclude them began nine days before it started.

The women adhered to strict customs that included completely abstaining from sex. On the first day of the festival, women came to the gathering place (the Pnyx in Athens) and the second day was spent fasting and mourning, in imitation of Demeter's anguish at Persephone's abduction. During the second day, women would curse at

and insult each other in what was called the *aischrologia*. On the third day, they rejoiced.

Prophetic priestesses

The Greek women who became priestesses had authority and independence outside of marriage. The most famous of these was the priestess who delivered oracles on behalf of the god Apollo in Delphi,

◄ **Symbol of aristocracy**
Mirrors, usually small enough to hold in the hand, were a status symbol in ancient Greece because only elite women could afford to buy them. This fifth-century example is made of bronze.

BIOGRAPHY
SAPPHO

A lyric poet from the Greek island of Lesbos, Sappho wrote sensual hymns of poetry which were primarily concerned with deep love and yearning. The word "lesbian," meaning a woman of Lesbos (and used to refer to women of her school of thought), is derived from her birthplace. Her verses were unique for the time in that they spoke from one person to another. She composed nine volumes of works, but the only text to survive in its entirety is her *Hymn to Aphrodite*. Sappho is believed to have died around 570 BCE.

a place considered by the Greeks to be the centre of the world. This woman was called the Pythia and a new woman would be chosen to fill the role upon her death. By the 8th century BCE, Pythias were recognized for their prophetic powers. According to mythology, the first Pythia was a young virgin, but after she was raped, only older, less desirable women were chosen. The Pythia did, however, dress in a young woman's clothes. People flocked from all over Greece to ask the Pythia questions. She sat atop a tripod and entered a trancelike state, giving answers and predictions that were often ambiguous. The Pythia filled one of the most powerful female roles in the Classical world and shaped history by guiding men on matters of politics, religion, and warfare.

"THE **MALE** IS ... **SUPERIOR** AND THE **FEMALE** [IS] **INFERIOR**; ... ONE **RULES**, AND THE OTHER IS **RULED**."

ARISTOTLE, *POLITICS*

▼ **Domestic scenes**
These scenes copying ancient Greek terracotta show wealthy women and their female servants undertaking a variety of domestic tasks, including gathering olives, spinning, and dressing.

> "Everyone should be extremely pleased that ... such **great love** could **reside** in a **woman's heart in** the **bond of marriage**.

CHRISTINE DE PIZAN, *THE BOOK OF THE CITY OF LADIES*, 1405

EXPERIENCES OF MARRIAGE

Tying the knot

Love and marriage have not always gone hand in hand. Traditionally, marriage was often a far less romantic affair, serving as a way to join two families for economic or political reasons, in which a woman was passed from father to husband as property.

ALTHOUGH MARRIAGE is an ancient custom, until modern times it had little to do with love or being equal partners. Historically, a woman's family often selected her husband, particularly among social elites. Until the early 20th century, the marriages of nobility and royalty were about forging diplomatic and dynastic alliances. Such matches were often made while the bride and groom were children; in 1464 Louis XI of France arranged for his daughter Joan to marry her cousin, Louis of Orléans, just after she was born. Despite Joan being disabled and possibly sterile, the wedding itself took place when Joan was just 12 years old. Arranged marriages are still prevalent in some countries, such as India, despite the recent rise in "love matches" in which parents are not involved. Indian arranged marriages require both spouses' consent, unlike forced marriages, which still occur in sub-Saharan Africa, Latin America, and South Asia. In forced unions it is most often the woman who is coerced into marrying, often at a young age.

Paying the price

A traditional pillar of a marriage contract has been the dowry – wealth that is given to the groom or his family by the bride's parents. In medieval Europe, the dowry was money or property, whereas in Tsarist Russia it often consisted of linens and clothing for the bride herself to wear. Conversely, in some cultures, a "bride price" was paid by the family of the groom. This is still the case in Islamic marriages, in which the groom or his father

FLEMISH WEDDING IN ILLUSTRATED MANUSCRIPT, 1515–20

> A **maid marries according** to the **will** of her **parents**; a **widow decides** her **marriage by herself**.

CHINESE PROVERB

> "From the **wedding day**, the **young matron** should **shape her life** to the probable and desired **contingency of conception** and **maternity**. Otherwise she has **no right** or **title to wifehood**."
>
> **EMMA FRANCES ANGELL DRAKE**, *WHAT A YOUNG WIFE OUGHT TO KNOW*, 1902

▲ **Bridal coat**
In Qing China, wedding attire was embellished with motifs such as pomegranates, which were a symbol of fertility. The phoenix and dragon represented the bride and groom, respectively, while the colour red was associated with luck.

pays *mahr* – money, gifts, or possessions – to his bride. The form that bride price and dowry take has varied across cultures; men of the Maasai tribe in Kenya, for example, pay the bride's mother in goats, cows, and sheep, which are precious commodities within the community.

A clandestine affair

If a marriage choice did not gain parental approval, lovers often eloped or married in secret. In 18th-century England, the most popular venue for clandestine weddings was London's Fleet Prison. Due to a legal quirk, the debtor's prison was not subject to the usual regulations, meaning that couples could marry there with no questions asked and at very little cost. Other English couples wishing to evade the constraints of the 1754 Marriage Act, which introduced an age of consent of 21, eloped to Scotland, where boys could marry at 14 and girls at 12 without parental consent. In the slave-era American South, marriage between slaves was viewed with suspicion by slave owners who thought it could threaten their authority or decrease productivity. As a result slave marriages were not legally binding and could be overruled by owners. Slave weddings were often informal and conducted with little ceremony. The couple would jump over a broom to symbolize their union, a custom now practised in fun.

Wedding customs continue to vary widely across different societies. For a month before their wedding, Tujia brides in central China must cry for one hour a day to show gratitude to their family. Elsewhere, in the northwestern African nation of Mauritania – in contrast to the pre-wedding diet cultures of the United States and elsewhere – brides are sent to "fattening camps" before marriage so that they gain weight, because obesity is seen as a symbol of the family's prosperity.

When Britain's Queen Victoria wore a white bridal gown at her nuptials in 1840 it was an unusual choice for the era. She set a tradition that continues to modern times, although, outside Western cultures, white is not the traditional colour of choice – in China, for example, it is typically red, whereas in Africa bright patterns are often preferred. The "white wedding" has its roots in the belief in a bride's purity. Across history, marriage dictated people's sexual behaviour: intercourse was only allowed between spouses. This was important for women to uphold, as premarital virginity ensured the paternity of any children.

> "**All marriage** is such a **lottery** … though it may be a very happy one, still the **poor woman** is **bodily** and **morally** the **husband's slave**."
>
> **QUEEN VICTORIA** TO HER DAUGHTER, MAY 16, 1860

WIVES AND
workers

ANCIENT IRAN

The first Persian Empire, known as the Achaemenid empire, was founded by Cyrus II in 550 BCE and lasted until Alexander the Great defeated the Persians in battle in 331 BCE. The kings of Ancient Persia were polygamous, and their wives lived within a strict hierarchical structure headed by the king's mother and his main wife, who was likely the mother of his named heir. Elite women lived together in a household that some historians called a harem – a term also used to describe the women themselves. In addition to wives, Persian kings also took concubines, who came to court as war captives or tribute gifts. A king's polygamy served a major political purpose. His wives produced children – sons to inherit the throne or become governors, and daughters to marry high-ranking courtiers and local dynasts. Polygamy was therefore integral to the rule of the Achaemenids, helping to ensure the king's continuing authority across his empire.

Powerful landowners

Records of women's estates survive in cuneiform texts found at Persepolis, the ceremonial capital of the empire, which allow a glimpse into life in the ancient Persian world. Evidence from these texts suggests that elite women had a degree of economic independence, and could amass great amounts of land and personal property. One such woman was a particularly wealthy landowner named Irdabama, who the texts reveal oversaw vast personal estates. She received and distributed food supplies, and commanded a huge entourage of workers. Her largest workforce, at Tirazziš (near

◀ **Woman in blue**
This bust made from lapiz lazuli – a precious blue stone – is thought to depict a boy, eunuch, or woman of the Achaemenid period.

Shiraz), had groups of up to 480 people in her employ. Irdabama's seal on records for dispensing wine, grain, flour, and barley shows that not only did she feed her workers from her own estates, but that she also took an active role in the administration of her financial affairs.

Workers and rations

The Persepolis texts also include lists of rations allocated to various workers, explicitly recording their sex. One type of worker appeared to earn more than any other: a female *arrašsap* (chief) received 30 quarts of wine, 50 quarts of barley, and meat each month. Women with this title were even occasionally mentioned by name in the records, leading scholars to believe they were important. Such women were in charge of large groups of workers called *pašap*, and the texts show that, in these groups, men and women received equal pay for doing the same job. Records from a distributor named Iršena, for example, show that male and female attendants were both given 40 quarts. However, not all women were so fortunate. Within a group of workers known as *harrinup*, some women earned just two-thirds of what their male counterparts did for the same work. However, after childbirth, both *harrinup* and *pašap* women seem to have been supported by employers; they were provided with extra food rations (called *kamakaš*) for the following month, suggesting that the Achaemenids placed some value on mothers even outside of elite circles.

▼ **Adorned in gold**
Men and women alike wore lavish jewellery and makeup. This earring depicts the Persian god Ahura Mazdā and "Bounteous Immortals", three of whom were female.

BIOGRAPHY
PARYSATIS

Born around 436 BCE, Queen Parysatis was the formidable wife and half-sister of King Darius II. She held sway over the Persian court during the reign of her husband and into that of her son, Artaxerxes II. Parysatis was very wealthy, with estates in Iran, Syria, and Mesopotamia. She was also ruthless: she ordered her opponents to be crucified, flayed, and hung. Parysatis championed her son Cyrus the Younger to become king in place of his elder brother. When Cyrus' plot to take the throne failed, Parysatis was exiled in Babylon, but later returned to court, where she poisoned Artaxerxes' main wife to secure her own power.

360
Greek concubines
were at court at one time

◀ **Queen of Persia**
The story of Esther – a Jewish wife of Persian King Xerxes I who saved her people from getting massacred – is an ancient tale mentioned in several religious texts, including the Hebrew Bible.

THE DAUGHTERS OF THE
Republic

ANCIENT ROME

The Roman Republic, which lasted from 509 BCE to 27 BCE, ascribed little value to women, who lived under the authority of male guardians – their father or their husband. At birth, men and women alike had a short average life expectancy of about 30 years, but people often lived into their sixties if they survived childhood. Girls usually married in their teens, and had to remain chaste until then, but after marriage were expected to produce children. Roman women inhabited a domestic sphere; they were responsible for running the household and taking care of the family – all the while staying modest and loyal towards their husbands.

Roman marriage

There were two types of marriage in ancient Rome, known as *cum manu* and *sine manu*. The difference between the two depended on who would act as the woman's guardian. In a cum manu marriage, the wife and her property came under her husband's legal control, whereas in a sine manu marriage, the wife remained under her father's guardianship. *Sine manu* marriages emerged at the end of the Republic and became more common in the Empire (see pp. 38–39).

Marriages among the elites were often political alliances, and it was customary for the bride's family to pay a dowry – which might include land, slaves, clothes, toiletries, and jewellery. The dowry provided for the marriage, and often included items ensuring that the woman remained beautiful and well-dressed. A dowry was traditionally recognized as a woman's property, and so returned to her family in the case of divorce (a common practice among the ancient Romans, and an equal right amongst men and women), and it was hers to pass on after death as she chose.

Vowed to Vesta

The Vestal Virgins' lives were in stark contrast to those of other Roman women. Vestals were priestesses of the cult of Vesta – virgin goddess of the home and hearth – and it was considered a high honour to be a Vestal Virgin. Rome's chief priest, the *pontifex maximus,* selected them. He chose noble girls between the ages of six and ten. Service lasted for 30 years, the first ten of which were spent learning their duties. Six maidens were granted the responsibility of tending to the sacred fire of Vesta and ensuring that it never burned out. The fire was symbolic of Rome and its existence, and Romans believed that if it went out, it would have disastrous consequences for all aspects of life. Vestals were therefore punished harshly if they neglected their duties. Sworn to chastity, they symbolized the purity of Rome. A priestess who broke her

◀ **Sports for all**
Although ancient Rome is not associated with women's freedom, this 4th-century mosaic of a female athlete being crowned suggests that women did have opportunities to engage in sports.

celibacy and endangered the health of the city would be put to death. Since it was forbidden to spill the blood of a Vestal, she was buried alive in an underground chamber. Notably, only ten convictions for unchastity were recorded during the Roman Republic, including a Vestal named Marcia in 114 BCE. All such convictions took place during periods of crisis in the Roman state.

For their devotion to the city, Vestal virgins were awarded privileges, including the power to free slaves or imprisoned men simply by touching them. Throughout the Roman Republic, Vestal Virgins enjoyed rights that were not open to single women of a similar social status, free from male guardianship and allowed to manage their own property. The Vestals were disbanded in 394 CE by the Christian Emperor Theodosius I, who also extinguished the fire.

> "IF YOU **ALLOW** [**WOMEN**] TO ACHIEVE ... **EQUALITY** ... THEY WILL BE ... **MASTERS**."
>
> **CATO THE ELDER,** AS RECORDED BY LIVY, *HISTORY OF ROME*

▼ **School of Vesta**
The priestesses of Vesta held an exalted status in ancient Rome's state religion. Their lives were seen as being spiritually tied to the fate and health of the city itself.

"They saw her stone-dead, lying upon a **bed of gold ... in all her royal ornaments**."

PLUTARCH RECOUNTS THE DEATH OF CLEOPATRA IN *LIFE OF ANTONY (LXXXV.2-3, DRYDEN TRANS.)*

DYING WITH HONOUR

Queen Cleopatra VII was the last ruler of Ptolemaic Egypt. Politically astute and beautiful, she became the lover of the Roman politician, Julius Caesar; later, after the death of Caesar, she became the ally and lover of his supporter, Mark Antony. In 30 BCE, Roman forces led by Octavian, Caesar's heir, invaded Egypt and defeated the armies of Cleopatra and Marc Antony at Actium. After Marc Antony killed himself, Cleopatra, wishing to avoid the humiliation of being paraded as a prisoner when Octavian's victory was celebrated, also took her own life (the aftermath of which is depicted here). While many accounts claim that Cleopatra poisoned herself by letting an asp (Egyptian cobra) bite her, it is medically unlikely that such a bite would have killed her. Some historians have theorized that she was murdered by Octavian, who saw the powerful queen as too great a threat.

> " I have in **sincerity pledged myself** to **your service**, [just] as so **many of you** are **pledged** to **mine**. "

ELIZABETH II, CORONATION SPEECH, 1952

THROUGH THE AGES

Royalty

Most kingdoms and empires favoured male heirs when it came to passing on the crown. However, in spite of this, some remarkable women rose up to reign as queens in their own right, while others wielded considerable power as regents or wives of rulers.

TO ENSURE CONTINUITY, monarchies put laws and customs in place to determine the line of succession. Historically, the most widespread system was primogeniture, in which the firstborn, legitimate son of the ruler inherited, even if he had an older sister. However, if a ruler had only daughters, under this system the eldest became queen (or empress) regnant, ruling in her own right – as opposed to a "queen consort", the spouse of a ruling king, or a "queen regent", temporarily in charge on behalf of a king who was too young or too ill to make decisions for himself.

Many kings went to extreme lengths to secure a male heir, because it was believed that women were less fit to rule and would create instability in the line of succession. Most famously, in the 16th century, Henry VIII of England broke away from the Catholic Church in Rome to grant himself a divorce from Catherine of Aragon (the first of his six wives), so he could marry Anne Boleyn and

try to have a son. Henry eventually sired a male heir, Edward VI, who died childless and was succeeded by his older half-sisters: first Mary I, then Elizabeth I (see pp. 108–09). Other monarchs have changed laws to secure the succession for their daughters. Emperor Charles VI, ruler of the Austrian Habsburg realms, had no sons. Under the Pragmatic Sanction of 1713, he made concessions to other European powers so that they would recognize his daughter, Maria Theresa, as heir to his lands. However, when he died in 1740, Austria and its allies were forced to go to war against these powers to ensure her succession.

▲ **Crown of Russia**
This was the crown of Catherine the Great, who ruled Russia from 1762 to 1796. An enlightened monarch who corresponded with prominent thinkers of her day, she sought to modernize Russia through arts and education.

Elsewhere, some women have seized the throne for themselves. Empress Catherine I of Russia – a commoner from what is now Latvia – rose in station by marrying Peter the Great, then oversaw a coup after he died in 1725 to take power for herself. Although she only ruled for two years, she was the first female Russian ruler, setting a precedent for those that followed, such as Catherine II, the "Great", who became the country's most influential leader and its longest-ruling female monarch.

Patrilinies and matrilinies

Some countries followed (or still follow) the law of agnatic primogeniture, which skips royal women in line to the throne in favour of the nearest male relative. Even in these cases, however, it has still been possible for queen regents (usually the spouse or mother of the monarch) to govern. For example, in France, where women could not legally ascend to the throne, there were queen regents. Two of the

▲ **Habsburg Empress**
Maria Theresa, shown here at her coronation, was the Habsburg Empire's only female leader. She ruled for four decades. Although she made her husband coruler, she never let him manage state affairs.

most renowned were Italian noblewomen from the House of Medici, a powerful and wealthy dynasty. The first, Catherine de'Medici, ruled in the place of her young son from 1560 to 1563 and continued to be a major influence on the country for the remainder of her life; and her relative, Marie de'Medici, acted as regent for her son Louis XIV from 1610 to 1617, and ruled France until the "Sun King" came of age.

In contrast, a small number of states practise matrilineal succession, in which titles are inherited through the female line. In the African Ashanti Kingdom, for example, the queen mother is an incredibly important and powerful figure. Today, many monarchies have reformed their succession laws and instituted a system of absolute primogeniture, whereby the monarch's oldest child inherits the throne, regardless of gender. The first to do so was Sweden in 1980; most other European monarchies have since followed, including the UK in 2015.

THE ASHANTI QUEEN MOTHER IN GHANA 2001

PROFILES
INFLUENTIAL RULERS

Ku-Baba (b.c. 24th century BCE) was the only woman listed on the Sumerian King List, a tablet recording those endowed with the divine right of kingship. According to the list, Kubaba was a tavern-keeper before she became queen of the city of Kish (near modern Tell al-Uhaymir, Iraq). The Mesopotamians worshiped her as a goddess.

Empress Theodora (c. 497–548 CE) was the daughter of a bear trainer. She became the mistress of Justinian, heir to the Eastern Roman Empire, and married him in 525. When Justinian ascended in 527, Theodora became his chief adviser and was made empress. She had her own court and seal, and her influence led to divorce law reforms.

Margaret I (1353–1412) was a Danish princess who married the King of Norway when she was ten; they had one son, Olaf. After her father and husband died in 1375 and 1380 respectively, she secured the Danish and Norwegian crowns for her son, and ruled in his name. When Olaf died in 1387, Margaret became regent of Denmark and Norway, and in 1388 became ruler of Sweden, thereby laying the foundation for the later union of the three kingdoms in 1523.

Amina of Zazzau (1533–1610) was queen of the medieval African kingdom of Zazzau, now part of northern Nigeria. A great military tactician, Amina led her people to conquer many surrounding Hausa lands during her 34-year rule and created trade routes for her empire. Amina has been cited as the inspiration for the 1990s television show *Xena: Warrior Princess*.

Maharani Ahilyabai Holkar (1725–1795) married the Maharaja of Malwa (a Hindu kingdom in India) as an eight-year-old. After the deaths of her husband, father-in-law, and son she became ruler of Malwa in 1767. She led armies against invading forces to maintain her state's independence.

Catherine the Great (1729–1796) married the heir to the Russian throne in 1744. Ambitious and clever, she regarded her husband as unfit to rule. When he became emperor in 1762 she led a coup against him and became empress. During her reign, Catherine expanded Russia's territory by over 520,000 sq km (200,000 square miles).

ACROSS THE
Empire

LIFE UNDER ROMAN RULE

In 27 BCE, having won a civil war, Octavian (later given the title Augustus) became the first ruler of the Roman Empire. Until its fall in 476 CE in the West, its vast territories were ruled by emperors, first in Rome and later in Constantinople. This brought a diverse range of peoples under the control of Rome, whose laws were enforced across its empire. Defining issues such as slavery, concubinage, and marriage, Roman laws affected the lives of millions of men and women.

During the period of the empire, Roman women remained unable to vote or hold political office, but progressively gained some independence; girls from aristocratic families could receive an education at home and women could write their own will and also appear in court as their own advocate. With the abandonment of *cum manu* marriage (see pp. 32–33), husbands no longer gained control of their wife's property; wives remained under the control of their *pater familias* – the oldest male in their family. When a woman's father died, she became independent and could inherit property as her brothers did.

Citizens and slaves

Although women did not have any political power, some still exerted influence as a result of their high social status. Born in 58 BCE, Livia Drusilla was the third wife of Emperor Augustus, and often gave him advice. He gave her the right to manage her own affairs in 35 BCE, raised a public statue in her honour, and granted her the title of Julia Augusta (a great woman of the

▶ **Sabine women**
In Roman mythology, its soldiers abducted and forcibly married women of the Sabine tribe. However, in reality, soldiers of the Roman Empire raped women in the lands they conquered and saw them simply as spoils of war, not potential brides.

17.9
years was the average life expectancy for a female slave in Rome

Julian family) in his will to secure her position after his death. Livia, however, was an unusual case in a culture ruled by *patres familias*.

The average woman probably spent her days cooking; caring for and educating the children; and sewing or spinning, which was an important part of women's lives. With the advent of the empire, upper-class women could now leave textile work to their slaves, who were typically war captives from lands conquered by Rome, such as Britain, Greece, Syria, and North Africa. Male slaves from educated backgrounds tended to work in skilled professions, whereas women were typically domestic servants. How female slaves were treated depended on the temperament of their owners. Some suffered at the hands of predatory masters and bore their children. Any child born of a slave by her master was a slave; the master could free that child but not acknowledge or adopt it. Enslaved women

◀ **Equal partnership**
This fresco of a baker named Terentius Neo and his wife was painted in 55-79 CE in Pompeii. The wife holds a stylus and writing tablet, indicating that she was literate and probably helped to manage her husband's business.

BIOGRAPHY
BOUDICA

Born into a royal family in c. 30 CE, Boudica married King Prasutagus and became queen of the Celtic Iceni tribe that revolted against the Romans occupying Britain in c. 60 CE. After being flogged, having her property seized, and her daughters raped, Boudica led the uprising, but her people lacked the skills and tools to drive the Romans from Britain. Boudica may have poisoned herself to prevent being taken alive by the Romans, or died from an illness in c. 61 CE.

could enter into an informal marriage which had none of the rights of a legal marriage. If a woman had children, they became the property of her owner – also as slaves.

Early Christian women

Christianity became a legally recognized religion after the death of Constantine the Great in 337 CE, who had converted to the faith. Theoretically, the move to Christianity improved the status of women of Rome, who were encouraged to participate more actively in religion. For example, Constantine's mother, the Empress Helena, played an important role in spreading Christianity, even travelling to Jerusalem to search for biblical relics. In reality, however, Christianity proved even more patriarchal than the pagan faiths, lacking a female deity and closely prescribing women's roles in Church and society.

MOTHERHOOD AND
marriage

MESOAMERICAN SOCIETY

In the ancient societies of Central America and Mexico – known as Mesoamerica – the value of women was associated with their role as mothers. However, while women generally occupied a subservient role to men, they performed vital functions in society. This reality was reflected in the pantheon of Mesoamerican deities, which included beings such as the jaguar goddess Ix Chel, who was associated with childbirth, medicine, and weaving, and had the power to raise storms and floods. In Mesoamerican societies, many everyday tasks were imbued with spiritual significance. For example, spinning and weaving, carried out by women using a back-strap loom, were seen as ritual reenactments of creation.

Mesoamericans believed that motherhood granted women divine favour. Those women who died in childbirth were believed to ascend directly to the heavens, and Mesoamericans saw the physical effort (including the risk of death) involved in childbirth as analogous to the dangers of warfare experienced by men. Their reverence of creation and motherhood even extended to women's appearances. While both sexes had tattoos, it was also common for women to decorate their faces and bodies with red

3 in 4
people in the Mesoamerican world worked in agriculture, which revolved around corn.

paint, a colour that the Mesoamericans associated with the east, the rising sun, and rebirth.

Living and loving

In most civilizations, such as the Olmec and Maya – which flourished in the region from around 1200 BCE – men usually worked in the fields and hunted, while women focused on tending kitchen gardens, foraging, and preparing food. Some women also made pottery, or worked as healers or midwives. Mesoamerican rulers were nearly always male, but women could wield political power as widows or consorts of leaders, or as regents for underage sons. Lady K'Abel, even became *kaloomté* (supreme warrior) of the Wak Kingdom (in modern-day northern Guatemala) after marrying its king in 672, and this title gave her higher authority than him. While it was rare for a woman to rule in her own right, there were a few examples – such as Lady Six Sky, who ruled the city-state of Naranjo (in present-day Guatemala) from 682–741 CE, fighting off many enemy attacks, and acting as regent for her son until he came of age. Monuments commissioned by the queen show her standing triumphantly over prisoners of war – an unusual depiction for a woman at the time.

Archeological evidence suggests the extremes to which Mesoamericans went to alter their physical appearance. Carvings and sculptures show that for both men and women, the most desirable physical features were a long nose, being crosseyed, and a sloping forehead. The first was achieved by wearing

◀ **Goddess of childbirth**
Ix Chel, the jaguar goddess, was a powerful figure in Mayan folklore. The goddess, depicted as an ugly old woman, presided over the sweat bath, where women often gave birth.

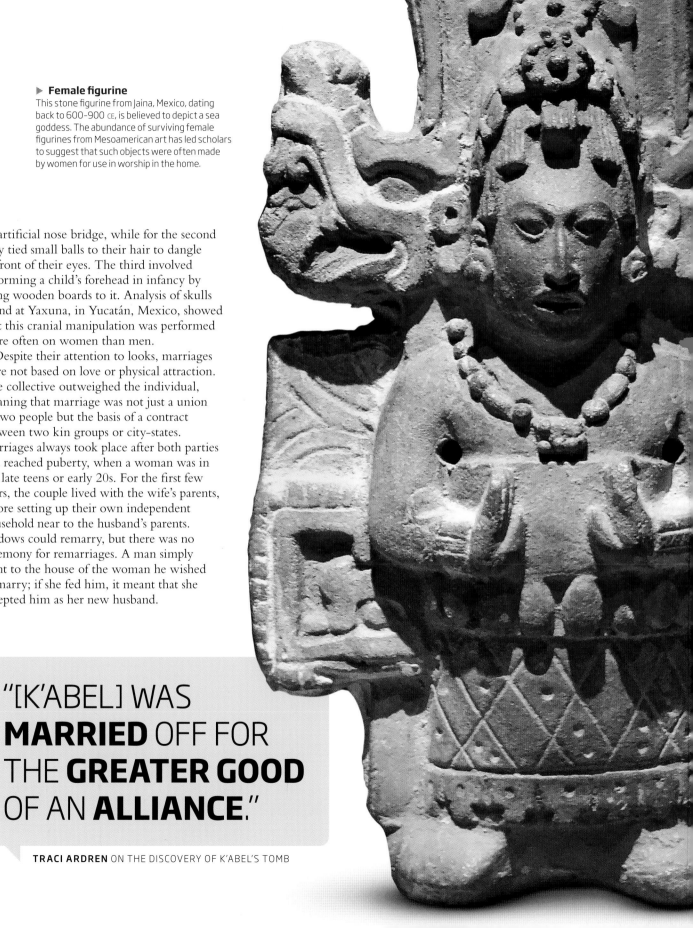

an artificial nose bridge, while for the second they tied small balls to their hair to dangle in front of their eyes. The third involved deforming a child's forehead in infancy by tying wooden boards to it. Analysis of skulls found at Yaxuna, in Yucatán, Mexico, showed that this cranial manipulation was performed more often on women than men.

Despite their attention to looks, marriages were not based on love or physical attraction. The collective outweighed the individual, meaning that marriage was not just a union of two people but the basis of a contract between two kin groups or city-states. Marriages always took place after both parties had reached puberty, when a woman was in her late teens or early 20s. For the first few years, the couple lived with the wife's parents, before setting up their own independent household near to the husband's parents. Widows could remarry, but there was no ceremony for remarriages. A man simply went to the house of the woman he wished to marry; if she fed him, it meant that she accepted him as her new husband.

"[K'ABEL] WAS **MARRIED** OFF FOR THE **GREATER GOOD** OF AN **ALLIANCE**."

TRACI ARDREN ON THE DISCOVERY OF K'ABEL'S TOMB

WARRIOR
queens

ANCIENT AFRICAN KINGDOMS

While the dominant deity in the sub-Saharan Nubian kingdoms was the god Amun – known to the Nubians as Amani – the goddess Isis (see pp. 18–19) also inspired great dedication. The Nubians built many temples solely for this mythological mother and wife of kings. Her cult enabled Nubian women to take on key roles in the priesthood. Many scholars have suggested that Nubian royal succession may have followed the female line, and some have attributed this to the influence of Isis in ancient Africa. Even if succession was not matrilineal, evidence shows that women played an important role in selecting the next ruler.

Queens of Kush

The Nubian empire of Kush, located on the western banks of the Nile in modern-day Sudan, emerged around 1000 BCE. By 300 BCE, the capital had moved to Meroë,

ushering in a period of strong female rulers. While a king's mother and sisters were given the title of *kandake*, women who ruled in their own right were called *qore* (meaning "king"). One such *qore* was Shanakdakhete, who ruled in the late second century BCE. Her husband was regarded as her consort, rather than as a coruler. The Nubian queens were as formidable as kings: they fought wars, founded temples, and built monuments. Some presided over the most prosperous periods in Nubian history. Even a *kandake* could be fierce; relief carvings at the Temple of Apedamak at Naga show the Kandake Amanitore dressed for battle.

▼ **Status symbol**
The jewellery found in Queen Amanishakheto's pyramid, such as this ornate gold armlet, testifies to the wealth and status of Nubian queens. Worn by Amanishakheto in the 1st century BCE, the armlet is decorated with a depiction of the winged goddess, Mut.

10
sovereign queens ruled Kush from 300 BCE to 200 CE

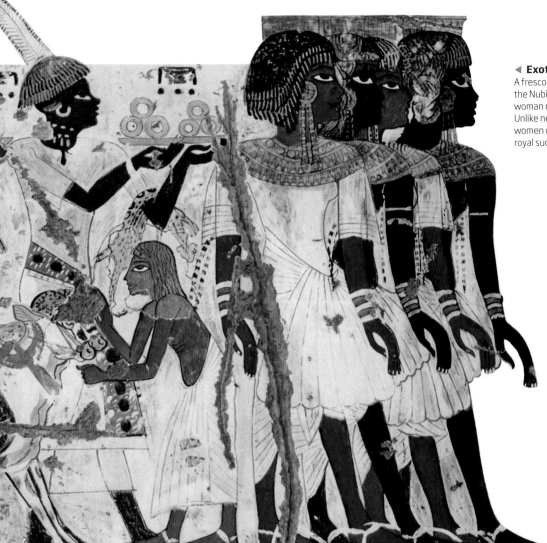

◀ **Exotic foreigners**
A fresco illustrates how Egyptians saw the Nubians. A high status woman woman rides in a cart drawn by oxen. Unlike neighboring Egypt, Nubia gave women control in governance and the royal succession.

BIOGRAPHY
AMANIRENAS

Queen Amanirenas ruled from the battlefield as much as the throne. In 24 BCE, when Roman emperor Augustus tried to levy taxes on the Nubians, she led a 30,000-strong army to sack the Roman fort at Aswan, losing an eye in the ensuing battle. In response, she mutilated a statue of Augustus, burying its head at the threshold of the fort, so that all who came and went would tread upon it as a sign of disrespect. Even Greek writer Strabo said of her, "This Queen had a courage above her sex."

The public trust placed in African warrior queens is likely to have lifted the status of women in general. While there is far more evidence about the life of Nubia's ancient monarchs than about the condition of everyday women under their reign, there are indications that women across the social scale took an active role in public life. This included the right to own and sell property, and manage their own businesses. There are even instances of women, albeit with royal connections, rising to positions of administrative power as district governors. As household managers and food-producers, women not only undertook the labour, but also made key decisions about what to cultivate, where, and how. This level of control – over matters so pivotal to the wellbeing of the entire community – supports the idea that even non-regal women enjoyed a degree of authority. This is substantiated by matrilineal naming customs, whereby children took their mothers' names rather than their fathers'.

Matriarchal structures decline

With so little evidence to draw on, it is vital not to overemphasize the position of women in these ancient African kingdoms, and pay too much attention to such exceptional examples as the ruling queens. Even so, it is clear that the matriarchal structures of ancient African societies were important. However, they did not last and were eroded gradually by external forces, largely in the forms of Christianity, Islam, and colonialism.

> We **shoot** with **bows** and **hurl javelins** and **ride horses**.

AMAZON WARRIORS,
HERODOTUS' *HISTORIES*, 440 BCE

▶ **Warlike women**
A bronze sculpture of an Amazon warrior conveys the athletic strength and skill the legendary tribe were said to possess.

THROUGH THE AGES

Warfare

Throughout ancient and medieval history, women seldom fought in battles in large numbers. However, while warfare was predominantly a male activity, across many cultures exceptional individual women fought on the battlefield – and a handful even led armies of their own.

◀ **Pictish woman**
In the time of the Roman Empire Scottish tribes had both male and female warriors. The Romans called them "Picti", or "painted ones", due to their body decorations.

ALTHOUGH WOMEN WARRIORS were rare, the war goddess features repeatedly across the world's mythologies. In ancient Egyptian lore, Sekhmet appeared in the form of a fierce lioness and protected the pharaoh in battle, while in the Hindu pantheon, Durga is often shown riding a tiger and clutching weapons in her ten hands, valiantly fighting the forces of evil. The Amazons are perhaps the best-known female warrior figures, and are immortalized in Greek legends.

A tribe of warlike women, they cut off their right breasts to fire their bows and throw their javelins better, but protected their left breasts so that they could breastfeed their babies.

Though such fighting women were mythological, they are thought to have some basis in reality. The Amazon myth may have been founded on the Scythians, a nomadic people from Central Asia who migrated to Eastern Europe by the 7th century BCE. They fought on horseback and were highly skilled with the bow. Archaeological analysis of Scythian burial mounds has found that over one-third of female remains were interred with weapons and their bones showed evidence of fighting, suggesting their warriors were women.

Asia's most famous legendary female fighter was Hua Mulan, who is said to have lived in China in the 4th or 5th century CE. Disguised as a man, she joined the army and fought for over a decade. She was promoted to general, winning a great victory after revealing her true identity to her soldiers. Her legend, the inspiration for many books and a 1998 Disney film, probably has no basis on any single historical individual. However, there are real examples of women fighting while disguised as men, such as Fannu, a 12th-century Moroccan princess who disguised herself to fight off an invading army in Marrakesh. Some women in ancient and medieval times fought openly, even leading armies – such as Chinese Empress Fu Hao, who was a general in her own right.

Taking command

Ancient and medieval women did lead armies across the world. Among those queens who personally commanded their forces was Rudrama Devi, an Indian monarch who died fighting an enemy kingdom in the late 13th century. Women could also hold command in the absence of a male leader. Blanche of Castile, for example, who served as French regent from 1226–1236 CE personally led the royal army. Such women were exceptions, however – for the most part, even female monarchs left military leadership, and the fighting itself, to male generals.

▼ **Fearless Samurai**
Tomoe Gozen was a female warrior (*onna-bugeisha*) who rose to fame fighting in the Genpei War, a civil conflict between Japan's clans. She led male warriors into battle and was accomplished with both the bow and the sword.

PROFILES
VALIANT WARRIORS

Artemisia I of Caria (c. 5th century BCE) ruled the city-state of Halicarnassus (present-day Turkey) and several Aegean islands. When the Persian Emperor Xerxes launched an invasion of Greece in 480 BCE, she joined his forces. She advised Xerxes not to engage the Greek fleet at Salamis but he ignored her, and suffered a major defeat. Artemisia commanded a squadron of ships and survived the battle, ruling Caria until her death.

The Trung Sisters (d. 43 CE) , Trac and Nhi, were born in northern Vietnam at a time when it was dominated by the Chinese Han Dynasty. After the Chinese executed Trac's husband, she and her sister began to agitate against their foreign overlords. In 39 CE the sisters led a popular rebellion against Han rule, gaining control of much of northern Vietnam. The Han quashed the uprising, and in 43 CE the sisters drowned themselves to avoid defeat.

Dihya al-Kahina (c. 7th century CE) was the daughter of a Berber chieftain. In the 680s she emerged as leader of the Berber tribes who joined together to resist the Arab Empire in its expansion into the Maghreb. Dubbed "Queen of the Berbers", she inflicted a major defeat on the Arabs, forcing them to retreat. They returned, and in around 702 Dihya was defeated and possibly killed in battle.

Olga of Kiev (d. 969) was married to Igor, King of the Kievan Rus', an East Slavic state. When her husband died in 945 Olga became regent. Refusing to remarry, she led military campaigns against opposition tribes and defeated rebels. In 968, while her son was away campaigning, she defended Kiev from invasion by nomads from Central Asia.

Matilda of Tuscany (1046-1115) was the daughter of a powerful northern Italian prince. After he was assassinated in 1052 she inherited his lands, which she successfully fought to maintain control of–even donning full armour to lead her armies in person.

Joanna of Flanders (c. 1295-1374), Duchess of Brittany, was a fierce military leader in the War of the Breton Succession from 1341 to 1365. She took up arms to secure the position of first her husband and then son, riding into town and encouraging local women to cut their skirts and join the fight. After leading the charge to burn down an enemy camp, she was known as "Jeanne la Flamme".

Purity, Piety, and Property

600–1485

Modern impressions of medieval women, especially in Western societies, highlight their chastity, obedience, and lack of autonomy. Limitations were placed on women by religion, custom, and law, and many women's lives were dominated by their duties as wives, mothers, and workers, with any earnings for their labours often going to their husbands. Yet women did not always fulfil the image of pure, meek, and subservient wives and daughters that has been painted. In some medieval societies, women had a surprising amount of freedom, and the historical record is littered with stories of strong female warriors, religious leaders, and property owners.

PRIVILEGES UNDER
Tang rule

CHINA'S GOLDEN AGE

▲ **Female attendant**
Pairs of terracotta figures depicting spirits, guardians, and officials stood at the doors of Tang burial chambers. This figurine from a woman's tomb was one of a 9th-century pair representing court ladies-in-waiting.

The Tang Dynasty (618–907 CE) is often called a golden age of Chinese civilization. During this period, women, particularly elites, enjoyed many rights and privileges, and they played a major political role. The most notable was Empress Wu, the only reigning female emperor in Chinese history, who ruled under titles such as Sacred and Divine Empress Regnant from 690–705.

Women could wield great influence at the imperial capital of Chang'an (now known as Xi'an). In the early eighth century, imperial princesses had the right to independently establish their own offices of staff, which could be highly lucrative. Princess Anle, Empress Wu's granddaughter, sold off over 1,400 appointments at court and in addition fraudulently ordained 12,000 monks and priests. Part of the proceeds may have gone towards an extensive pleasure park she constructed for herself, which featured an artificial lake with a circumference of 250 km (16 miles). Excesses such as Anle's may have led to the imperial austerity edict of 714, which forbade women at court from wearing rich brocades, embroidery, pearls, or jade.

A number of less fortunate women became part of the "Flank Court," which was made up of relatives of men sentenced to death for rebellion. They were responsible for looking after the imperial mulberry trees and making silk. Many women received an education and some became renowned scholars – the most famous was Shangguan Wan'er (664–710 CE), who organized and judged poetry contests, as well as being one of Empress Wu's

"A CHILD ... WITH HEAVENLY GRACES ... WAS CHOSEN ONE DAY FOR THE IMPERIAL HOUSEHOLD."

BAI JUYI ON YANG GUIFEI, ONE OF THE GREAT BEAUTIES OF TANG CHINA

advisors. Furthermore, all women had hereditary privileges so they could pass down property and titles to their heirs.

Marriage and divorce

During the Tang Dynasty, marriage laws gave women legal protection. Men were only allowed to take one wife (although there was no limit to the number of concubines they could buy or sell). A man could only divorce his wife under certain conditions: the failure to bear children (once the wife was 49); adultery; refusal to obey her in-laws; theft; or contracting an incurable disease. However, a man could not divorce his wife if she had married him when he was humble and they had later become rich, or if she had no family to return to. If a husband tried to divorce under such conditions he was given 100 blows with a thick rod. If a wife tried to leave her husband without his consent, she was given two years of penal servitude.

Chinese culture overall was still patriarchal. Confucianism stressed that a woman's place was in the home, and that she was subordinate to her father, husband, or some other male relative. However, despite this view, many women in Tang China enjoyed freedoms and influence unparalleled in most other contemporary societies, meaning the country's golden age was not just limited to men.

BIOGRAPHY
WU ZETIAN

Born in 624 CE, Wu Zetian was claimed as a concubine by Emperor Taizong at the age of 13. Wu rose to power by eliminating other powerful women at court; some sources even suggested that she killed her own child and framed the emperor's first wife to gain her position. After the death of Taizong's son, Gaozong, Wu quelled a revolt and usurped the throne. She ruled alone as empress until she was forced to abdicate her throne to her son in 704. Wu died just a year later.

◀ **Imperial ensemble**
Court women play flutes during the reign of Emperor Li Yu (937–978 CE), in this detail of *The Night Revels of Han Xizai*. As well as the flute, the fiddle and another stringed instrument called the pipa were popular during the Tang Dynasty.

THE RISE OF
Islam

7TH-CENTURY ARAB WORLD

▲ **The hand of Fatima**
This design, also known as the *khamsa*, is a stylized representation of a hand. A popular amulet in the Islamic world, its name may refer to the protection provided by devout women such as Fatima, the daughter of Prophet Muhammad.

Among the tribes of the Arabian peninsula in the 6th century CE, societal attitudes to women were complicated by traditions. Arab pagan men could take as many wives as they wanted and, in some tribes, newborn girls were valued so little that they were buried alive; early Islamic sources contain some harrowing accounts of Muslim converts lamenting their parts in such crimes.

The rise of Islam fundamentally improved women's lives on the Arabian Peninsula. The faith originated there in 610 CE, when the Prophet Muhammad is said to have begun receiving revelations from God in a place called Makkah. During the next 23 years of his life, his teachings spread across the peninsula and, after his death the Islamic faith expanded rapidly thanks to invasion and conquest throughout North Africa, and as far as present-day Pakistan.

Rights and property

The new religion enshrined women's rights in its laws and also gave them privileges and freedoms. God declared in the Qur'an, Islam's sacred text, that women were spiritually equal to men, and the Prophet Muhammad treated women with reverence. However, these laws were also affected by the male-dominant cultures brought under Islamic rule.

The Qur'an prescribed laws that protected the social position of women. While polygamy was not outlawed, a man was permitted a maximum of four wives, with the proviso that, "if you fear you will not be fair, then only one". The limitations on polygamy were considered radical by many early followers of the Prophet. Women's property rights were also enshrined in the Qur'an. Women inherited half of a brother's

Muhammad's
11
wives were called Mothers of the Faithful

share on the death of her parents, but whereas a man had to use his share to care for his family, a woman was able to keep hers entirely for herself. Qur'anic law gave women the right to consent to marriage and also the right to

divorce. The Qur'an reveres several women. Unlike in the Hebrew bible, Eve is described as Adam's mate and helper – she is not created from his rib, but, like Adam, is one half of a single soul that was split into two. Other notable females recognized by the Qur'an are Asiya, the pious wife of the tyrannical Pharaoh in the time of Moses; Mary, mother of Jesus; and Fatima, the daughter of the Prophet.

The Prophet is recorded in both early Sunni and Shia Arabic sources as having shown a particularly high degree of respect for his daughter. Fatima, known as the "Shining One" is praised in both the Qur'an and *hadith* (records of the Prophet's words and actions) for her purity and devotion to her father and faith. Today, Muslims continued to honour Fatima and her descendants – such as her daughter, Zainab, who played an active role in teaching women the new religion, travelling widely in the Islamic world with her male relatives. Zainab was also a witness to the defeat and martyrdom in 681 CE of her brother Husain at the battle of Karbala, after which she was imprisoned by the victors. The Qur'an encourages women to emulate the Prophet's female descendents, such as Fatima and Zainab, in faith and works.

BIOGRAPHY
KHADĪJA BINT KHUWAYLID

Khadīja was the first wife of the Prophet Muhammad. Muhammad often described her as the love of his life. She was the mother of his beloved daughter Fatima. Khadīja was not only slightly older than Muhammad but she was also his employer. Historical sources confirm that her wealth surpassed that of any male trader in the Arabian Peninsula. In the years when the pagans imposed sanctions on the Muslims, it was her wealth that saved them.

◀ **Guardian of the Qur'an**
Initially recited from memory, the teachings of the Qur'an were written down in the 650s to be preserved and distributed. Some scholars suggest that Hafsa bint 'Umar – one of the Prophets' wives – acted as its first editor, and as a guardian of the original documents. This manuscript was created in Morocco in the 12th century.

LIFE AND LEADERSHIP IN
the Pacific

ISLAND TRADITIONS

▲ **Sound of music**
The tone of the Maori putorino - a flutelike wooden instrument - was said to represent Hineraukatauri, a female ancestor spirit who personified music. Use of the putorino died out in the mid-1800s, but Maori musicians have begun to reintroduce it.

The island cultures of the Pacific Ocean stretch back tens of thousands of years before European contact was first made. Migration to the islands started from Southeast Asia between 3000 and 1000 BCE. People first settled across Melanesia (from Papua New Guinea to New Caledonia, Fiji, Santa Cruz, Vanuatu, and the Solomon Islands), then Micronesia (Marshall Islands Palau and Mariana Islands), and finally the Polynesian islands (New Zealand, Tonga, Samoa, Tuvalu, Hawaii, Cook Islands, Marquesas Islands, French Polynesia including Tahiti and Bora Bora, and Easter Island).

Due to the remoteness of the islands, contact with other islands was infrequent and each island society flourished individually. However, although they grew into diverse cultures, many of the islands shared common gender roles. Men did most of the deeper sea fishing and cultivation of trees such as coconut and breadfruit, while women cultivated the land, did inshore fishing, and manufactured the valuables that were used for trade – loom-woven clothing, mats, medicine, and ornaments. The role of women in these groups was also to bear children and to teach and care for them in their formative years.

> In 1890,
> # 4 of 5
> **chiefs** in **Rarotonga** were **women.**

Female leaders

One commonality in Pacific societies is the lack of historical, written documentation on the everyday lives of women. When European contact first occurred, explorers expected to meet with male leaders and not women, and those who wrote about their encounters minimalized the high rank and power women held. In Pacific societies, rank and family lineage was the deciding factor in the distribution of political and social power. In pre-contact Hawaii, for example, the status of women was higher than men. Women were chiefs as early as 1375, when Kukaniloko ruled Oahu.

Other island cultures also have long histories of female leadership. Before colonization, more than half of the recorded rulers of the island of Huaine (French Polynesia) were female, and Pōmare IV ruled Tahiti for 50 years as its last major monarch before the French took control. Powerful women, however, were maligned by Europeans – for example, Tupoumoheofo, an 18th-century Tongan leader, was characterized as a scheming, tyrannical, "meddling wife".

▲ **Polynesian skirt**
This striking dancing skirt known as a *titi saka* was made in Tuvalu from pandanus leaf and plant fibre. The artistry used to make a dance costume is as important as the dance itself in the Pacific islands.

◀ **Romanticized view**
Paul Gauguin's 1892 work
Mata Mua (In Olden Times)
depicts an idyllic view of
the Pacific landscape. His
sexualized depictions of
Tahitian beauties exemplify
how many of the white
explorers characterized
island women.

> The **foetus** is attached to the **womb** just like **fruit to a tree**, which when it proceeds from the flower is **extremely delicate**.

TROTULA, 12TH-CENTURY ITALIAN TEXTS ON WOMEN'S MEDICINE

EXPERIENCES OF CHILDBIRTH

Hard labour

No matter how rewarding the result, throughout history childbirth has been dangerous and often unavoidable. In many communities, women worked together to ease the way for mothers bringing new lives into the world.

THE HISTORY OF LABOUR often begins with a look at who was present, or absent, from the birthing room. For thousands of years, it was midwives, fellow women, who were the traditional birth partner of the labouring woman. Australian Aboriginal women traditionally left their home camp with female elders to labour in a secret place. They believed that giving birth among nature was a spiritual experience that created a bond between mother, child, and the world.

In the 19th century, Inuit tribes in northern Canada involved anyone who was present to help with the birth of a child. Older children were not shielded from birth, as this was seen as a way for them to gain experience, and husbands might just as easily serve as midwives as the woman's mother or female relatives. In Nigeria today, many women choose to give birth in their local church, with the pastor as a birth attendant. They believe that in this sacred space, women can pray without hindrance, and their physical closeness to God will bring them a complication-free birth.

Pain relief

While sacred texts such as the Bible say that labour pains were a punishment visited on the first mother, ways to alleviate them have long been a focus for both birth attendants and mothers themselves. In medieval Europe, women commonly wore protective amulets and special prayers were written for the labouring woman. With the invention of laudanum in the 16th century by the Swiss physician Paracelsus, and chloroform – used by Queen Victoria in 1853 – Western women increasingly sought to lessen labour pains by chemical means. Other cultures had different

WOMAN IN LABOUR MINIATURE 500-1500

> A pregnant woman is in more **serious danger** than sailors and horsemen.

CHINESE PROVERB

> "For far too many, **pregnancy and birth** is still something that **happens to them** rather than something they set out **consciously** and **joyfully to do** themselves."
>
> **SHEILA KITZINGER**, *THE EXPERIENCE OF CHILDBIRTH, 1962*

approaches to pain relief. Arabic women learned Raqs Sharqi (known in the west as belly dancing) from puberty. This dance had a threefold purpose: it increased abdominal strength from a young age; the movements reduced pain by helping the baby move more smoothly into the birth canal; and other women would also join the dance, attempting to hypnotize the mother into following their movements and keeping time. Women in West Micronesia began dilation artificially around a month before the mother's due date, using tightly rolled leaves. This decreased the pain, and shortened labour considerably.

Pushing through

Throughout history, one of the greatest concerns about childbirth has been the survival of both mother and child. Many factors also influenced a baby's chance of survival. Infants born to poor women and slaves had a higher chance of fatality because of maternal malnutrition and disease. In the 18th century, the mortality rate for children born to African American slaves was as high as 50 per cent, although some sources suggest that women smothered their babies to spare them a life in bondage. In some societies, infant and maternal mortality have been seen as punishments. On the Yucatán Peninsula, husbands are still expected to witness the suffering of the woman during labour and, if absent, are blamed for deaths.

Advances in medical equipment have contributed to a decrease in infant death rates. A common cause of infant mortality was becoming stuck in the descent into the birth canal. In the 16th century, French obstetrician Peter Chamberlen developed forceps to help

extract the baby from the birth canal, thereby preventing suffocation. His family kept the invention a secret until the 17th century, when its use became commonplace.

Other birth procedures have a much longer history. Evidence suggests, for example, that the caesarean section took place as many as 3,000 years ago in China and 2,200 years ago in India. At first the procedure was practised to save the infant if the mother had died during labour because, before 1500, surgical techniques and hygiene practices were not sophisticated enough to allow the mother to survive the operation. Today, increased knowledge of hygiene and anatomy has made childbirth safer than ever before, but infant mortality rates remain high in less developed parts of the world.

▲ **BIRTHING CHAIR**
Many women in history gave birth sitting down with the aid of furniture such as this 17th-century French chair. It could also be folded out flat to become a bed or an operating table.

> "[My husband] **cut a hole in the wooden bed** and placed a caribou skin over it for me to **release the baby**."
>
> **APPHIA AWA**, INUIT WOMAN FROM NUNAVUT, CANADA, 1992

PROPERTY AND
equality

▲ **Ornate object**
Women's brooches, worn on each shoulder to hold back a cloak or shawl, were more embellished than those of men. This example was found in the grave of a woman from the kingdom of Kent, southeast England.

ANGLO-SAXON SETTLEMENT

Anglo-Saxon women in England enjoyed a surprising degree of equality. A seminal study published in 1984 described females of this period as "near equal companions to males in their lives… much more than in any other era before modern time." The Angles and Saxons were Germanic tribes who had migrated from northwestern Europe and displaced the Romans in Britain. By about 600 CE, a "heptarchy" of seven Anglo-Saxon kingdoms arose that lasted until Wessex emerged as the leading kingdom in the early 9th century. Anglo-Saxon rule continued until the Norman invasion in 1066.

Property rights

Not a great deal of information survives about the lives of Anglo-Saxon queens, although a few, like Margaret of Wessex and Ealhswith (wife of Alfred the Great) were pious enough to be venerated as saints. Legal documents and archaeological evidence, however, do give valuable insights into women's status. Women had property rights, and many landowners were female. A number of English place-names reflect this; Wolverhampton, for example, was named for its founder Wulfrun,

▲ **Streaking in protest**
Lady Godiva was an 11th-century noblewoman who, according to legend, rode naked through the streets of Coventry to protest against the oppressive taxation imposed by her husband, the earl of Mercia, on his tenants.

a 10th-century noblewoman. Women brought matters to court to settle disputes, and could make binding oaths. One-quarter of surviving Anglo-Saxon wills were made by women. Married women retained a separate legal identity and property rights independent of their husband. After the wedding the husband paid his wife a *morgengifu* (morning-gift) in money, livestock, land, or jewellery which she retained full control over. A widow could not be forced to remarry, but if she did she would sometimes have to give up part of her late

"SHE WAS CALLED MARGARET … PRECIOUS IN FAITH AND WORKS."

BISHOP TURGOT, *LIFE OF ST. MARGARET*, 12TH CENTURY CE

husband's estate. Divorce, which is an important indicator of women's rights, was common among upper-class Anglo-Saxon women. Divorce laws also granted women full custody of their children. Women's roles in this period were symbolized by girdle-hangers, many of which have been found in Anglo-Saxon female graves. These were long, distinctive, key-shaped pieces of metal that hung from women's girdles (or belts). They were not actually keys, but represented the woman's control of her household.

The Norman Conquest changed everything. Under William the Conqueror, land-holding was linked to a promise of military service to the crown, so he and his successors preferred that land be held by men and women's property rights were taken away. Women's property came to be controlled by their husbands, and widows wanting to retain ownership of their lands had to pay a fine to the king and seek his approval. This loss of rights lasted hundreds of years, and it was not until the 19th century that women in England regained independent property rights.

BIOGRAPHY
ÆTHELFLÆD

The oldest daughter of Alfred the Great, Æthelflæd was born around 870 and later married Ethelred, the ruler of Mercia. The kingdom was bordered by Vikings to the north, leading to constant warfare. Unusually for the time, Æthelflæd became involved in governing Mercia, and when her husband died in 911 she became the sole ruler. She launched several campaigns to take back the lands under Danish control, but died in 918 before completing the reconquest.

◄ **Working companions**
Anglo-Saxon women were mainly responsible for spinning yarn, weaving cloth, and embroidery. In communal weaving houses women could work and socialize at the same time.

COURT LIFE IN
Kyoto

HEIAN-ERA JAPAN

The Heian period (794–1185) saw Japan break away from China's influence to establish a distinctly Japanese way of life. The era is celebrated for its poetry, art, and literature, and female poets played a central role in what became a golden age of Japanese culture. Women writers of the period, untrained in Chinese, wrote in Japanese – the language of the people. The work of female poets and their observations of daily life were therefore the texts that became most widely known, and heralded some of Japan's great literature.

Politics of marriage

Court marriages in the Heian capital of Kyoto were arranged, and elite women were instrumental in the associated marriage politics. Women of the courtier upper class stayed with their own families after marriage; husbands and wives either lived separately or the wife's family would adopt the husband as a son. This meant that Heian women could inherit property, unlike in societies where couples settled with the husband's family. Only Japanese men could be polygamous but, if discreet, women could take lovers. They could also petition for divorce and remarry. Women were fully involved in raising children, and ran their own households if married to a noble or government official. Aristocratic families used the marriage of their daughters to further their political position, notably within the Fujiwara clan who married their daughters into the Imperial House of Japan and produced many emperor sons. Daughters of court officials and lesser nobles could advance their status by becoming concubines of high-ranking noblemen.

Women who could write elegant calligraphy or recite poetry attracted many admirers. Physical beauty was also important; practices such as whitening the face with powder (*oshiroi*), blackening the teeth (*ohaguro*), painting the mouth small and red, and removing the eyebrows to redraw them higher on the forehead (*hikimayu*) are described by Heian women writers. *Ohaguro* had become a custom during the Nara period (710–794). Initially, the practice was used to indicate that a girl from an aristocratic family had reached puberty, and in her later years that she was married. On a superficial level, *ohaguro* was thought to enhance sex appeal.

> Heian's most **important writers were women** between the years
> # 950–1050

Writers and leaders

Many Heian literary works throw light on the lives of noblewomen and courtesans at the Kyoto court, the most famous being *The Tale*

◀ **Folk heroine**
Japanese 12th-century heroine Kesa Gozen, pictured in a domestic scene, having washed her hair. Kesa sacrificed her life to protect her family's honour, and the story is told in a text that reflects the morals of the period.

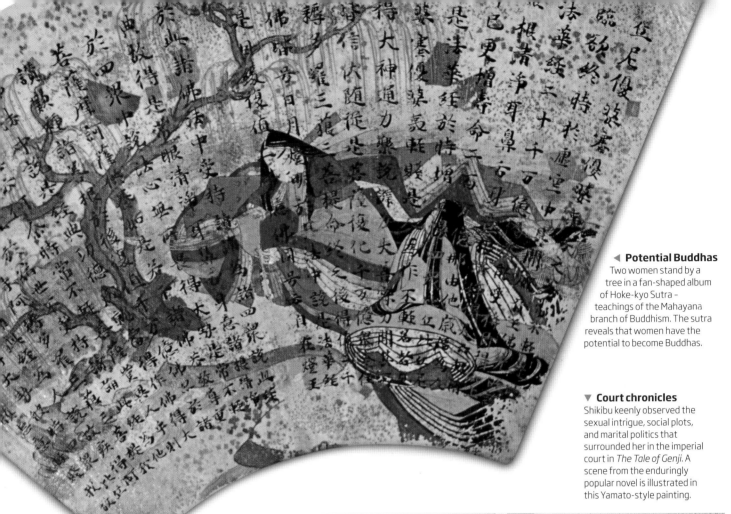

◀ **Potential Buddhas**
Two women stand by a
tree in a fan-shaped album
of Hoke-kyo Sutra –
teachings of the Mahayana
branch of Buddhism. The sutra
reveals that women have the
potential to become Buddhas.

▼ **Court chronicles**
Shikibu keenly observed the
sexual intrigue, social plots,
and marital politics that
surrounded her in the imperial
court in *The Tale of Genji*. A
scene from the enduringly
popular novel is illustrated in
this Yamato-style painting.

of Genji. Composed in the 11th century by
Murasaki Shikibu, it is widely considered the
world's first novel and a masterpiece of world
literature. Sei Shōnagon, a contemporary of
Shikibu, also vividly captured Heian court life
in *The Pillow Book* (c. 1002). In brilliant and
original prose, she makes witty, insightful
observations of Japan's late 10th-century elite.
Fujiwara Michitsuna's *The Mayfly Diary*
(c. 974) is a haunting record of the author's
unhappy marriage to a Fujiwara courtier.

Despite women's prominence in Heian
culture, their role in politics was limited.
Earlier in Japanese history, men and women
had reigned in equal numbers, but by the start
of the Heian era, female sovereigns yielded
less power in government. However, they
remained influential as mothers of emperors,
and were formally designated as empress
mother or empress dowager (*kōtaigō*).

"To be pleasant, gentle, calm ... this is the basis **of good taste and charm in a woman**."

MURASAKI SHIKIBU, *THE DIARY OF LADY MURASAKI,* JAPAN, 11TH CENTURY

LESSONS IN PROPRIETY

Women during Japan's Heian period were expected to be beautiful and to be quiet. Written by lady-in-waiting Murasaki Shikibu (left), the *Tale of Gengi* is not only a novel but a key insight into Heian-era courtship. Shikubi's work, which spans 53 chapters, describes the intrigues of Heian court life and gives a sense of the propriety and good taste that governed courtship and seduction. The exchange of poetry, for example, was an essential part of courting etiquette, and men and women disliked seeing each other naked – even during intercourse. Noblewomen like Murasaki lived meekly and respectably, their silk-draped bodies hidden from male eyes behind veils and screens.

NORSE MYTH AND
reality

Medieval Icelandic sagas are filled with strong female characters, which suggests that Scandinavian women during the Viking Age (c.800–1100 CE) could command respect and exercise considerable influence. However, in reality, women had few legal rights and no formal role in public life. They could not be a witness in a legal case, and did not have the right to speak at the *thing* (assembly) – the main political institution – so women's authority depended to some extent on force of character. Viking society was hierarchical; although an aristocratic woman might have lower status than an aristocratic man, she did have the advantage of being seen as superior to everyone of lower social rank, regardless of their gender.

Divided roles

Gender roles in Viking Age Scandinavia were clearly defined. Men ploughed, hunted, traded, fished, and fought. They also monopolized physically demanding crafts like blacksmithing and carpentry. Women's lives, on the other hand, were centred on the home and family farm: they baked and brewed; spun thread; wove cloth and made clothes; milked the cows; and churned butter. They also cared for children and the sick.

In wealthy households, women managed the servants and slaves, and looked after the whole family estate if their husbands were away on business or fighting. Women wore the keys to the house and to the family's strongbox on their belts as a symbol of their domestic authority, and a wife would expect her husband to consult her on decisions affecting the family's welfare. Females also had a special role in pagan religion as practitioners of *seiðr*, a dangerous magic said to be gifted by the fertility goddess Freyja, which endowed them with the power of prophecy.

▲ **Remnants of a bygone age**
Brooches – such as this example found in Norway – have been crucial for identifying graves of Viking women. They were not only decorative, but also held layers of clothing in place.

IN BRIEF
VIKING EXPANSION

As Viking men explored and plundered foreign lands, women took charge at home. Raiders often brought female slaves back to lessen the load – or for their own pleasure.

700 CE

793 The English monastery of Lindisfarne is sacked in the earliest recorded Viking raid – an event defining the beginning of the Viking Age.

800 CE

820 The Oseberg burial takes place in Vestfold, Norway. A Viking queen is buried in a longship with a sacrificed female slave.

870 The Viking settlement of Iceland begins.

892 Viking chief Hastein invades England; he brings his wife and children with him.

900 CE

922 Arab merchant Ibn Fadlan witnesses the sacrifice of a slave girl at a Viking chief's funeral in Russia.

945-963 Olga (Helga) rules the Viking Rus kingdom of Kiev on behalf of her infant son.

965 Harald Bluetooth, king of Denmark, converts to Christianity – as do his people. Norway follows c. 995 and Sweden by c. 1100.

1000 CE

1000 Thjodhild, wife of Erik the Red, founds the first church in Greenland.

1010 Freydis, sister of Leif Eriksson, becomes joint leader of an expedition to Vinland.

1100 CE

1117 Icelandic Grágás law code commits Viking marriage laws to writing for the first time.

◀ **WOMEN ARE TAKEN CAPTIVE** DURING A RAID BY THE VIKINGS IN 994 CE.

»

▲ Lavish burial
Norway's Oseberg ship, one of the biggest finds relating to Viking women, was the final resting place for a very wealthy woman. Her body was buried with rich grave gifts, including carts, sleds, and textiles.

Gender distinctions were expected to continue into the afterlife. The Vikings placed gender-appropriate offerings in the graves of the deceased: weapons and tools in male graves, compared with grave gifts of jewellery, needlework, weaving equipment, and household utensils for women.

Weapons have been found in a small number of female graves, but historians dispute their significance. Although Valkyries and other supernatural female warriors appear in Viking mythology, there is no historical evidence that real women took up arms. However, women are known to have accompanied Viking armies on campaign, providing domestic comforts for the warriors in camp, and they also took part in voyages of exploration. For example, spindle whorls, ring pins, and other artefacts associated with women, found in excavations of the Viking settlement at L'Anse aux Meadows in Newfoundland, confirm saga accounts of women joining the expeditions to Vinland.

Legal status

In Viking society, unmarried women fell under the authority of their fathers. Marriage itself was a contract between the father and the prospective bridegroom – the woman's

BIOGRAPHY
AUD THE DEEP-MINDED

The central character of the 13th-century *Laxdæla Saga*, Aud the Deep-Minded was the only woman among the leaders of the Viking settlement at Breiðafjörður in Iceland. As the daughter of a Viking chief living in the Scottish Hebrides, and the widow of Olaf, the king of Dublin, Aud was a woman of natural authority. However, faced with opposition from the native Gaels, her position became insecure. She commissioned a ship to be built secretly in the forest, and sailed it first to Orkney and then on to Iceland with 20 men under her command. Aud settled in Laxardale where she claimed land for her people.

consent was not required. The bridegroom paid a bride price for his spouse, while her father provided a dowry. After marriage, both remained the property of the wife. In this respect, Viking marriage laws were more favourable to women than those in Christian Europe, where a woman's property passed to her husband after marriage. Also in contrast with contemporary Christian practice, both partners had equal rights to divorce if a marriage proved unsuccessful. These rights, however, were gradually eroded after Christianity was adopted across Scandinavia.

Although Viking men were not expected to be faithful, a wife's adultery was deemed a serious matter as it dishonoured her husband. If a husband found his wife and a lover together, he had the right to kill both of them on the spot. While Viking raiders became associated with rape and plunder, a man who raped a freewoman was outlawed for his crime. Slave women, on the other hand, had no legal protection: they were viewed as property and their owners did not need to seek their consent before having sex with them. Slave women were sometimes sacrificed as grave gifts to follow their owners into the afterlife – as was the case in the Oseberg ship burial near Tønsberg, Norway.

"... IT'S **NOT A MAN'S BUSINESS** TO BOTHER ABOUT **KITCHEN MATTERS.**"

NJÁLS SAGA, ICELAND, 13TH CENTURY

▼ **Reconstructed picture**
A tapestry from the Oseberg burial – a richly detailed and expensive grave gift – depicts mythological scenes, including women carrying spears.

THROUGH THE AGES

Religion

Most world religions are based on a patriarchal view of society that marginalizes the role of women. However, religious communities of women are still important across many faiths, and in some, females take a leading part as priests, pastors, ministers, and rabbis.

▲ **Literate nuns**
This fresco shows the Poor Clares, a Franciscan order founded in 13th century by Clare of Assisi, reading their missals. At this time, convents were one of the only places where women could be educated.

FROM THE VESTAL VIRGINS of the Roman Republic (see pp. 32–33) to priestesses in the Ryukyu Islands in Japan, women often served in significant ways in many ancient religions. In contemporary religions such as Hinduism, there is a long tradition of female priests, sages, and gurus. However, monotheistic religions have historically discouraged or prevented women from joining the priesthood. Judaism's first female rabbi, Regina Jonas, was only ordained in 1935, and most branches of Christianity, such as the Catholic and Orthodox churches, still do not allow women to join the priesthood.

Protestant churches differ. Quakers have ordained women since the faith's founding in the mid-17th century, and by the later 20th century there were female priests in many other denominations including Anglican, Baptist, Methodist, and Lutheran. However, the most prominent role that women play in Christianity, and in Buddhism, too, is as nuns. Although there are wide variations between (and within) religions, most nuns live in a community, often enclosed, and abide by vows of poverty, obedience, and chastity.

Early nuns

Ordained nuns, known as *bhikkhuni*, have existed since Buddhism began in the 5th century BCE. The Buddha himself is said to have ordained the first *bhikkhuni* – his aunt and foster-mother Mahapajapati Gotami. Within Buddhism, women may join the *sangha* (monastic community). However, in some branches of Buddhism, nuns have to take more vows than monks to make them subordinate to male authority, as well as to increase the difficulty of being fully ordained.

> " Taking **this road** … we gain … **treasures** … no wonder if … [the] **cost** seems … **high**. "

SPANISH NUN ST. TERESA OF AVILA, *WAY OF PERFECTION*, 1577

▲ Indonesian rituals
This Toraja priestess is dressed for a religious ceremony. Women play an essential role in the rituals of the Toraja, an ethnic group that lives in the Sulawesi province of highland Indonesia.

By the 6th century, there were groups of Christian women across Europe, North Africa, and West Asia who had withdrawn from the secular world to devote themselves to religious life. Over time, different religious orders developed, each with their own rules and customs. These women often faced suspicion from church authorities, who believed their gender made them more susceptible to sin. It was also feared that nuns were mentally and physically unable to live by the same guidelines as men, although in practice they often did.

Freedom in the convent

Before the 19th century, convents were one of the few places where women had some responsibility for their own governance and, in the double monasteries of the Middle Ages, could even have powers over monks. In convents, communal obligations were placed above individual ones; there was time set aside for private prayer, but it could not interfere with other duties, the most important of which was the daily schedule of prayer and singing hymns. In many convents nuns made goods for sale outside the community to help pay for day-to-day expenses. Nunneries were also active as centres of education (today the largest order of nuns is the teaching order of Salesian Sisters), medical care, and charitable works. Nunneries remain important in both the Catholic and Orthodox branches of Christianity. However, they are less significant in Protestantism, despite a small resurgence since the mid-19th century.

THE "PINK" NUNS OF MYANMAR, THE KEEPERS OF MORALITY

PROFILES
NUNS AND PRIESTESSES

Hildegard of Bingen (c. 1098–1179) experienced religious visions from a young age, and by her teens had entered a cloistered community of nuns at a Benedictine monastery in western Germany. The nuns elected Hildegard as their leader, and in 1147 she founded a separate convent nearby. She wrote works of theology and science, and also composed music.

Sun Bu'er (c. 1119–1182) became a Taoist priestess at the age of 51. She travelled throughout China, splashing hot oil on her face to disfigure herself and deter molesters, and found inner enlightenment. She became a prominent religious leader with a group of female followers. After her death, she is said to have become an immortal.

Herrad of Landsberg (c. 1130–1195) came from a noble Alsatian family and entered Hohenburg Abbey, France, then famed as a centre of learning. She was elected its abbess in 1167, and held the office until her death. Herrad also compiled *Hortus deliciarum* (*Garden of Delights*) – an encyclopedic work about science and theology.

Catherine of Siena (1347–1380) decided to devote herself to a religious life at the age of 16, when she refused to marry her late sister's widower. She joined the Dominican order, but lived at home and worked to help the needy. Following a religious vision when she was 21, Catherine took on a more public role, travelling across Italy, preaching peace and religious reform.

Regina Jonas (1902–1944) was born in Berlin. After studying the Torah, Talmud, and other sources, in 1935 she persuaded a liberal rabbi to ordain her, and led services. In 1942, the Nazis deported Jonas to Theresienstadt (in what is now Terezín, Czechia) concentration camp; two years later she was murdered at Auschwitz.

Tenzin Palmo (b. 1943) was born in England, but moved to India, where she took a new name and was ordained a novice Tibetan Buddhist nun. A decade later she was fully ordained, and lived as the only nun in an all-male monastery.

CHIVALRY AND
courtly love

MEDIEVAL EUROPE

Part of the pageantry of noble and royal life, the concepts of chivalry and courtly love arose in the courts of medieval Europe. Both ideas helped to govern the behaviour and relationships of the elite. The word "chivalry" came into use in the late 11th century. It means "horsemanship" in Old French but can refer to brave deeds in battle or a group of knights. Chivalry's most important role was as a social code of behaviour for knights to follow. Its main features included believing in and defending the Church, championing good causes, protecting the weak, and remaining faithful to one's overlord.

Intermingled with chivalry was courtly love. Developed in present-day France during the late 11th and early 12th centuries, the idea of courtly love emphasized that a knight should honourably serve his paramour by following her every command, even if it meant death. In the many poems and songs

◄ **A culture of romance**
A scene of romantic courtly love is captured on this embroidered 14th-century French purse. The wreath the young girl holds in her left hand symbolizes her virginity.

inspired by courtly love, knights would be as obedient to their lover as their king. In the tales of King Arthur, which experienced a resurgence in popularity during the age of chivalry, the knight Lancelot does the lady Guinevere's bidding, betraying his king. Love was thought to inspire skill and great deeds in battle, improving a knight's character.

Courtly love placed romance and mutual attraction above all else, but this was at odds with the reality of the medieval era – a time in which elite relationships were based on strategic marriage alliances. The chivalric code urged knights to show respect towards women. In practice, they often failed to live up to the ideal, especially when it came

"ANY ... **LADY** OF **NOBLE DISPOSITION** ... **DESERVES** TO BE **SOUGHT AFTER**."

MARIE DE FRANCE, "EQUITAN," 12TH-CENTURY POEM

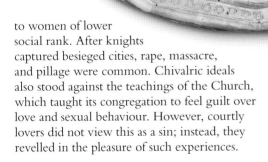

◄ Amorous games
The Garden of Love, a 14th-century birthing tray, was used to carry gifts and food to new mothers while they recovered from childbirth. The painting shows male and female musicians around a well, in a scene of courtly love.

to women of lower social rank. After knights captured besieged cities, rape, massacre, and pillage were common. Chivalric ideals also stood against the teachings of the Church, which taught its congregation to feel guilt over love and sexual behaviour. However, courtly lovers did not view this as a sin; instead, they revelled in the pleasure of such experiences.

Women's experiences of chivalry

Courtly love was usually recorded in song. Stories were told in courts and in taverns by itinerant musicians – known as a Minnesinger in German, or a troubadour in Occitania (part of modern Italy and France), Spain, and Italy. The existence of the female term *trobairitz* shows that women also made music in this way, and *trobairises* such as Tibors de Sarenom and the Comtessa de Diá became some of the first female composers in the history of secular music.

Only a small number of works about courtly love by women have survived. Among these are the narrative poems of Marie de France, who lived in England in the late 12th century. Her work skewered male attitudes that fighting solved all problems. In "The Unfortunate One", three knights hold a tournament to win a lady, ut two of them die and the survivor is left impotent by a lance wound – proof that the glamorized ideals of courtly love did not live up to the brutal realities of medieval life.

BIOGRAPHY
ELEANOR OF AQUITAINE

Eleanor was the most powerful woman of the Middle Ages. In 1137, she inherited the French Duchy of Aquitaine. That year she married Louis VI of France, and introduced his court to the rules of courtly love. The marriage was annulled in 1152; two years later Eleanor married Henry II of England, 11 years her junior. As queen she played a prominent part in politics, and she promoted courtly love and chivalry at the court in Poitiers.

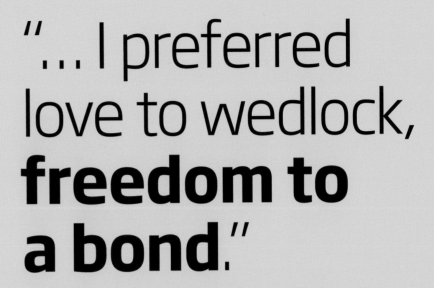

"... I preferred love to wedlock, **freedom to a bond**."

HÉLOÏSE D'ARGENTEUIL'S THOUGHTS ON MARRIAGE AND CHILDREN, IN THE FIRST LETTER TO PETER ABELARD

SPURNING CONVENTION

Héloïse d'Argenteuil was a 12th-century French nun and scholar. Her correspondence in the form of letters to her husband and former tutor Peter Abelard, a monk, chronicle their tragic love story. The letters are noted for Héloïse's erudition and her disdain for convention, and have found a place in feminist literary history. Despite having wed to satisfy social mores, Héloïse wrote that she would still prefer to be Abelard's mistress. She felt theirs was an ideal union to which marriage added nothing, and personally viewed marriage to be a form of contractual prostitution through which a woman might become richer. Héloïse saw her love for Abelard (pictured left, tutoring her) as pure, in the sense that she loved him for himself rather than anything he could give her.

NOMADS AND
empire

MONGOLIAN SOCIETY

Renowned as fine horsemen and for creating a vast empire in the 13th century, the Mongols are a nomadic people of Central Asia. They once moved around in search of pasture for their livestock and lived in round tents called yurts (known as *gers* in Mongolian). Men and women contributed to the household economy. Women loaded the yurts onto horse-drawn carts and drove them to the next campsite. They also took charge of childcare, making felt, sewing, cooking, and processing dairy. In addition, they herded and milked all of the livestock with the exception of horses, which were cared for by the men. Mongol women enjoyed more freedom than women in the countries the Mongols conquered, and they refused to adopt the Chinese practice of foot-binding.

Polygamy was permitted in Mongol society, although the practice had declined by the 19th century due to the breakdown of patrilineal clans. If a husband had multiple wives, each wife had her own yurt, which was lined up west to east behind the husband's tent, according to who he had married first. Marriages, particularly among the elite, were arranged in order to link clans. However, warrior princess Khutulun, a niece of Kublai Khan, only agreed to marry a suitor if he would gamble 100 horses for the chance to beat her in a test of physical strength. It is said that through these tests she accumulated a herd numbering 10,000. Sometimes prospective brides were kidnapped by the groom's family and exchanged for livestock – in return all resulting children belonged to the husband's

◄ Portable art
Mongols prized ornamentation highly, such as this 13th-century silver-handled shell with a panther figure. Women probably used such items to decorate their yurts.

▼ Influential wife
Empress Chabi, the favourite wife of Kublai Khan, was a valued adviser during his reign. Here she wears the headdress known as the *boqta*, said to be in the shape of an inverted boot.

"THEY **BEAR EQUALLY** THE **TITLE OF EMPRESS**, AND **HAVE** THEIR **SEPARATE COURTS**."

MARCO POLO DESCRIBING KUBLAI KHAN'S MULTIPLE QUEENS IN *THE TRAVELS OF MARCO POLO*, 13TH CENTURY

clan. Once a woman married she could wear the *boqta* – a unique headdress reaching over five feet in height. When Marco Polo took the *boqta* back to Europe, fashion-conscious medieval women eagerly imitated it and wore cone-shaped headdresses known as hennins.

Creating an empire

For centuries the Mongols fought among themselves and raided neighbouring areas. Genghis Khan united all the tribes under his leadership in 1206, thereby founding the Mongol Empire, after which he was hailed as "Great Khan." Genghis Khan and his descendants embarked on a series of campaigns in which they conquered over 9 million square miles of territory extending from the Pacific to Central Europe. The majority of the Mongol Horde was male, although some women did go on campaigns and a few even served as commanders. Most women stayed at home and, while their men were

away, some elite females became highly influential in Mongol society. Börte, the senior wife of Genghis Khan, was the first Grand Empress to help govern in her husband's absence. Sorghaghtani later became the most prominent Mongol woman (see right); her son Kublai became Great Khan in 1260 and, through conquest, Emperor of China in 1271. Kublai's wife Chabi was his most trusted adviser; she helped integrate China into his realms, promoted Buddhism, and may have helped advance the career of Marco Polo in China. Chabi epitomized the high status of Mongol women and played a major role in the creation of the largest contiguous land empire in history.

▼ **Sharing the throne**
Even though men were dominant, women had a considerable degree of power and freedom in Mongol society. This 14th-century miniature depicts Emperor Ghazan seated on his throne with his principal wife Kököchin beside him.

▶ **Devout queen**
Indian poet Mirabai was born into a Rajput royal family but left her husband to devote herself to Krishna, to whom she became an ideal "wife" or devotee.

POETRY AND
power

EASTERN POETRY

Women have been writing literature in China since about 600 BCE, yet it was not until the 16th century when the number of female poets saw a dramatic increase. This can be in part attributed to the rise in female readership at the time; amongst the Chinese elite, female education became increasingly popular. Their literacy inspired many women, elite and non-elite alike, to think far beyond the confines of the traditional female sphere. Women felt empowered to express themselves in ways they had been unable to before.

Female poets offered fresh and contemporary voices in contrast to the static male classics. Diverse poets, from maids, concubines, and courtesans to hermits and grandmothers wrote of marriage, lost loves, motherhood, adultery, unhappiness, and the banality of the everyday, with varying degrees of desire to incite change.

In spite of this shift, women still faced barriers, and those writing were very aware of the limitations placed on them by society. Many 16th century female poets referenced classical stories, such as that of the 1st-century BCE poet concubine Ban Jieyu, who was replaced by a dancer in the affections of the father of her children, the emperor. The tale

▶ **Japanese wordsmith**
This woodcut from the Edo period shows a Japanese courtesan doing calligraphy. The artistic accomplishments of courtesans were admired as well as their beauty.

acted as a bitter reminder that female scholarship still took second place to physical beauty.

Sexual odes

In India during the eighth to 17th centuries, women poets emerged from the *bhakti* movement, which emphasizes an individual's intense devotion to a Hindu god and challenged existing hierarchies, with many poets writing in regional languages. Many *bhakti* poets were women and male poets also wrote from the female perspective. *Bhakti* poetry is usually erotic, with writers using the form to praise their god (who was cast in the role of a husband or lover). The most revered of the *bhakti* women poets is the 15th-century mystic and saint, Mirabai, who composed up to a hundred songs or *bhajans*.

In contrast, in Japan, the activity of female poets (see pp. 58–59) decreased from the 14th century with the rise of poetic forms such as *renku* and *haiku,* which were written in men-only groups and considered too coarse for women. However, in the 17th century, *haiku* came to rely less on obscene references, and the genre became open to female poets via its focus on classical allusion and wordplay.

"UNDER MOONLIT CURTAINS, AS THE **SONGS SUBSIDE** I SEARCH ..."

LIU RUSHI, CHINESE COURTESAN AND POET

APOCALYPSE AND
aftermath

In 1347, 12 ships sailing from the Black Sea docked in Sicily, with sailors dead and dying from a fatal plague on board. This plague had already struck the trading nations of the East, including China, India, and Persia. Over the next four years, the disease spread across Europe, killing at least one-third of its population in what became known as the Black Death. No subsequent outbreaks were as devastating as that of the 14th century, but plagues would ravage Europe until the 18th century, particularly across its dirty and densely-packed cities.

Many characterized the Black Death as a divine punishment for the sins of the people. Some monastic chroniclers claimed that women in particular were to blame for the plague due to their "immodest" clothing. Thousands of men took to naked self-flagellation as an act of penance for society's sins, hoping to repel the plague. The whippings were public events, and female onlookers supposedly screamed encouragement and smeared their eyes with the blood that flew through the air, believing that it contained healing properties. Writers were equally quick

▼ **Dying woman**
This detail from the 1411 Toggenburg Bible, depicts a woman dying of the Black Death. Female victims were shown naked, just like men, suggesting that the plague stripped them of any need for modesty.

▲ **Female producers**
Even before the plague, women worked alongside their husbands to produce and sell goods. This 14th-century illustration from Lombardy, Italy shows women making cheese.

"FAIR **LADIES** BREAKFAST WITH THEIR **KINFOLK** AND THE SAME NIGHT **SUPPED** WITH THEIR **ANCESTORS**."

GIOVANNI BOCCACCIO ON THE BLACK DEATH

to condemn women in the post-Black Death period. One Italian author wrote that women who survived in Florence became more likely to commit sexual sins, because they had been attended to by men in the plague years. In England, plague widows, who were deemed too quick to move onto new lovers after their husbands died, were the focus of criticism.

A golden age?

Some historians argue that the Black Death led to a "golden age" for women, particularly in England. In cities, women's economic power increased. Widows were encouraged to continue running their late husbands' businesses. Girls and young women were allowed to take on skilled apprenticeships and join trade guilds, while married women traded as *femmes soles*, a status that gave them

an independent legal and economic identity. However, during the 15th century, once the supply of male labour recovered, many gains made by women were reversed, and by 1500 economic opportunities for women had returned to pre-plague levels.

Other historians argue that women had no golden age of their own at all. Women remained under the legal authority of their male relatives and were generally excluded from civic and political life. In some cases, the plague led fathers to name daughters as their heirs after the death of their sons, but under the legal systems of the time, any inheritance would nonetheless be managed by the daughter's husband. While after the Black Death, those who survived enjoyed the prospect of greater mobility, higher wages, and reduced land prices, this was true for men and women alike.

▲ **Afflicted woman**
The plague affected men, women, and children alike. Studies suggest that men and woman were equally at risk of dying from the disease. This 15th-century fresco from Rhône-Alpes, France, shows a doctor treating a noble lady by lancing a bubo (a swollen lymph gland).

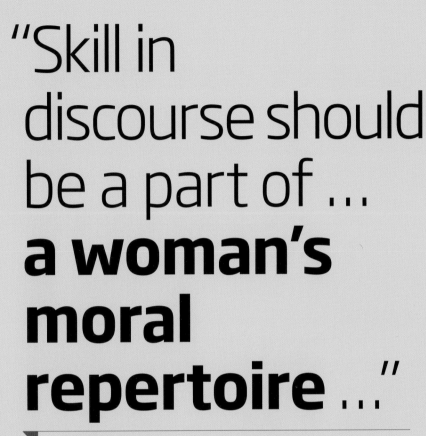

"Skill in discourse should be a part of ... **a woman's moral repertoire ..."**

CHRISTINE DE PIZAN, *THE BOOK OF THE TREASURY OF LADIES*, 1405

CHALLENGING MISOGYNY

The French-Italian writer Christine de Pizan was Europe's first professional female author, and is considered to have written some of the earliest pieces of feminist literature. She began by writing love ballads, which attracted the attention of wealthy patrons including Isabella of Bavaria, the queen of France (shown, left, receiving a manuscript of Pizan's works). Pizan, who believed that she had been chosen by God to challenge the misogyny of the French court, published her popular *The Book of the City of Ladies* in 1404–1405, and *The Book of the Treasury of Ladies,* an education manual, in 1405. Her works presented women in a positive light and denounced her male contemporaries for their sexist treatment of women implicit in their writing.

EXPERIENCES OF EDUCATION

Life lessons

In many societies of the past, women were not expected to be academic. Those who did receive an education found that their lessons were designed to prepare them for religious or married life, rather than the pursuit of knowledge for its own sake.

▲ **Writing slate**
From the 18th until the 20th century, it was common for girls to use erasable slates – such as this example from the 1890s – in the classroom to learn how to write and do arithmetic.

FOR MUCH OF HISTORY, women did not have the same access to education as men. Women were expected to marry, have children, and, if they were poor, help their husbands by working; they needed no formal schooling for tasks such as farming, doing laundry, or housework. Literacy was often tied to a woman's class and station, and varied greatly between cultures. In ancient Athens and Rome, for example, many women were educated in numeracy because the economies revolved around commerce, and even some slave women were literate.

Assessing female literacy across time does not reveal a simple rising progression – rather it shows that it rose and fell, the latter notably in the medieval period, when levels of female literacy plummeted. Increased urbanization from the 10th century onwards was one of the major factors in improving women's education

> Education deserves **emphatically** to be termed **cultivation** of [the] **mind**.
>
> **MARY WOLLSTONECRAFT**, 1792

> I am **convinced** that we must **train not only** the **head**, but the **heart** and **hand as well**.
>
> **CHIANG KAI-SHEK**, 1940

once more, as women in towns began to need to read, write, and do basic calculations as part of their daily lives. Some women set up small schools – called *Winkelschule* (backstreet schools) in Germany – to teach boys and girls how to read (but not write or do arithmetic). Coeducational schooling like this was especially popular during the Reformation, when such schools taught children to read the Bible.

Finishing schools

In many cultures, women's education focused on what was deemed necessary to make a girl a suitable wife. In the ancient Zhou Dynasty of China, boys and girls were separated in education at the age of 10, after which girls would go on to study the "Three Obediences and Four Virtues". These virtues were based around how girls should behave once they married; girls were taught how to speak,

> The **education** and **empowerment** of **women** throughout the world **cannot fail** to result in a more **caring**, **tolerant**, **just**, and **peaceful life** for all.

AUNG SAN SUU KYI, KEYNOTE ADDRESS TO THE NGO FORUM ON WOMEN, 1995

act, dress, and work to please their future husbands. Similar practices occurred in societies more than a millennium later, and even into the 20th century, upper-class girls in the West were sent to "finishing schools", where they learned deportment and skills that would help them to enter high society. These schools taught girls social graces, such as how to make polite conversation, and emphasized being "ladylike"; one example was the Institut Alpin Videmanette in Switzerland, where students – including Diana, Princess of Wales, in the 1970s – learned how to cook, ski, make dresses, and speak French.

Academic education

The 18th century saw a blossoming of institutions for girls that had academic curricula. New schools were often established by nuns or female rulers. The oldest girls' school in the United States, the Ursuline Academy in New Orleans, was founded by Sisters of the Order of Saint Ursuline in 1727, and in 1786, Queen Catherine the Great allowed girls to receive free primary and secondary education in Russia. In the West, women's participation in higher education dates back to the 11th century; women were permitted to study and teach at the University of Bologna, Italy, from its founding in 1088. In 1237, a woman called Bettisia Gozzadina earned her law degree there, and taught at the institution from 1239. Many universities, however, did not admit women. This problem persisted until the 19th century, when women's colleges were founded in the US and elsewhere. Mount Holyoke Female Seminary, founded in 1837, is the oldest women's college still operating for that purpose.

Today, the majority of schools and colleges are coeducational. Yet while studies suggest that girls do better in school than boys, at the highest levels of academia women are still outnumbered by men. Women in academia are also more likely than their male counterparts to be offered temporary or part-time positions, and to be given contracts with a heavy teaching load. On the other end of the spectrum, inequality at the most basic level also persists, especially in developing countries; today, two-thirds of the 750 million illiterate adults in the world are women.

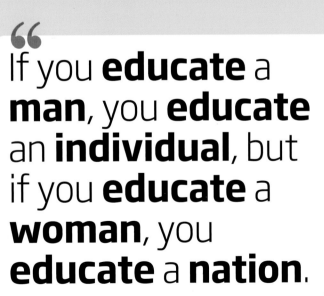

HOME SCHOOLING IN 18TH-CENTURY GERMANY

> If you **educate** a **man**, you **educate** an **individual**, but if you **educate** a **woman**, you **educate** a **nation**.

FANTI PROVERB, AFRICA

FREEDOMS IN
decline

JOSEON KOREA

When Neo-Confucian beliefs glorifying men and the first-born son were adopted in Korea and Japan (see pp. 124–125) it led to the widespread oppression of women. The Joseon Dynasty (1392–1910) was Korea's longest-ruling Confucian dynasty, and the era when Neo-Confucianism was established as state and social ideology. Yet, despite increasing patriarchy, the dynasty was also a period of cultural development that produced female intellectuals, poets, and heroes.

Korean women had enjoyed considerably more liberty and influence during the preceding Goryeo Dynasty. The advent of the Joseon Dynasty and the ideological and legal changes it brought greatly affected women's lives. When a woman married, she no longer remained at her natal home as women had done previously, but went to live with her husband's family, who received a dowry. This meant that having girls was expensive – for this reason, a daughter was called a *todungnyo*, or robber woman. To save a woman's share of inheritance from being given over to in-laws, it was reduced or removed entirely and male family members came to inherit most of a family's wealth.

◀ **Palanquin to patriarchy**
Due to Confucian ideas about modest, women travelled by palanquin and wore headdresses when they left their homes to hide their faces from passersby.

Maintaining her chastity became a woman's greatest responsibility to the extent that women were customarily given a *p'aedo* or suicide knife, and expected to use it if their family's honour became compromised. Royal and noblewomen were not exempt from these strictures. When the 15th-century Joseon king Seongjong discovered his cousin, the widowed princess Yi Guji, had been cohabiting with a slave after her husband's death, she was ordered to kill herself.

Almost nameless

Later in the 15th century, the Joseon king Yeonsangun took thousands of women from the provinces to serve as palace entertainers, called *gisaeng*. Although they were technically slaves, and provided sexual services, the *gisaeng* had more freedom than most women. They had no family constraints, could converse with men, and were schooled in literature, the arts, and polite conversation, as well as medicine and acupuncture. Most of the real names of *gisaeng* have been forgotten and indeed, by the end of the Joseon period, women in general were almost nameless. They were invariably referred to by their husband's or children's names, as "such-and-such's wife" or "such-and-such's mother."

◀ **Palace women in power**
This silk painting from the Joseon period depicts the court women or *gungnyeo*. They were royal slaves and, if favoured by the king, could achieve rank and even wield some political power.

BIOGRAPHY
HWANG JIN-YI

Born around 1506, renowned entertainer Hwang Jin-Yi is one of Korea's most famous *gisaeng*. Celebrated for her outstanding beauty, intellect, wit, and strong character, she composed verse and wrote music for the zither. Her poetry comments on the beauty of the landscapes she encountered, and her own lost loves. She continues to inspire writers and filmmakers today, with popular and award-winning literature, film, and television shows telling her story.

◀ **Dressed for work**
As entertainers, *gisaeng* were expected to be beautiful and accomplished for their owners to show off to government officials and their guests. They are shown here getting ready.

CHIEFTAINS, QUEENS, AND
kinswomen

PRECOLONIAL AFRICA

BIOGRAPHY
QUEEN ELENI OF ETHIOPIA

Born in 1450, Queen Eleni was among the many African women who played key political roles during the precolonial period. From the Muslim state of Dawaro, she converted to Christianity after her marriage to the Christian king, Zara Yaqob. After he died in 1468, she became regent queen to three successive young kings, including her son Na'od. She possessed exceptional diplomatic skills, and maintained good relations with neighbouring Muslim empires via intermarriages and peaceful negotiations.

The women of precolonial African kingdoms commanded great respect. They had roles as queen mothers and queen sisters, princesses, chiefs, and other high-ranking positions in villages and towns, and as warriors and healers. Women were also visible in the economic life of their societies, in areas such as farming, trade, and crafts.

Kinship and power

Societies were based around familial lines and kinship groups. African women had particular responsibilities towards their kinsmen and kinswomen; they offered assistance to their close relatives and performed important rites, such as ceremonies, marriages, and funerals. Within the kinship family, women could occupy various roles – not only as mothers and daughters but also wives and cowives in polygamous marriages. In matrilineages (where bloodlines are traced through the mother), women held formal leadership positions. They generally did not have such key roles in patrilineages (in which lineage is traced through the father), but the more advanced in age women became, the greater their influence was. In both patrilineages and matrilineages, seniority was determined by order of birth rather than gender, so older sisters outranked younger brothers.

Precolonial Africa was notable for the presence of women in key positions in formal governmental structures, as well as for its parallel chieftaincies, which comprised one line of males and another of females. In the West African Yoruba political culture, the Alafin's council (judiciary body) included the *Iyalode*, a female representative who was responsible for women's issues. In 19th century Sierra Leone, women could be the heads of towns and subregions.

Queen Amina of Zazzau commanded an army of
20,000
Hausa warriors

◄ **Mother of the kingdom**
This is a Nigerian sculpture
memorial of a queen mother.
Such cast-brass heads were used
to decorate altars dedicated to
these influential women.

Women often created
their own organizations
that served them in
public and private spheres.
In Owan, Nigeria, they
formed *idegbe* groups (for
married and unmarried daughters)
and *ikposafen* (for wives of the family and
married women) of a particular lineage.

Women of precolonial Africa also fought
in armies. Among the Sotho of South Africa,
daughters of subrulers often joined women's
regiments, and the Amazons of Dahomey
(see left) were famed warriors. Women led
conquests and migrations to new territories
for their people, too. For example, in the 16th
century, Queen Amina of Zazzau (see pp. 36–
37) conquered North African lands to bring
the Hausa kingdom to the height of its power.

Since land was mainly community owned,
no single individual had rights over it. In
certain regions of Africa, such as Ghana, land
came with clans, and marriage played an
important role in keeping land within them.
Because of this, families encouraged unions
within the kinship group. Land was mainly
cultivated by women; consequently, women
were essential to land development. The
Bambara women of West Africa, for example,
controlled certain forest products and had
customary rights to the land. Since most
African states were agrarian and because
women played such a large role in food
production and processing, they were
considered to be crucial players in the
development of African economies.

◄ **Warriors of Dahomey**
The Amazons were an all-female military
regiment of the kingdom of Dahomey, now
Benin, which lasted until the end of the 19th
century. Pictured here in 1897, they were the
only female combat troops at the time.

"My body, clean and whole, never ... corrupted ... **today must be ... burnt to ashes**!"

JOAN OF ARC, AS QUOTED BY JEAN TOUTMOUILLE AT HER POSTHUMOUS RETRIAL, 1449

HEROINE OF WAR

Born in 1412 to a peasant family in Domrémy, France, Joan of Arc believed she had been chosen by God to defeat the English in the protracted Hundred Years' War. Acting on this divine guidance, she led the French to victory against the English at Orléans in 1429. However, two years later Joan was captured in Compiègne and burned at the stake by the English. They accused her of sorcery, which constituted a charge of heresy. Despite her short life, Joan's bravery later inspired many artistic works, such as Hermann Anton Stilke's 1843 oil painting of her in battle (right). Joan became a symbol of France and was canonized as a Roman Catholic saint in 1920.

LA GRAN
Nusta Mama
Occollo. de dico en
Birginidad al Sol. quise
biolar sus botos un Indio Noble
deszendiente de Manco Capac
y como fue degollado por mis
proprias manos y fue la
primero Christiana

SUN WORSHIP AND
sacrifice

INCAS AND AZTECS

Both Inca and Aztec societies were known for practicing human ritual sacrifice in the 15th and early 16th centuries. The Inca Empire ruled much of western South America, while the Aztec Empire was the most powerful force in present-day Mexico. Both worshiped sun gods, and women played significant roles as priestesses of their religions. Indeed, the Inca high priestess, the Coya Pasca, was believed to be Inti the sun god's earthly consort.

Aztec priestesses, *cihuatlamacazqui*, were celibate, and were responsible for decorating the temples and making preparations for rituals. In the Inca religion, *Aclla* ("chosen women") played a similar role. *Aclla* were selected aged 8-10 and sent to schools called *acclahuasi* to learn to make textiles and *chicha* (alcohol used in rituals). They took vows of chastity, tended sacred fires, and prepared food for ceremonies. After their service ended, a select few became *mamaconas*, known by the Spanish as "Virgins of the Sun". *Mamaconas* never married, but worked at temples and trained girls to be "chosen women". Former *aclla* were given as wives to nobles to cement alliances, or were ritually sacrificed. "The Maiden", a frozen mummy found in Argentina, was thought to have been an *aclla*. She had been left at the top of a volcano to die at the age of 13, and studies of her body suggest that she had been sedated over time with *chicha* and cocoa.

Entering womanhood

Women's roles in Inca households were not dissimilar to their roles in temples. They were in charge of preparing meals, cleaning, making clothing, collecting fuel, and

◄ **Aclla figurine**
The "Chosen Women" were poor Inca girls who lived and served at the temples. They were chosen based on their talents and attractiveness, then spent about six or seven years unable to leave the temple.

childcare. Gender roles were also clearly defined in Aztec society; when a girl was born, a midwife placed a miniature distaff, spindle, staff, or broom in her hand. This was then buried with the umbilical cord under a metate (a stone for grinding corn) to symbolize a woman's household duties.

In Inca society, a girl became a woman at her first menstruation. She was house-bound for three days, then her relatives assembled and the girl was sent out to serve them food and drink. She got her first haircut, received gifts, and was given a permanent name by her most senior uncle. Inca women typically married between the ages of 16 and 20. The ceremony was simple: the groom and his family travelled to the bride's house and placed a sandal on her foot – made of wool if she was a virgin and grass if she was not.

While the Inca did not expect all women to stay chaste, the Aztecs believed that pre-marital sex was dangerous and led to diseases. Aztec girls married at around 15, and had an elaborate ceremony in which they were decorated with feathers and bright colours. A bride spent four days in a bedchamber with her husband, emerging to make offerings at the family altar, before they finally consummated the marriage.

◄ **Brutal punishment**
This Spanish colonial portrait of an Inca princess likens her to Mama Occollo, the first queen of the Inca dynasty, who allegedly beheaded all men who attempted to violate her sacred vow of chastity.

The largest acclahuasi housed

1,500

chosen girls

Crime

Cast in their role as nurturers, women are depicted as far less likely to commit the most serious of crimes. Female offenders have often been harshly punished, not only for the crimes they commit but for the unwritten social codes that they break.

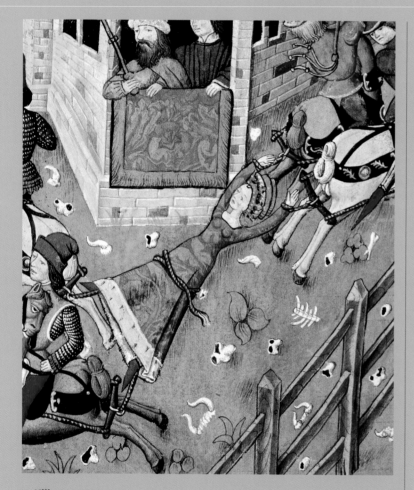

▲ Killer queen
Brunhilda, Queen of Austrasia (a 6th-century European kingdom), was put to death because of her feud with Fredegund, the murderous Queen of Soissons. The queen's son later had Brunhilda executed by being pulled apart by four horses.

WITH THE EXCEPTION OF prostitution, women have lower arrest rates than men for virtually all categories of crime. Between 1750 and 1815 in Europe, the majority of crimes committed by women – solicitation, robbery, and theft – were linked to their need for money, food, or resources. In the Victorian era, women were harshly punished: Emily Brennan, for example, twice received seven years of penal servitude for shoplifting.

The ultimate crimes

Female murderers have a distinct role in criminal history because many societies see killing as against women's supposedly innate nurturing nature. Consequently, when women have committed murder, they have been more severely condemned than men. Like men, women have killed for various reasons: some "black widows" married and then killed a

> " I have **no remorse** ... I **ain't killed** nobody. I never **took anything** I **regretted**. "

DORIS PAYNE, AMERICAN JEWEL THIEF, 2015

string of husbands, such as Belle Gunness and Ottilie Klimek; others, such as Japanese midwife Miyuki Ishikawa, took in babies from struggling mothers for a fee, then murdered them rather than take them to a new home as promised. Murders by women have most often taken place in their capacity as caregivers – to children and the elderly – or to lovers (or rapists) as "crimes of passion," with motives from jealousy to self-defence. Unusually, in the 1930s the notorious Ma Barker, supported the Barker-Karpis gang, a murderous band of bank robbers led by her four sons that operated across the US.

Since the 1980s, historians have highlighted the gendered nature of crime, with some acts designated as "male" or "female," and punishments divided along gender lines: women, for example, received the most convictions for witchcraft (see pp. 120–121), whether or not they were guilty. The means by which women have killed have differed from those of men. From the 1st-century Roman Locusta to the "Lonely Hearts Killer" Nannie Doss in the 20th century, women often used poison, a silent weapon that is easy to slip into food while it is being prepared. Others have used more "male" methods of brute force – such as Juana Barraza, who was imprisoned in 2008 for bludgeoning or strangling to death between 42 and 48 elderly women.

Historically, some women only committed crimes with a male accomplice. American outlaw Bonnie Parker was tempted into a (much-romanticized) life of robbery and murder when she met Clyde Barrow in the 1920s. Later, in the 1960s, notorious female killer Myra Hindley was imprisoned for her part in the abduction, torture, and killing of children on the British Moors. Hindley blamed her actions on her "abusive" partner Ian Brady; however, while she might not have killed without Brady's influence, she was an active participant in the murders.

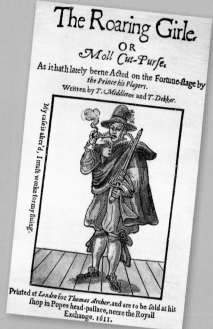

▲ The roaring girl
Mary Frith, known as "Moll Cut-Purse," was a pickpocket and fence operating in London at the turn of the 17th century. She was cross-dresser who wore men's clothes, and also a bawdy entertainer, both of which helped her to distract her targets.

BONNIE PARKER AMERICAN ROBBER, 1934

VILLAINS AND MURDERESSES

Lucrezia Borgia (1480-1519) was the daughter of Pope Alexander VI and was born into a fiercely ambitious family. Depicted by her enemies as a seductress who poisoned to achieve her ends, she was also accused of incestuous relations with her brother, Cesare. Her two arranged marriages ended badly for the grooms (the first in annulment, the second in death by murder), but it is questionable whether she was involved except as a pawn.

Elizabeth Báthory (1560-1614) was called the "blood countess" because she tortured and killed hundreds of girls at her castle of Čachtice, Hungary. She started with servants and peasants' daughters - supposedly bathing in their blood to stay beautiful - but was caught after she started killing the daughters of the lesser gentry, sent to her to learn etiquette. She was convicted of 80 murders in 1611 and held in solitary confinement until her death.

Amelia Dyer (1837-1896) may have been the most prolific serial killer in British history. A baby farmer (who accepted custody of a child in exchange for payment), she is said to have murdered 200-400 infants in her care over a 20-year period. She killed the children she was paid to look after, substituting the dead child with newer charges if the mother wished to see them, frequently moving premises. She plead guilty to murder and was hanged.

Aileen Wuornos (1956-2002) was sexually abused as a child and was a prostitute at the age of 14. She worked on Florida's Interstate 75, picking up clients on highways and in motels. She killed seven men between 1989 and 1990 by shooting them at point blank range, and became America's most prolific female serial killer. At trial, Wuornos claimed all of the killings were in self-defence as the men were trying to rape her. She was executed by lethal injection in 2002.

Griselda Blanco (1943-2012) was a Colombian drug lord, who was often referred to as the "Cocaine Godmother." She was a key figure in the drug wars that took place in Miami, Florida, in the 1970s and 1980s. She became known for ordering the executions of her enemies in drive-by shootings from motorcyles, but was assassinated by her own method in 2012, after her supposed retirement.

A STRUGGLE FOR THE
English Crown

THE WARS OF THE ROSES

From 1455–1485, two rival branches of the Plantagenet dynasty battled for the throne of England. Many noble women participated in the political intrigues and negotiations behind the scenes of a series of battles known as the Wars of the Roses. The warring factions were allied to the descendants of two sons of Edward III: the Dukes of Lancaster and York.

For more than a decade the leader of the Lancastrian faction was Margaret of Anjou, who Shakespeare famously called the "She-Wolf of France." Margaret married Henry VI of England in 1445, but Henry's mental instability soon created a power vacuum. She stepped into it; with Henry incapacitated, she fought fearlessly to secure his kingship and the succession of their son, Edward of Westminster. Their cause, however, was dealt a severe blow when Edward died in battle in 1471. Henry was executed, and Margaret was captured and exiled to France.

Peace through marriage

The majority of records from the Wars of the Roses that pertain to women are about noble women and the gentry. During this period, women's lives were determined by not only their social status, but by their allegiances, and they succeeded by cultivating relationships with those who were more wealthy and influential. Women were expected to marry in their early 20s and produce children to inherit their husbands' estates, but as many as 20 per cent died in childbirth. During the period of civil war, women also dealt with the vulnerability of a changing political landscape, struggling to keep royal favour as the faction they supported came in and out of power.

Marriages among the nobility at this time were important alliances, formed for ambition rather than for affection. Many of the noble women became embroiled in the wars to secure their legacy, putting their sons and daughters on the throne or in advantageous positions to ensure the family's continuing success. Elizabeth Woodville (wife of the Yorkist King Edward IV) was widely disliked for her Lancastrian family and nepotism, and remained a dominant force in court politics even after her husband's death. When the wars finally ended – with the Lancastrian Henry Tudor defeating Richard III in battle in 1485 – Woodville's influence continued. She secured the marriage of her daughter, Elizabeth of York, to the new king Henry VII in a symbolic union of the two factions. Despite this, however, Woodville and her supporters continued to work against the crown to restore Yorkist control. She even worked alongside her sister-in-law, the Duchess Margaret of Burgundy, to send young pretenders (posing as her dead Yorkist sons) to claim her son-in-law's throne – with little success.

"**SHE** IS **KEPT IN SUBJECTION** BY THE **MOTHER** OF **THE KING**."

THE SUB-PRIOR OF SANTA CRUZ ON ELIZABETH OF YORK, TO FERDINAND AND ISABELLA OF SPAIN, 1498

BIOGRAPHY
ELIZABETH WOODVILLE

Elizabeth was the daughter of Sir Richard Woodville and Jacquetta of Luxembourg. Her first husband was a Lancastrian noble who died in battle in 1461. Elizabeth then married the Yorkist king Edward IV in secret in 1464. This marriage angered many Yorkists and some even accused her of practising witchcraft. After Henry VII married her daughter, she was given the title Queen Dowager, but was disgraced and sent to a convent for her treasonous behaviour.

◄ **French queen**
Henry VI's ineptitude facilitated Margaret of Anjou's rise to power, as she effectively ruled for him. Here, she is depicted receiving a betrothal gift.

WARRIORS, WIVES, AND
widowhood

THE SPANISH RECONQUISTA

During the early 8th century, Muslim Arabs invaded the Iberian Peninsula (Spain) from North Africa, establishing a territory called Al-Andalus. It became one of the most cosmopolitan and culturally advanced states in Europe, with freedom to practise their religions generally extended to Christians and Jews. Meanwhile, Christian kingdoms that survived in the north (mainly León, Castile, Navarre, Aragon, and Portugal) fought to regain control in a process that lasted nearly eight centuries: the Reconquista.

The near-constant warfare of the Reconquista made widowhood common. Women who wished to remarry faced particular challenges, such as being sure their husbands had actually died (given the difficulty of communication then, this was not always easy). Some states had heavy penalties for bigamy – a law introduced in the kingdom of Castile in 1241 stated that if a woman remarried while her first husband still lived, she and her new husband could both be sold into serfdom (tied to landowners as peasants).

By the 15th century, after years of fighting, most of the Iberian Peninsula was once again in Christian hands. The final surviving Muslim state was the Emirate of Granada, in what is now southern Spain. Queen Isabella I of Castile and her husband Ferdinand II of Aragon – joint rulers with equal powers – were determined to conquer it and bring all of Spain under Christian rule. In 1492, following a decade of hard fighting, Granada finally surrendered. The Reconquista laid the foundations for Spain to become Europe's most influential power in the 16th century, but the process was a long and bloody one, and left behind a legacy of religious intolerance and violence.

Fewer than
1%
of the people tried by the **Spanish Inquisition** were executed

The Inquisition

Isabella and Ferdinand initially agreed to grant freedom of religion to the Jews and Muslims who lived in Granada, but soon went back on their promise and demanded compulsory conversion to Catholicism. In March 1492, the monarchs put out an edict expelling all practising Jews, and in 1501, Muslims were ordered to convert or leave. Tens of thousands of people left Granada and resettled elsewhere in Europe, North Africa, and the Americas.

Just as they did in Castile and Aragon, Jews and Muslims who had converted – known as *conversos* and *moriscos*, respectively – still faced persecution, as Ferdinand and Isabella sent out Inquisitors to identify heretics. *Morisco* women were made to give up their traditional language and dress, and *converso* women were given special attention by the Holy Inquisitors, who suspected them of carrying on customs such as observing the Sabbath or making kosher food. Some were even thought to have washed holy water off their babies after baptism in order to de-Christianize them. Along with other suspected heretics, such women were put on trial and, if found guilty, were burned at the stake.

▼ *Converso* **woman**
During the Spanish Inquisition, the civil tribunals used different execution methods for false converts. A woman who truly converted to Catholicism after receiving her death sentence might be executed by garrote, (seen as a merciful death), rather than by burning.

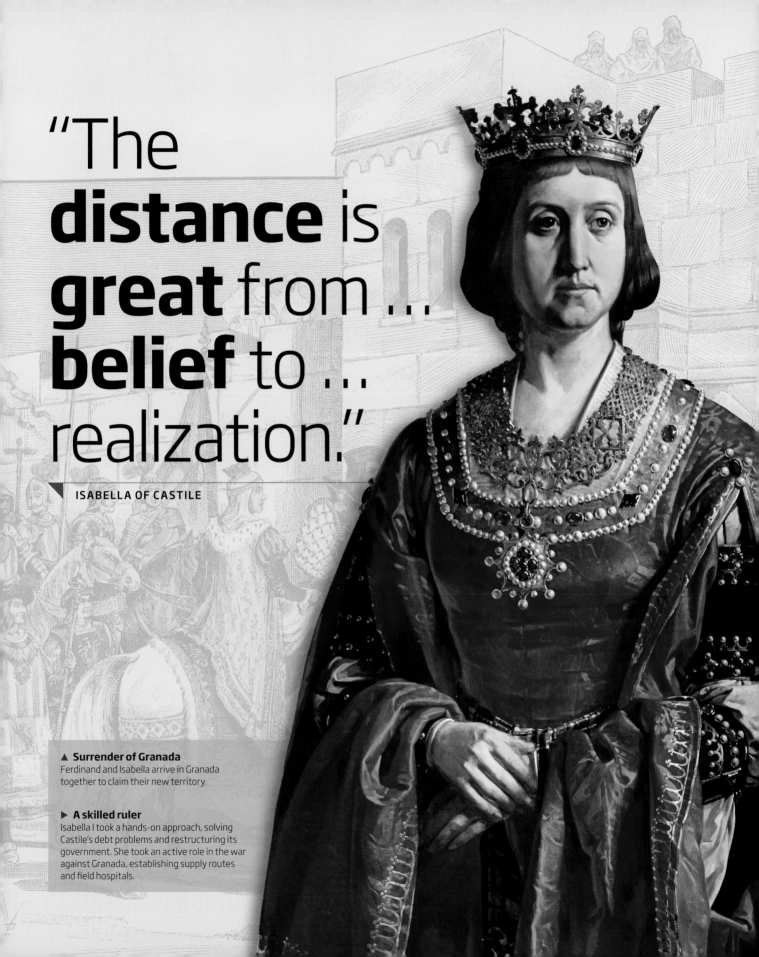

"The **distance** is **great** from … **belief** to … realization."

ISABELLA OF CASTILE

▲ **Surrender of Granada**
Ferdinand and Isabella arrive in Granada together to claim their new territory.

▶ **A skilled ruler**
Isabella I took a hands-on approach, solving Castile's debt problems and restructuring its government. She took an active role in the war against Granada, establishing supply routes and field hospitals.

From Empire to Enlightenment

1500–1800

The expansion of empires in the 16th century transformed the world. Trade routes developed, distant islands were connected by ships, and power shifted. Such changes challenged traditional values, and women's lives were increasingly bound up with the political and military battles of the time. Many women became powerful or influential figures. However, for every woman driving change, there were dozens more fighting for their basic rights in the newly forming classes of society. Local cultures and practices were constantly under threat, and many changes had a negative impact on women, imposing strict limitations on their lives.

CULTURAL
clashes

THE NEW WORLD

When the Europeans began to arrive in the Americas at the end of the 15th century, they brought new ideas that threatened traditional ways and challenged native gender roles within the diverse indigenous populations. Under attack were such things as matrilineal structures (where children belonged to their mother's clan, not their father's), which some Native American nations followed. These included the Choctaw, the Haida, the Hopi, the Navajo, and the Tlingit nations of North America, and the Carb and Kogi nations of South America. In some nations, such as the Haudenosaunee of New York, women had a

▶ **False narratives**
Europeans often depicted indigenous people as barbaric. This 16th-century woodcut showed native Brazilian men and women half-naked as they feasted on human flesh, exaggerating the difference between Old and New World beliefs.

▶ Folk tales

Storytelling was the realm of women in many indigenous tribes. Inuit women in western Alaska wore these masks on their fingers during dances, and used their hands to relay stories of the cosmos – represented by the mask's circle.

say in choosing the leader of their tribe, could divorce their husbands, and determine how many children they had. In the Cherokee nation, a Ghigau, or "war woman", sat in council meetings with war chiefs, while Blackfoot tribes had just as many female shamans as male.

The earliest clashes between European and Native American cultural practices revolved around agriculture. Many native people on the East Coast of North America considered farming to be women's work. Native American women planted and tended corn, clearing land, and moving when necessary to avoid depleting the soil. In Europe, however, farming was a man's job. The settlers paid little attention to native agricultural practices. As a result, many of the colonists did not survive the first winter because they had not adapted their farming methods to suit the American landscape.

Sexual contact

Differing sexual mores between Europeans and indigenous nations led to conflict. Many settler accounts describe Native American women as being sexually lascivious. Jesuit accounts condemned the Huron nation (in what is now Ontario, Canada), describing a healing ceremony in which a group of Huron women slept with the young men of the town in a group ceremony. However, some colonizers' descriptions of women as sexually aggressive were made simply to hide their own sins. When Spanish conquistador Hernán Cortés arrived at Mexico's Yucatán Peninsula, local leaders gave him women dressed in gold as gifts to breed with. Cortés and his men baptized these women, taking them as slaves and concubines. Calling them "horse-hair savages", the men refused to acknowledge *mestizo* (mixed-race) children born of such unions, and often abandoned these women when they returned to Spain.

BIOGRAPHY
MALLINALI

Born in Coatzacoalcos, central Mexico, in 1502, Mallinali was given to conquistador Hernán Cortés by a Mayan prince. Cortés saw her intelligence and took her as a translator, guide, and concubine in his conquest of Mexico (1519–1521). Her knowledge of Náhuatl and multiple Mayan dialects made her a big asset to the Spanish colonizers, and she was both vilified as a traitor to her people and seen as a victim, symbolizing all such unequal relationships between conquerors and natives.

▶ Subjects of curiosity

Explorers often made paintings and sketches of the native people they encountered. John White created this illustration during his time in Ossomocomuck, coastal South Carolina, depicting the wife of a chief with her daughter.

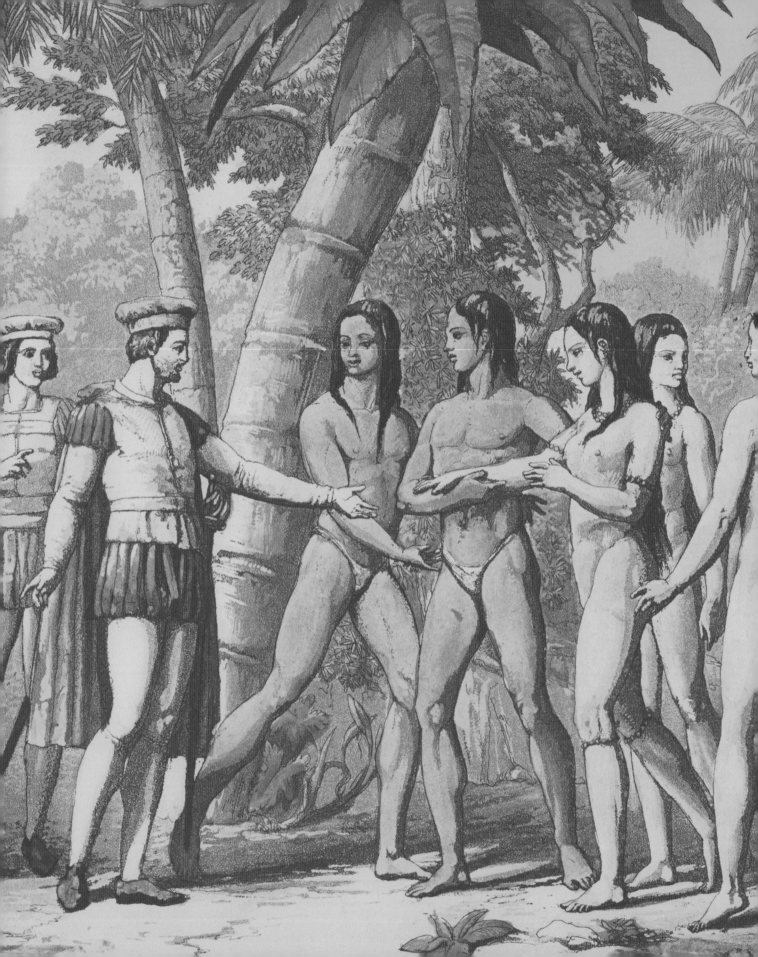

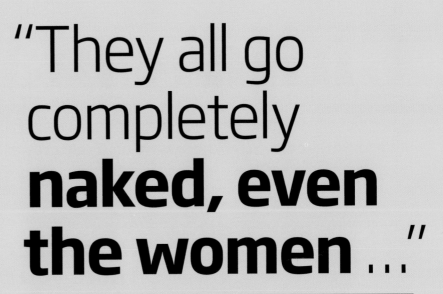

"They all go completely **naked, even the women** ..."

CHRISTOPHER COLUMBUS ON THE TAÍNO WOMEN OF SAN SALVADOR, 1492

THE CRIMES OF COLUMBUS

At the end of the 15th century, Ferdinand and Isabella of Spain (see pp. 94–95) commissioned explorer Christopher Columbus to sail west, in search of a new trade route to Asia. During his voyage, in 1492, Columbus landed in the Caribbean, laying the foundations for subsequent European exploration and colonization of the New World. Columbus's reports home falsely depicted the women he met on his travels – who, in truth, were not fully naked – as both promiscuous and naive; according to Columbus, this made them the perfect candidates to be Christianized and turned into servants. Columbus and his men treated the native women as little more than sexual objects. Accounts by his crew claimed that they were so overcome by desire for the women that they took them against their will, and also contained evidence that girls as young as nine or ten were sold into sexual slavery. The print (left) reflects the exaggerated fantasies of the colonists; it depicts the conquistador Hernán Cortés (see pp. 98–99) receiving a woman from the Tabasco Indians (in what is now Mexico).

EXPERIENCES OF MOTHERHOOD

Child's play

Motherhood has traditionally been portrayed as a woman's greatest role, often to the detriment of all other possible achievements. Even today, as most mothers work outside the home, mothers still tend to spend more of their time on childcare than fathers.

ALTHOUGH iconic mother figures have long featured in world mythology and popular culture, from Medea in ancient Greece to the Hindu mother god Kali, ancient laws recognized the father as head of the family. Bearing children is natural, but motherhood itself is a social construction that has been defined in various ways by societies over time. Most often women were assigned primary roles as wives and mothers but were still regarded as inferior beings.

Until the idea of the nuclear family – the basic social unit consisting of two parents and dependent children – became popular in the 15th century West, mothers were not expected to raise children alone. They had help from the extended family – grandmothers, aunts, or sisters; younger family members cared for siblings, too. For example, Enawenê-nawê Indians, in the Amazon rainforest, left infants to the care of ten-year-old children, with

> **Remember** that **nine months I bore you** in **my womb** … I **placed you** in your **cradle** … and with **my milk** I **nursed you**.

AN AZTEC MOTHER TO HER DAUGHTER, 16TH CENTURY

mothers returning from chores to breastfeed. Where extended families did not exist, they were created from the wider community. This practice continues today in southwest Siberia where "structural babushkas" invite young families to live with them. The older women provide childcare for the working parents, and in return are accorded a place in the family, and care in old age.

Feeding and nursing

If a mother was unable to breast-feed or died in childbirth, a wet-nurse, another nursing mother, was employed. The Qur'an stressed the importance of wet-nursing, and even today, under Islamic law one

> The **mother puts** a **breast** in the **child's mouth**, but not **sense** in its **head**.

FINNISH AND ESTONIAN PROVERB

◄ **Baby transport**
A Kootenai cradleboard made of wood, deer hide, glass beads, and conch shells. Portable baby carriers were important in allowing Native American mothers to work or travel.

CHILDMINDER WITH TWO CHILDREN, FRANCE, 1870

> " I looked on **child rearing** not only as a **work of love** and a **duty**, but as a **profession** as **interesting** and **challenging** as **any** ... in the **world**. "
>
> **ROSE KENNEDY**, POLITICAL FAMILY MATRIARCH, 1974

can be related by blood, family, or milk. From ancient times, some mothers fed their babies with "bottles." Devices included horns with leather teats and jugs with spouts, and rather than milk substitutes, mixtures such as wine and honey were fed to babies by the ancient Greeks.

However, until the discoveries of Louis Pasteur in the 19th century and new techniques to keep milk fresh for longer (pasteurization), bottle-feeding led to high infant mortality rates. The invention of infant formula in 1867 gave mothers another alternative to breast-feeding for the first year or two.

> " Deciding **not to** have **children** is a very, very **hard decision** for a **woman** to make ... we **call** these **women selfish**. "
>
> **CAITLIN MORAN**, *HOW TO BE A WOMAN*, 2011

In medieval Europe the upper classes outsourced child-rearing to wet nurses, nannies, and boarding schools, whereas the working classes often had a closer, nurturing experience with their offspring, who were often a necessity as future wage earners. Motherhood changed little up until the 18th century when enlightened ideas helped it become more highly valued, though women were still confined to family life in the home.

By the Victorian period, many Western societies began to reject wet-nursing, on anecdotal evidence that more infants died in a wet-nurse's care. With the rise of feminism in the 19th century, many women no longer wanted to be seen as just baby-making machines. However, until new contraception methods appeared in the 20th century (see pp. 278–279), they had limited control over reproduction. During World War II, with women in demand for factory jobs, nurseries sprang up in Britain, ensuring that mothers could work away from home.

The modern mother

During the 20th century, the increase in access to contraception and childcare, not to mention lower maternal mortality rates, meant that motherhood became a more positive choice for women in the West, rather than an expectation. The role of the mother has changed even more in the 21st century in terms of age, marital status, and sexual orientation. Nonetheless, women around the world still often find themselves caught between cultural expectations and the practical realities of mothering, such as arranging childcare and breast-feeding.

THE SULTANATE
of women

THE OTTOMAN EMPIRE

Women were influential in imperial Ottoman life. The mighty Ottoman Empire, founded in 1299 as a small principality in modern-day Turkey, endured for over 600 years, peaking in the 16th and 17th centuries, when it controlled most of the Middle East, North Africa, and Eastern Europe. The founder of the empire, Osman I, was succeeded by an unbroken chain of 36 direct descendants that reigned until 1922. Concubines – most of whom were slaves captured from Hungary, southern Russia, and the

Caucasus, as well as Africa and the Middle East – were central to this dynastic stability. Sons born to the sultan's concubines were regarded as legitimate and could succeed him.

The sultan's concubines, along with his wives and female relatives, lived in the imperial harem (women's quarters), secluded from the rest of his court. It was staffed and managed exclusively by women and eunuchs. The harem was not the

▶ **Western fantasy**
The idea of the harem fuelled the imaginations of Western artists, as in this stereotypical painting (c.1850) by British artist John Frederick Lewis.

◀ Turkish luxury
In this photograph from the end of the 19th century, a woman smokes a *nargile* (water pipe) – a pastime that emerged in Turkey in the 17th century as a status symbol among the elites.

place of unbridled passion that existed in the Western imagination. In reality, only a handful of sultans slept with multiple women, and European visitors observed that the harem shared similarities with a nunnery due to its strict hierarchy.

Power in the harem

Some women in the imperial harem became powerful political figures within the Ottoman court. This was most evident during the period known as the "Sultanate of Women", from around 1520 to the mid 17th century. Solomon Schweigger, a Catholic priest

30
of the Ottoman sultans were the sons of women from the harem

and translator of the Qur'an who travelled through Turkey in the 16th century, commented that "The Turks govern the world and their wives govern them." The sultan's favourite consort – the Haseki Sultan – was influential. The earliest recipient of this title was Hürrem (see right), who married Suleiman I the Magnificent – the first time a sultan took a concubine as his wife. Even more powerful was the mother of the reigning sultan. Known as the Valide Sultan, she was a custodian of power whose role was to guide her son, and act as regent for an underage sultan. One of these was Kösem Sultan, a slave concubine of Greek origin, who served as regent for her son Murad IV from 1623–1632 and from 1648–1651 for her grandson Mehmed IV.

Outside of the harem, women in Ottoman society also enjoyed independence and agency. Women were part of the waged labour force, often in the manufacture of textiles and clothing. Wealthy women could set up as money lenders or become silent business partners with a male merchant. Although legal, polygamy was rare in the Ottoman Empire by the 16th and 17th centuries. Divorce was common; a husband could divorce his wife without explanation, although he had to provide her with financial compensation. A wife could "purchase" a divorce by renouncing her claim to compensation. Although Ottoman men still had authority over women, the latter had rights (such as divorce) before women in other parts of Europe and Asia.

BIOGRAPHY
HÜRREM SULTAN

Born Aleksandra Lisovska in Ruthenia (modern Ukraine), in around 1520, Hürrem was kidnapped by Tatars and sold into the harem of Suleiman I. She converted to Islam and took the name Hürrem, but was also known as Roxelana. Hürrem became Suleiman's favourite concubine, and bore him five sons. In c.1533 they married, freeing Hürrem from slavery. Hürrem advised her husband and played an active role in state affairs. Her unprecedented rise led to rumours of witchcraft, but she remained influential at court until her death in 1558.

PROTESTANTS VERSUS
Catholics

THE REFORMATION

The Reformation of the 16th century was a revolutionary challenge to Catholicism, which led to the establishment of Protestant churches across Europe. The German theologian Martin Luther ignited the Reformation in 1517 with his Ninety-five Theses, which disputed many Catholic teachings. Luther had been a monk, and in 1525 married Katharina von Bora, a former nun who had become interested in reformist thought. While Protestantism was open to priests marrying, it still held a narrow view of women, who were confined to domestic roles. Von Bora managed Luther's extensive household, and became the role model of the supportive wife. Other Protestant priests followed Luther's example and also began to marry and start families, marking a clear contrast to the celibate Catholic clergy.

Another influential former nun was Elisabeth Cruciger, a poet who wrote some of the earliest Protestant hymns. However, the first known female Protestant writer

> **Between 1580 and 1675, Protestant Saxony saw 30% more schools for girls**

was a Bavarian noble, Argula von Grumbach, who published several pamphlets and letters that defended Luther and other reformers.

Catholic women also contributed to the Counter-Reformation – the intellectual response to Protestantism in the 16th century. Notable among them were Teresa of Avila, the Spanish religious reformer of the Carmelite order, and Angela Merici, who founded the Ursulines, one of the oldest Catholic teaching orders, in Italy in 1535.

Leading the reformation

Events in Europe helped spark an English Reformation, in which women played a central role, among them Anne Boleyn. Henry VIII instigated the Church of England's 1534 split from Rome so that he could divorce his first wife and marry Boleyn. She was interested in Luther's reformist stance and, due to her influence on the king and promotion of the vernacular Bible, Protestant thinkers gained prominence. Later, English queens also influenced religion. During Mary I's reign, hundreds of Protestants were burned for heresy, and these martyrs included over 50 women. When Mary died, her half-sister Elizabeth I came to the throne, overseeing a settlement that would permanently return England to the Protestant fold.

After the Reformation leader John Calvin settled in Geneva, Switzerland, the city became a centre of reform that also offered refuge to Protestant thinkers. One of these was Marie Dentière, a former abbess who left her convent to escape persecution, and moved to Geneva in 1528 after marrying a minister.

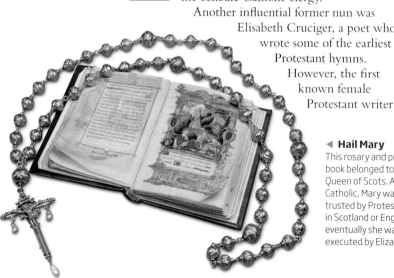

◀ **Hail Mary**
This rosary and prayer book belonged to Mary, Queen of Scots. As a Catholic, Mary was not trusted by Protestants in Scotland or England; eventually she was executed by Elizabeth I.

She argued that women should play an active role in religion. Dentière's is the only female name to appear on Geneva's Reformation Wall honouring the founders of Protestantism.

Despite such contributions, women were still marginalized from public roles in the Reformation. Luther and Calvin stated that a woman's place was to manage the household, and obey her husband and father. Women could not preach or act as ministers in most Protestant churches, although radical groups such as the Anabaptists had female preachers. In supporting the closure of nunneries, the Reformation removed some of the power women had held, as their abolition destroyed one of the few spaces in which women could be educated and have a degree of independence.

BIOGRAPHY
JEANNE D'ALBRET

The kingdom of Navarre on the Franco-Spanish border was ruled by Jeanne D'Albret from 1555–1572. Raised a Catholic and educated by humanist scholars, Jeanne announced her conversion to Protestantism in 1560. During the French Wars of Religion in 1562 Jeanne tried to remain neutral. However, she became leader of the Protestants, and in 1570 negotiated a truce that briefly ended the conflict. Jeanne died in 1572; it took until 1598 for her son Henry to bring the Wars to a close.

◀ **Nine-day queen**
Lady Jane Grey was proclaimed queen in 1553 in an attempt to secure a Protestant succession in England. Nine days later, Mary I claimed the throne and Jane was executed, at the age of just 16.

"I know I **have** the **body of** a **weak**, feeble **woman** but I **have** the **heart** and **stomach** of a **king**."

ELIZABETH I, AT TILBURY BEFORE THE ATTACK OF THE SPANISH ARMADA, 9 AUGUST 1588

RALLYING HER TROOPS

Elizabeth I ruled England from 1558–1603, her unmarried status leading to her nickname of the "Virgin Queen". Unlike Mary I, her predecessor, Elizabeth was a Protestant. Her persecution of Catholics led Mary's husband, Phillip II of Spain, to launch the Spanish Armada in July 1588, in the hope of overthrowing Elizabeth and restoring Catholicism to England. In August that year, the queen herself gave a rousing speech to her troops in which she promised to live or die along with her men. After a surprising English victory, Elizabeth's popularity rose, and *The Armada Portrait* (right) was painted to celebrate her success.

THROUGH THE AGES

The stage

Women's roles in the history of theatre have varied across cultures. Even when societies allowed women to tread the boards, most producers and writers tended to be men. Today, this inequality still persists.

▲ **Nara actress**
This figurine wears a replica of a costume worn by an actress from the musical theatre of the Japanese Nara Court (710–794 CE). The music performed at court was influenced by that of China's Tang Dynasty.

FEW OF THE GREATEST female roles of all time were written for women. Male actors, often young boys, played female roles from classical times, and iconic female parts – from Sophocles' Electra to Shakespeare's Lady Macbeth – were written for men. In Europe, the Church forbade women from appearing on stage until the Reformation, when papal authority was challenged. Women were finally allowed on stage in Spain in the 16th century, and early in the 17th century, Cervantes described a company of actors with a female lead in his novel *Don Quixote*. At the end of the 16th century, an actress named Marie Vernier starred in plays in France.

In England, playhouses were closed by the puritanical Oliver Cromwell after the Civil War of the 17th century and did not reopen until the restoration of the monarchy in 1660. Theatre-loving Charles II granted royal patents and women were invited to perform. The first English stage actress was Margaret Hughes, who in 1660 played Desdemona in Shakespeare's *Othello*. New "breeches" roles also enabled actresses to dress up as men. Female playwrights, too, found success at this time; Aphra Behn's first play, *The Forced Marriage,* premiered in 1670.

In Asia, it was very different. Female theatre groups are cited in Indian epics, the *Mahabharata* and *Ramayana*, and a treatise called the *Natyasastra* describes an all-female dramatic performance known as *lasyam*. There were no rules against female actors in the Sanskrit dramas at the end of the 7th century. Companies could be all male, all female, or mixed. When Islam started to spread eastward in the 10th and 11th centuries, however, the theatre was discouraged. In China, although

> " The **roles for women** in **theatre** are much **better** than they are in **film**. "
>
> **KIM CATTRALL**, ACTRESS, 2011

MARGARET HUGHES, ENGLISH ACTRESS, 1672

women performed in private theatre troupes during the Ming Dynasty (1368–1644), the status of actresses in imperial China was as low as that of prostitutes. Women became more visible as performers in Shanghai only in the 1850s, when theatres began to hire all-female groups, such as the *maoer xi* (Maoer opera troupe).

New roles

Since the 20th century, women have had more opportunities to write and produce their own plays. From the 1970s onwards, women have also worked together in collectives and all-female companies. Women have joined forces to stage feminist works and plays that focus on the female experience. One of the most notable feminist works was Eve Ensler's *The Vagina Monologues*, first performed in 1996, which she based on interviews with 200 women. Despite such initiatives, however, women today remain outnumbered two to one by men in most production and acting roles in Western theatre – while making up the majority in its audiences.

▲ **Black voices**
American feminist writer Ntozake Shange stars in her 1977 play, *For Colored Girls Who Have Considered Suicide/When the Rainbow Is Enuf.* The piece is made up of seven monologues by African American women, and emphasizes realistic speech patterns.

PROFILES
STARS OF THE STAGE

Hroswitha (935-1000) was a nun who spent most of her life in the Benedictine convent at Gandersheim, Lower Saxony. She wrote six comedies in Latin based on the works of Roman writer Terence. The rediscovery of her manuscripts around 1500 led to her recognition.

Peg Woffington (1714-1760) was an Irish actress who rose to fame at the age of ten in John Gay's *The Beggar's Opera* in Dublin. John Rich employed her at a salary of five guineas a week when she played Silvia in *The Recruiting Officer* at Covent Garden theatre in 1740, a role requiring her to appear in both petticoats and breeches. By 1745, she was earning an impressive £10 a week.

Sarah Bernhardt (1844-1923) was a French actress who became the first celebrity of her profession, performing in some of the most popular French plays of the 19th century. She was one of the first actresses to move from stage to screen, starring in silent films such as *Camille* (1911) and *The Loves of Queen Elizabeth* (1912).

Swanakumari Devi (1855-1932) was the first woman to write an Indian English drama. She was from the illustrious literary Tagore family of Bengal. Her play *The Wedding Tangle* (1904) deals with widowhood and remarriage. She also wrote novels, poems, essays, and even the first opera in Bengali, which addressed the position of women in Indian society.

Lorraine Hansberry (1930-1965) was the first African American woman to have a play produced on Broadway. Her play *A Raisin in the Sun* (1959) dealt with a family of black Americans living under racial segregation in Chicago. It was inspired by her own experience growing up on the South Side of Chicago.

Usha Ganguly (b.1945) is an Indian director who founded the Rangakarmee theatre group in 1976. She began directing in the 1980s, sparking a resurgence in Hindi theatre with works such as *Mahabhoj* (1984). Her play about discrimination against girls, *Beti Aayee*, was first performed with an all-female cast in 1996.

SPLENDOUR AND
seclusion

THE MUGHAL EMPIRE

The Mughal Empire (1526–1857) was synonymous with splendour, culture, power, and wealth. Its royal household held queens, mothers, and female elders in high regard, accommodating them in luxurious, female-only harems, or *zenanas*, along with concubines, servants, and slaves. Akbar I, the third Mughal emperor, reportedly had 5,000 women at his *zenana* in Fatehpur Sikri.

The *zenana* housed schools, playgrounds, bazaars, laundries, kitchens, and baths and was opulently decorated, furnished with verdant gardens, fountains, and pavilions. The lives of almost all its inhabitants revolved around the emperor – the greater a woman's proximity to the emperor, the greater her benefits and privileges.

Hierarchy of the harem

The *zenana* was very hierarchical. The *Padshah Begum*, or the Chief Queen, was the most senior figure. However, as the Mughal Empire allowed polygamy there could be more than one Chief Queen. The highest-ranking female officials, the *Mahaldars*, controlled the *zenana* and would often spy for the emperor; below them were the *Paristaran-é-hudur* (middle-ranking women); and lowest of all were the slaves who had entered the *zenana* as gifts or royal purchases.

The women were governed through strict rules of *purdah* – a Persian word meaning "curtain" that describes the practice of female seclusion – and were not free to wander outside the harem, which was guarded by *nazir,* or eunuchs. However, they were permitted to leave the *zenana* to accompany the emperor on hunting trips, excursions, or

◀ **Opulent riches**
Royal Mughal women were surrounded by treasures like this gem-encrusted box. One Mughal emperor was said to be wealthier than the emperors of France and Persia combined.

pilgrimages. Both the women of the *zenana* and the emperor himself were protected by *urdubegis*, women skilled in weapons and warfare.

Female education was confined to wealthy and royal families. Jahanara Begum, daughter of Shah Jahan and Mumtaz Mahal – for whom the Taj Mahal was built – headed the imperial harem from the age of 17, and patronized art and architecture. However, her brother, Emperor Aurangzeb, notably imprisoned his favourite daughter, Zeb-un-Nissa for daring to write poetry. She had been educated at court in mathematics, philosophy, and astronomy but her leanings towards poetry and music conflicted with her father's orthodoxy, and she spent the last 20 years of her life locked away in Salimgarh Fort in Delhi.

From far lowlier beginnings, Begum Sumru was a dancer in the Mughal court who went on to rule the principality of Sardhana at the age of 25, and to contribute to the arts, as well as trade, finance, and religion. She is famed for defending Emperor Shah Alam II against Sikh invasion in 1783, when she rode into battle on a stallion, despite being only 1.37m (4½ feet) tall.

▶ **Golden cage**
Although they lived a life surrounded by luxuries, women in the *zenana* were governed through strict and restrictive rules of *purdah*. This miniature painting depicts a Mughal court *zenana*.

▼ Age of the geisha
The Edo period gave rise to the geisha, an elite class of women providing companionship. The geisha system promoted independence and economic self-sufficiency for women.

CONFUCIAN
customs

EDO JAPAN

The military dictatorship that ruled Japan during the Edo period (1603–1868) based their ideology on neo-Confucianism, a philosophy which argued that women should be subservient to men. Attitudes were reflected in maxims designed to teach women moral principles. Educational texts such as the *Onna Daigaku* (Great Learning for Women) embodied the Confucian doctrine: "men superior, women inferior". However, women continued to hold responsibility within the household, and there were still some ways for them to exercise power.

Confucianism placed heavy emphasis on the importance of respect for one's elders and ancestors, an idea that became the pillar of a highly stratified society where patriarchal structures played a crucial role. Heads of household, or *ie*, were generally men. In the past it had been common for a husband to live with his wife's family, but wives began to live with their husbands' families instead. In the Edo period, bestowing property on a daughter meant sacrificing part of the family estate, and directly affected women's inheritance rights.

Buying pleasure

According to Confucian custom, romantic love in marriage was of little importance. Men, therefore, sought it from courtesans. In 17th-century Edo (now Tokyo), prostitution was rife and the government, therefore, established pleasure quarters to control the practice. These walled quarters, known as *yūkaku*, were also founded on the fringes of Kyoto and Osaka, and meant that women of pleasure, *yūjo,* were physically and legally separated from the rest of the city's female population. In contrast to the *yūjo*, the 1760s brought the rise of the geisha – by and large chaste, she entertained men with music, dance, and conversation. The *okiya* (the lodging house in which geisha live), and the *ochaya* (the teahouse where they work) were operated by women. These *okiya* looked after the geisha, and in return, her earnings went back into the house to pay for non-working geisha and other women in the household. Despite the patriarchal Edo society in which it existed, the world of the geisha itself was, at least theoretically, matriarchal.

▲ **Woman's kimono**
This garment would have been worn by the wife of a merchant. Before the Edo period, the kimono was mainly worn by samurais, but it was adopted by Edo merchants as they gained economic mobility.

◀ **Role reversal**
The restrictive Edo society forbade women from acting in kabuki theatre from 1629, so male performers began to play women on stage, as depicted in this print.

LIFE IN THE LAND OF
opportunity

COLONIAL AMERICA

The arrival of European settlers in North America changed the fortunes of the entire continent forever. In the late 15th and early 16th centuries, Europeans began to colonize the so-called "New World", sparing little thought for the people who already inhabited the Americas. Settlers went to America for a number of reasons – from the promise of land and money to the opportunity to be free from religious persecution. For European women, too, the building of the colonies allowed them a chance to be part of a new society, and to leave the old behind for what they perceived to be greener pastures.

Many Europeans were struck by the different roles that Native American women played in their societies (see. pp 98-99), compared to their own cultural norms. Among Eastern Woodland Indians in North America, who were among the first that British settlers encountered, women had defined gender roles and were in charge of rearing children and farming, while men hunted, fished, and conducted politics and

◀ **Chief's bride**
In native cultures, women played a more prominent role in society compared to their Western counterparts. In this 1591 engraving, a chief's new bride is carried to him in a ceremonial procession.

NEW BEGINNINGS

The colonization of the New World brought new opportunities for female settlers, but came at the expense of indigenous women, whose way of life came under attack.

1500

1503 Anacaona, a Taíno chief, is executed in Hispaniola when the Spanish massacre her people during a supposedly diplomatic visit.

1600

1608 Two female British colonists arrive in Jamestown, the first permanent English settlement in North America.

1613-1614 A year after she is captured by British settlers, Pocahontas is baptized as a Christian and marries John Rolfe.

1662 Virginia law makes slavery inherited upon the condition of mothers.

1663 King Louis XIV begins a programme to send about 800 *filles du roi*, or unmarried women, to New France to supplement the population of its Canadian colony.

1671 Awashonks, the female chief of the Sakonnet tribe in Seconet, Rhode Island, signs a peace agreement with Plymouth Colony and other Native American leaders.

1691 Virginia passes a law forbidding free white women from marrying non-whites, including Native American men.

1692 Hundreds of women are accused of witchcraft in Salem, Massachusetts, resulting in the execution of 14 women and 5 men.

1700

1756 Lydia Taft becomes the first woman to legally vote in colonial America at a town hall meeting in Uxbridge, Massachusetts.

1773 Phillis Wheatley publishes the anthology, *Poems on Various Subjects, Religious and Moral*, bringing her fame throughout the Atlantic World.

◀ **WOMEN ARRIVE IN JAMESTOWN** TO MARRY SETTLERS, AS DEPICTED BY WILLIAM LUDWELL SHEPPARD IN 1876.

diplomacy with other Native Americans and European settlers. Within many Native cultures, women played a prominent role in their communities and tribes as political and spiritual leaders. In addition, many families within native societies were structured along matrilineal lines, meaning that they traced heritage and tribe membership through their mothers. This was true for members of the Iroquois Confederation, in which women also held the power to select men for (or remove them from) the position of chief.

Colonial society

In the first English settlements in North America, men vastly outnumbered women. As the colonies were founded as economic ventures, colonial leaders often struggled to entice women to become settlers, and the imbalance led to much instability within the early years of settlement. Settlers also had to contend with local Native American tribes, many of whom were displeased at the permanence of the colonies and waged war against the settlements. One solution was the marriage of Pocahontas – daughter of the powerful Chief Powhatan – to English settler John Rolfe, which improved the relationship between early settlers and the Powhatan Indians. Pocahontas converted to Christianity, taking the name Rebecca after her baptism, and learned the language and customs to assimilate to English culture, earning her the name "Tamed Savage of the West".

BIOGRAPHY
SAINT KATERI

Born in c.1656 in present-day New York, Kateri Tekakwitha was the first Native American to be named a Catholic saint. A Mohawk woman raised by her uncle and the women of an Iroquoian longhouse, she was exposed to Christianity by French Jesuit missionaries. At 19, she converted to Catholicism and, in 1677, Kateri moved to a Christian Iroquois community in New France, where she took vows of chastity and self-mortification. Kateri died three years later, at 24, and was made a saint in 2012.

▲ **Mixed relations**
Some colonists had relationships with native women, resulting in children, as shown in this image of 18th-century Mexico. This led to laws forbidding the taking of non-white brides.

A decade after its founding in 1607, the first British colony – Jamestown, Virginia – was struggling. The first two women to arrive in the colony had been Mrs Forrest, a settler's wife, and her maid Anne Burras, who was to become the colony's first bride, in 1608. Yet the gender imbalance did not begin to tilt until the period from 1619 to 1621, when the Virginia company sent 150 women to the colonies as "maids to make wives". The company theorized that bringing women to marry the male settlers would make the settlements more permanent, as people would start families there, and the men would also be more satisfied and therefore work harder.

Some women also came to the colonies under contracts as indentured servants, exchanging a few years of work for passage to the New World, and food, clothes, and shelter during their service. In New England, where colonies were formed by religious separatists, many migrated and settled as families, which made for a more equal gender balance from the start.

The status and roles of women varied throughout colonial America, influenced by factors such as race, religion, and geography. The continued dominance of patriarchy was questioned and challenged by women like

"NOW HAVING **SEEN** … WHICH IS **INVISIBLE** I **FEAR NOT** WHAT **MAN CAN DO** UNTO ME."

ANNE HUTCHINSON'S TESTIMONY AT HER TRIAL, 1637

Anne Hutchinson – a Puritan who angered churchmen in the Massachusetts Bay Colony by preaching her own sermons. She was tried, convicted, and banished.

In Latin America, Spanish colonization was based on the Christianizing mission, and Catholicism was key to controlling the native peoples. Caste, gender, religion, and ethnicity were key determiners of a person's life and experiences. During the 16th and 17th centuries, the Spanish dismantled privileges previously enjoyed by indigenous women within their communities, such as owning land separately from their husbands, as part of their colonization efforts, and discouraged them from practicing traditional healing. Just as they did in North America, Christianization and the import of European culture conspired to lessen the authority of native women.

▼ **American princess?**
Pocahontas was first mentioned in the works of John Smith, who claimed that she saved him from her father. Many accounts of her life, however, were romanticized as she was made into an idyllic example of Indian assimilation.

"The Devil has my consent, **and goes and hurts them.**"

ABIGAIL HOBBS IN HER TESTIMONY, SEPTEMBER 1692

CONFESSING TO WITCHCRAFT

The Salem witch trials, a series of hearings for people accused of witchcraft (see pp. 122–123), took place in colonial Massachusetts between February 1692 and May 1693. While many of the women accused were innocent of any wrongdoing, prosecutors tortured or coerced them into confessing to practicing magic. Confession was one way in which accused women could delay their execution, as it led to them being questioned and asked to give up their companions. This was the case for teenager Abigail Hobbs, who admitted to giving her soul to the devil, taking part in the witches' sabbath, and killing her neighbours, but she also accused many others, including Salem's former minister George Burroughs. Her accusations led to a spate of trials, but Hobbs herself was granted a reprieve from execution in 1693 when the trials collapsed. Many depictions of the trials romanticized women who confessed–as in this example from 1892, showing a witch summoning powers to incapacitate her prosecutor.

Witchcraft

Although the idea of the witch is as old as humanity, it was first linked to gender during Europe's 15th-century Inquisition. By the 17th century, witch-hunting hysteria had peaked, and thousands of women had been unfairly persecuted and violently killed.

A VERSION OF WITCHCRAFT appears in most human cultures, and has usually been viewed with fear and suspicion. Accusations of its practice have mostly focused on women, particularly the aged and the poor. When medicine became the preserve of men, the "wise women" who administered traditional remedies to the poor were also targeted.

The powers ascribed to witches have varied over time and place. They were often thought to be able to fly and command demons, but other abilities assigned to them included using animals (called "familiars") to spy on and attack people, or turning into animals themselves. Witches were also thought to cause illness, impotence, and infertility, as well as make livestock fall sick or stop producing.

Persecutions

Between the mid-15th century and the end of the 18th century, by which time popular and learned opinion had become sceptical of the existence of witchcraft and witch hunts were nearly extinct, there were around 100,000 trials and 50,000 executions for witchcraft in Europe. About 80 per cent of the victims were women, and about half of the persecutions took place in German-speaking lands. Europe during this era was beset by near-constant warfare, religious controversy, and economic uncertainty. Such troubles contributed to an atmosphere in which people looked for a scapegoat for social ills, and trials notably peaked at times of recession. One case often created a chain-reaction of accusation — such as in Sweden from 1668–1676, where sorcery claims against a woman called Märet Jonsdotter spiralled into hysteria and resulted in around 280 executions. Overzealous officials led mass persecutions, too — as in England from 1644 to 1647, when Matthew Hopkins, the self-appointed "Witchfinder General", executed 300 women.

Paranoia about witches spread to the United States, helped by English Puritans who settled in New England. Such suspicion resulted in the Salem witch trials of 1692–1693, which began after a group of young girls, who had been telling fortunes, started to show signs of demonic possession and accused three women of bewitching them. The trials led to the execution of 14 women and five men.

> ## You're a **liar**! I **am no** more [a] **witch than you** are a **wizard**.
>
> **SARAH GOOD**, ONE OF THE FIRST VICTIMS OF THE SALEM TRIALS, 1692

▼ The Hammer of Witches
Witches were prosecuted based on treatises like the *Malleus Maleficarum* of 1486, which prescribed torture and encouraged execution. Such guides depicted witches as wanton women who consorted with demons.

▲ Ducking stool trial
Some women suspected of witchcraft were ducked into ponds and rivers to ascertain their guilt – if they swam, they were considered culpable.

Native Americans had their own ideas about witchcraft. It was believed that its practitioners could cause bad luck, and some communities thought witches could transform into or possess animals (called "skin-walkers" by the Navajo). Suspected witches, often older women, were captured and tortured before being warned, banished, or killed. Dislocation and disease caused by contact with western settlers increased accusation of witchcraft within indigenous communities.

Modern witches

Belief in witchcraft continues to exist in many places, especially in Africa, where tribal societies often make a distinction between "good" witch doctors and more malign witches, the latter being mostly women. While there has been sporadic persecution of witches in some African countries, the continent has never had a mass witch-hunt on the scale of those that occurred in Europe or the United States.

WITCH DOCTORS AT A HEALING SESSION IN UGANDA

PROFILES
ACCUSED WITCHES

Alice Kyteler (c.1263-1325) was a prosperous Irish woman who had been married four times. In 1324 she was accused of witchcraft by her stepchildren. The local bishop led an investigation against her, charging her with a range of offences: denying Christ, making offerings to demons, creating potions, and using sorcery to kill her late husbands. She fled the country to avoid execution.

Hwi-bin Kim (1410-1429) was the daughter of a senior Korean official, and in 1427 was chosen as consort for Munjong, the king's heir. Kim apparently used witchcraft to win Munjong's favour, as he was still interested in other women at court. She burned her rivals' shoes and tried to enchant Munjong by wearing a cloth covered with snake blood. When her actions were revealed, she was driven from court and relegated to the rank of commoner.

Merga Bien (d.1603) was from the German town of Fulda. In 1602, its ruler instituted a witch-hunt that led to the condemnation of over 200 people. Bien had been married to her third husband for 14 years but had only just become pregnant. She was accused of witchcraft as it was believed she had conceived through consorting with the Devil. Under torture she was forced to admit this, and to killing her second husband. Bien was then burned alive.

Catherine Monvoisin (c.1640-1680), known as "La Voison", was a French midwife, fortune-teller, and seller of aphrodisiacs. In Paris, she grew wealthy through telling the fortunes of the country's aristocrats, including the king's mistress. In 1679 she was accused of being at the centre of a poisoning and black magic ring; a year later she was burned at the stake for witchcraft.

Marie Laveau (c.1794/1801-1881) was born into a free black family in New Orleans. She was an acclaimed practitioner of voodoo, which was based on traditional beliefs brought to North America by enslaved Africans. Laveau sold lucky amulets called "gris-gris", performed enchantments, predicted the future, and even healed the sick. Due to her powers she became known as the "Voodoo Queen" of New Orleans.

LAND OF OBEDIENCES
and virtues

THE QING DYNASTY

▲ Status symbols
Most wives worked hard on domestic chores. Elite women of the Manchu court were an exception, and wore elaborate fingernail covers to show they did not partake in manual labour.

After the Tang Dynasty (618–907 CE), a golden age in China (see pp. 48-49), Chinese women experienced a setback in terms of freedoms and rights. Confucian ideology, which stressed the submission of women, became prevalent. According to the ideology, a virtuous woman was "she who hath no talent".

Moral lessons

By the time of the Qing Dynasty (1644–1912), women's virtue was directly linked to the well-being and authority of the state. The doctrine of the Three Obediences and Four Virtues (see pp. 80-81) developed in ancient China. Stressing patriarchal obedience and moral values, it formed the basis of female education from the age of around ten, when girls were segregated from their brothers. In line with the three obediences, girls were expected to obey their father, wives their husbands, and widows their sons. "Moral

1-1.5
million people worked in prostitution at the start of the Qing Dynasty

discipline, proper speech manner, modest appearance, and diligence" constituted the four virtues. Chastity for unmarried women was a central tenet of this doctrine and the foundation of a young girl's honour. Apart from these teachings, a girl's education consisted of lessons in household affairs, food and wine appreciation, deportment, and make-up. Women who possessed more than a basic level of literacy were often regarded with suspicion; literacy was traditionally associated with courtesans and learning was therefore seen as a corrupting influence.

The "cult of chastity" became a state-sponsored movement that ran from 1736 to 1795, honouring chastity martyrs with statues, memorial shrines, and canonization. This state valorization encouraged single women to kill themselves rather than lose their virginity, and, along with the practice of female infanticide, only

▶ Sensual pleasures
Qing China's complex relationship with sexuality was the result of Confucian puritanism, which began to trump the more libertine Daoist philosophy of the previous period. Erotic artworks, however, continued to be commissioned during the Qing era.

"VEHEMENT IN HER CHASTITY, [SHE] SACRIFICED HER LIFE."

QING MAGISTRATE RECOMMENDING THE CANONIZATION OF AGUAN, A CHASTITY MARTYR, 1752

exacerbated the dearth of available women for men to marry. Meanwhile, widows who remarried were viewed with disapproval by society, as a woman was expected to live a celibate life after her husband's death. Many widows instead of remarrying or remaining celibate also chose to commit suicide. Qing emperors tried to ban the practice but were unsuccessful, and so settled for enforcing more stringent rules on who could be martyred.

In the late 19th and early 20th centuries, towards the end of the Qing dynasty, the intellectual classes began to challenge the traditional Confucian view of women and to demand female education. The writer and philosopher Liang Qichao championed the establishment of girls' schools, albeit arguing that a better education would make girls better wives and mothers, and therefore be of benefit to the whole of Chinese society.

▼ "Go" girls
The Qing view of virtue was not limited to sexual behaviour. The ancient strategy game weiqi was seen by some as a way to avoid gluttony and idleness, so was an approved pastime for Qing women.

"Put your hands to work **and give your hearts to God**."

MOTHER ANN LEE, FOUNDER OF THE SHAKER MOVEMENT,
AS QUOTED BY CHARLES NORDHOFF, 1875

THE SHAKER MOVEMENT

The Shakers (a name given to the United Society of Believers in Christ's Second Appearing due to their euphoric practices of worship) are a Protestant sect that was brought to the US in the 18th century by British immigrant Mother Ann Lee. She formed the first congregation in Albany, New York, in the 1770s, and the movement flourished into the mid-19th century before it began to decline. The sect lived a communal life, and emphasized hard work, simple living, and celibacy. Shaker communities also believed in duality – that God was both male and female – and their doctrine therefore promoted the equality of the sexes. Shaker men and women engaged in set dances (one depicted right, in an 1870's woodcut) such as the "Square Order Shuffle" and the "Quick Step Manner" in order to receive the "gift"– prophetic powers or the ability to heal diseases.

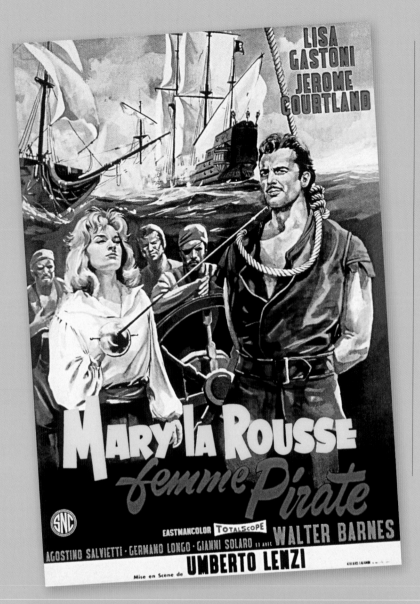

PIRATES ARE SEAFARERS who take goods, ships, or people with violence, and then usually share their spoils within a male-led collective. Since piracy relies on seafaring and combat – traditionally skills that women were excluded from – female pirates have been rare. In the past, there was great resistance to women being allowed on ships at all as they were seen as unlucky and a distraction for male crews. Although occasionally a few women were accepted on the seas as the captain's wife or widow, many female buccaneers cross-dressed as men to gain admittance to a pirate crew.

Historically, the term "pirate" when used in relation to women often described a tough female associated with any bloody, sea-related adventures. For example, Artemisia (see right), the 5th-century BCE

> " No warlike chief or Viking … had bolder heart than she. "
>
> SONG OF GRACE O'MALLEY, 1798

◀ **Pillaging the high seas**
A 1961 movie poster for *Mary La Rousse, Femme Pirate (Queen of the Seas)* about the cross-dressing English pirate, Mary (Mark) Read, who was convicted of piracy in the early 18th century.

THROUGH THE AGES

Piracy

There have been few female pirates, but those that have lived as ruthless, sometimes cross-dressing, buccaneers are surrounded by myths. Popularly regarded as liberated, transgressive heroines, today they are more likely to be based in an office.

queen of Halicarnassus (modern-day Turkey), commanded five ships during the second Persian invasion of Greece. Medieval female pirates of any form were rare, and mostly Scandinavian, including the Danish queen Alfhild. Norse sagas refer to female longship captains such as Hetha, who became queen of Zeeland in the 8th century. She was one of several maritime heroines with "bodies of women and souls of men", who were cast by male writers as acceptably loyal rather than outsiders.

Renowned pirate Grace O'Malley (see right) assumed leadership of a 16th-century seafaring dynasty in west Ireland after her father died. Previously he had refused to allow her to accompany him on an expedition because her long hair could get caught in the ship's ropes, so she had cut off all her hair (earning the nickname Granuaile, meaning cropped hair).

The "Golden Age" of piracy (1650–1726) featured around eight known women pirates. Most were British or American – all were white. Operating in the Caribbean and off America's east coast, they heisted lucrative cargoes during piracy outbursts against Britain, France, and Spain. Anne Bonny and Mary Read achieved the greatest notoriety thanks to the romanticized bestseller *A General History of the Pyrates* (1724).

Modern piracy

In the late 19th and early 20th centuries, Chinese women pirates came to the fore. At least two rose from poverty to command large fleets of junks after their husbands died. Female and male pirates alike were hard-hearted towards captives – Lo Hon-Cho's 64 junks captured young women then sold them as sex slaves in the 1920s. Today, women are mostly involved in piracy from land, away from the Somali-dominated business at sea. Office-based, these women pass on intelligence about cargo ships, fence goods, and process ransom emails.

▲ **Marauder queen**
A picture of the 18th-century Irish American pirate Anne Bonny, who joined the crew of "Calico Jack" Rackham in the Caribbean. She did not disguise her gender from her shipmates but dressed as a male when pillaging.

CHING SHIH 19TH-CENTURY CANTONESE PIRATE

PROFILES
NOTABLE WOMEN PIRATES

Artemisia (c. 480 BCE) is often regarded as the first woman pirate. As a widow, this Greek Queen of the ancient city-state of Halicarnassus led five ships in the Greco-Persian wars. Her daring manoeuvres led her ally, Persian king Xerxes I, to praise her courage and declare she was made of the substance of a man.

Jeanne de Clisson (1300–1359), the daughter of a French nobleman, led a fleet against the merchant vessels of King Philip VI of France to avenge her husband's execution. Known as the Lioness of Brittany, she attacked French ships in the English Channel, raided French villages, and carried supplies for the English army.

Sayyida al Hurra (1485–1561) was a 16th-century Moroccan queen who turned to piracy/privateering against Christian enemies to avenge the ousting of her Muslim family from Granada. The acknowledged leader of piracy in the western Mediterranean - but seemingly not seagoing - she was well-respected for her capabilities.

Grace O'Malley (c.1530–c.1603) was known as the Pirate Queen of Ireland. The chieftain of a wealthy Irish clan, she plundered at land and sea over four decades of privateering (licensed piracy), sailing as far as Portugal. She never hid her gender, wearing dresses and even giving birth at sea. After she promised Queen Elizabeth I she would reform her ways, her son was made a viscount.

Mary Read (c.1690–c.1720) dressed as a boy from a very young age in order to wangle payments from her dead father's family, join armies, and live as a man. In her twenties she became a privateer, then a pirate, under Captain "Calico Jack" Rackham. She and her shipmate Anne Bonny sailed for about two years. When captured, they evaded execution by claiming they were pregnant. Mary died in prison from illness or in childbirth in 1721.

Ching Shih (1775–1844) was a former Canton sex worker in Qing China who married pirate Cheng I, leader of the Red Flag Fleet, and sailed with him in the South China Seas. When he died in 1807 she assumed leadership and commanded 70,000 men and 400 junks (traditional Chinese sailing ships). She negotiated an amnesty with the Chinese authorities and later ran a gambling house.

THE FIGHT
for liberty

The period between 1775–1848 in Europe and the Americas is often called the "Age of Revolution" by historians. During these tumultuous years, many nations experienced social and political movements that led to major domestic conflict; other nations were dragged into international warfare. The two most famous revolutions occurred in North America and in France, both inspired by the Enlightenment – an ideological movement that promoted liberty and freedom. Caught up in the revolutionary atmosphere, many women saw the changing times as a chance to better the lives of their sex.

Fighting for freedom

Early revolutionary efforts in North America relied on the cooperation of women, especially for the boycott of British goods. For example, in 1774, the women of Edenton, North Carolina, refused to buy British products until its Parliament repealed the punitive legislation that restricted trade by the colonists. Once armed hostilities began to rage between the Patriots and Loyalists, women also joined the military effort in a variety of capacities. Some became camp followers, travelling with the armies as wives, laundry women, or prostitutes; others carried messages. Famously, in 1777, a 16-year-old girl called Sybil Ludington rode 65 km (40 miles) to warn the colonists about an imminent British raid on Danbury, Connecticut. In South Carolina,

◀ **Lady Liberty**
This banner of Lady Liberty was likely made by women to carry at a Philadelphia public parade in the 1790s. Her liberty pole and Phrygian cap are both symbols of revolution.

FREEDOM FIGHTERS

Revolution was not just a man's business; women were eager participants. However, the sweeping societal changes many women hoped for never came.

1700

1774 The American revolution begins; women come together to boycott British goods.

1775 Lord Dunmore's Proclamation offers freedom to slaves who flee their masters to join the Loyalist (British) cause; one third of the people who respond are women.

1776 Abigail Adams writes to her husband, a member of the Continental Congress, to ask that they "remember the ladies" when drafting new law codes for the Thirteen Colonies.

1783 The American Revolution ends; many Loyalist women leave the US to begin new lives in Canada or Great Britain.

1789 The French Revolution begins; women march on the Palace of Versailles in October.

1791 Olympe de Gouges publishes her *Declaration of the Rights of Women and of the Female Citizen*.

1792 British writer Mary Wollstonecraft publishes *A Vindication of the Rights of Woman: With Strictures on Political and Moral Subjects*. Sisters Félicité and Théophile Fernig enlist in the French revolutionary army as men.

1793 The "Reign of Terror" begins in France; Queen Marie Antoinette is executed, as are several moderately republican women.

1797 State law gives women in New Jersey the right to vote.

1800

1813 The Serbian uprising fails; the victorious Ottomans enslave many women and children.

1848 Women take part in the revolutions that sweep across Europe and South America.

◀ **MOLLY PITCHER**, A REVOLUTIONARY US HEROINE, FIGHTS AT MONMOUTH IN 1778.

▶ **Rallying cry**
Women and men marched together to the Bastille on July 14, 1789. The fall of the prison signified the toppling of the king's authority and the beginning of the French Revolution.

18-year-old Emily Geiger was captured by British forces in 1781 while taking a message to General Greene on the front lines. No evidence was found among her belongings – she had memorized the message and eaten the paper – so Geiger was released.

In both the French and American revolutions, some women were so determined to join the war effort that they disguised themselves as men. Anna Maria Lane of Virginia dressed as a man and fought for the rebels alongside her husband in the Continental Army. When she was wounded at the Battle of Germantown, Lane refused treatment for her injury. This was understandable, since most of the women caught serving as men were discovered while receiving medical treatment. Like their American counterparts, women who fought in the French Revolutionary Wars also went to great pains to hide their bodies from scrutiny, binding their breasts and cutting their hair in order to enlist as men.

Enlightened women

The French revolution began in 1789 and was followed by years of warfare as the rest of Europe fought to contain its antimonarchist spirit. Women were involved from the very beginning. In July 1789, women joined men in storming the Bastille (a Parisian fortress that held political prisoners) and in October,

24
demands for equal rights were made by radical Hungarian women in 1848

marched to the royal palace of Versailles (see pp. 134–135). Educated in the philosophy of the Enlightenment, female intellectuals wrote bold treatises advocating women's rights, or joined political clubs such as the Society of Republican and Revolutionary Women. Women in both France and the US wrote pamphlets and novels about the role of women in a republic.

This political opposition was as dangerous for women as it was for men, if not more so. In 1793, the National Convention in France banned women's political associations. Olympe de Gouges, writing under the name "Polyme", criticized Robespierre and his Jacobins (the extremist faction in power) and was executed during the Terror of 1793–1794, in which critics of the regime – particularly women – were

BIOGRAPHY
CHARLOTTE CORDAY

Marie-Anne Charlotte Corday d'Armont was born in 1768 into a poor but noble family in Caen, France. She later became involved with the moderate Girondists. In 1793, horrified by the brutality of the Jacobin Terror, Corday travelled to Paris. There, she tricked her way into a meeting with Jacobin leader Jean-Paul Marat by promising to betray the names of fellow Caen Girondists, and stabbed him in his bathtub. Corday was executed by guillotine for the murder that same year.

killed. Another victim was Marie-Jeanne Roland, a member of the Girondist faction (a moderate republican group). She was executed for her Girondist sympathies, but her memoirs – written during her time in prison – testified to her bravery and unwavering faith in Enlightenment ideology. The writings of both Roland and de Gouges not only inspired their compatriots but also women across the Atlantic.

Some women, on the other hand, actively supported the radical revolutionary regime that held power from 1792–1795. During the many executions, women known as "tricoteuse", or knitters, sat beside the guillotine, making objects such as the Phyrigian cap, a long-standing symbol of liberty.

Year of revolutions

During the Age of Revolution, rebellions and uprisings also swept Haiti, Serbia, Ireland, and Latin America. The year 1848 saw a wave of revolutions sweep across Europe. As in earlier revolutions, women came together to form political clubs, advocate for equality, raise money, shelter insurgents, and take part in boycotts. Women in Elberfeld, North Rhine-Westphalia, for example, pledged only to wear clothing purchased in a German state, because their "hearts beat stronger and faster at the hope of a unified Germany".

Despite contributing to revolutions across Europe and the Americas, women's actions rarely led to significant changes to their own position. The Code Napoleon – French laws codified after the revolution – denied women most civil and political rights, and the new US Constitution did nothing to improve their status. While revolutionary declarations stated that all men were created equal, it was clear that this ideology did not yet extend to women.

◀ **Patriotic blockade**
A female rebel leads fellow nationalists as they use furniture to block the waterways of the Rhine during the Baden Revolution of 1849, an uprising to make the Grand Duchy of Baden a republic.

"Women! ... What have you **received from the Revolution**?"

OLYMPE DE GOUGES, FRENCH WRITER AND ACTIVIST,
DECLARATION OF THE RIGHTS OF WOMAN, 1791

QUESTIONING THE REVOLUTION

In 1789, rioting began in Paris over the price and scarcity of bread. As the mob grew more agitated and violent, nearly 7,000 women stole weapons from the city's armoury and marched to Versailles. There, they besieged the palace, forcing the king and his ministers to return to Paris. This signalled the beginning of the end for Louis XVI, who was now called upon to answer to his critics. The writer Olympe de Gouges saw that while women played an active part in the uprisings, after the revolutionaries came to power women were still excluded from active citizenship. This inspired de Gouges to write her *Declaration of the Rights of Woman*, which set out a list of rights that all women should have. For example, since women could be executed at the guillotine, she believed they should also have the right to speak publicly about political matters. However, de Gouges was punished by Jacobin revolutionaries (see pp. 130–133) for airing these views, and like many other well-known political women, she was executed in 1793.

Knowledge and Power

1800-1914

In the 19th century, Western nations were gripped by a desire for knowledge and exploration. The period saw a number of women traversing the globe and educating themselves, breaking free of societies that sought to confine them to a domestic role. Furthermore, the Industrial Revolution required immense labour mobilization, and more women entered the waged workforce. The revolutionary spirit of the preceding era persisted: women engaged with change but also fought it when it harmed them, which change often did. Women were frequently exploited in the workplace and the growth of the European empires set back women's rights in many colonized countries.

CONVICTS AND
colonization

The history of women in Australia and New Zealand reflects the impact of colonization on the lifestyle, identity, and freedom of both the colonized (the Aboriginal and Māori indigenous peoples) and the colonizers (the European settlers – not all of whom were willing migrants).

Prior to European arrival, Australia had been inhabited for more than 60,000 years. Aboriginal and Torres Strait Islanders lived in small communities, often moving around, and had a strong sense of kinship and responsibility for the land. Aboriginal people have an oral tradition for sharing their history

12,500
women were shipped to Tasmania as punishment for their crimes, mainly theft.

and traditions, while the first Europeans to visit Australia recorded their impressions of the Eora women of Sydney in journals and drawings. A number of the women featured in these journals are remembered today. Patyegarang, for example, helped British marines officer William Dawes to record the Eora language. Barangaroo, a fisherwoman and hunter, is recalled for refusing to wear European clothes and for her compassion when she witnessed a white convict being flogged for stealing – she tried to grab the whip out of the flogger's hands.

Colonization had a devastating impact on the indigenous Australian women. The "stolen generations" (the forced removal of children from their mothers) is just one shocking aspect of their experience. Women also encountered violence at the hands of the

▲ **Ritual fishhook**
This 18th-century carved *matau* fishhook is characteristic of Nagati Tahu of South Island. The Māoris used such hooks to catch fish for gods, priests, and chiefly women.

IN BRIEF
SETTLEMENT HISTORY
The colonization of Australia and New Zealand has informed women's activism, in particular that of indigenous women who have had to fight racism and patriarchy.

1700

1769 James Cook lands at Poverty Bay, North Island.

1788 About 192 female convicts arrive in New South Wales on the First Fleet.

1800

1806 Convict Charlotte Badger escapes from New South Wales and is one of the first European women to live in New Zealand.

1814 Jane Kendall, Hannah King, and Dinah Hall help their husbands found the first settlement of the Church Missionary Society at Rangihoua, North Island.

1840 Māori women are signatories for the Treaty of Waitangi with the British government.

1861 Propertied women are awarded the vote in local elections in South Australia.

1888 Kate Sheppard publishes *The Ten Reasons Why the Women of New Zealand Should Vote*.

1890s Māori women join the Women's Christian Temperance Union and the fight for suffrage.

1900

1901 The state of Queensland criminalizes informal marriages between Aboriginal women and non-Aboriginal men.

1962 Aboriginal women and men are given the right to vote in Australian federal elections.

1967 Aboriginal women and men are allowed to become Australian citizens.

1975 Whina Cooper leads the first Māori land rights march. It starts the land movement.

1997 The *Bringing Them Home* report into the stolen generation reveals that between one in three and one in 10 indigenous children were removed from their mothers from 1910–1970.

◀ **MAORI WOMEN** CELEBRATE THEIR HISTORIC MIGRATION FROM POLYNESIA TO NEW ZEALAND AT A FESTIVAL, 1950.

colonizers. Some were murdered in cold blood by settlers, and others were kidnapped by seal hunters and forced to become unpaid domestic workers.

Indigenous Australian women have a history of activism and they continue to be recognized in many areas of public life. Poet Oodgeroo Noonuccal campaigned successfully for the 1967 abolition of discriminatory, anti-Aboriginal sections of the Australian constitution. Tracey Moffatt is regarded as one of Australia's top artists; her work often focuses on how Aboriginal people are understood culturally.

Māori women sign treaty

Before the Europeans arrived, Māori status was determined by descent from ancestors, not by gender, and women often had important roles. Māori women, for example, were signatories to New Zealand's founding document, the Treaty of Waitangi. However, the Europeans, believing that the differentiation between civilization and savagery was partly determined by how a society treated and protected its women, imposed their perception of gender roles on the Māori people. After colonization, Māori women lost their equal status, a grievance that continues to motivate Māori women's activism today.

Prominent female Māori activists include women's suffrage campaigner Meri Te Tai Mangakahia. In 1893, she not only requested that Māori women be given the vote, but that they be eligible to sit in the Māori parliament, thus going a step further than her contemporaries in the European suffrage

▼ **Passage to Australia**
Passengers pose aboard the SS *Sobraron*, which plied the England-Australia route from 1866-1891. The vessel catered to first- and second-class passengers only.

movement. The Māori queen and longest reigning Māori monarch, Te Atairangikaahu, (reigned 1966–2006) is noted for raising the profile of the Māori at home and abroad. She also worked to revitalize Māori culture and language, and promoted better education and welfare among her people. Another woman, Whina Cooper, led a coalition of Māori groups in their first protest against the loss of Māori land in 1975.

Emancipists and founders

In the early days of Sydney, women were in short supply. Female convicts were highly sought after both as domestic servants and as companions (see pp. 192–193). From 1788 to 1852, about 20,000 women were transported to Sydney but they were outnumbered by men by seven to one. More than 80 per cent of those women transported had been convicted of petty crimes. Prostitution was not a transportable offence, and only a few women had been found guilty of violent crimes. Former convicts were known as emancipists, and while such a label was once considered a social stain, they are now seen as the founders of the state of Australia. Among them was Mary Reibey. She was convicted of stealing a horse at the age of 13 and arrived in Sydney from England in 1794. She became a successful businesswoman and property owner, and was a cofounder of the Bank of New South Wales. She has been featured on the Australian $20 note since 1994.

The first settler women arrived in the 1790s with their husbands or families. The journals of these women give a particular insight into domestic life in the colony, including urban Sydney society, life in remote pastoral locations, and the settlers' interactions with indigenous women. Notable women include Elizabeth Macarthur, who landed in Sydney in 1790 and became a pioneer of Australia's merino wool industry, and Caroline Chisholm, who arrived in Sydney in 1838 and is known for her philanthropic work for the welfare of female immigrants.

From 1814, settlers started to arrive in greater numbers, along with missionaries. The men among them greatly outnumbered the women, so they were advised to bring a wife, and from the 1860s there were government incentives to encourage single British women to emigrate too. Large families were common and the white population grew rapidly. Among them were free thinkers who championed a number of social causes, such as Jane Atkinson, who arrived with her brother in New Zealand in 1850. A Unitarian and progressive thinker, she was active in the suffrage movement. Ellen Hewett arrived in New Zealand in 1854 with her family. Her memoir *Looking Back* (1914) is a vivid account of life for settler women during this period, and details the long separations, hard work, illnesses, and dangers of pioneer life.

▲ **From prison to prosperity**
Mary Reibey was an Australian merchant and trader in the 19th century. Originally a convict deported to Australia, she became legendary as a successful businesswoman in the colony.

"ALL THAT **SEPARATES**, ... **RACE** ... OR **SEX**, IS **INHUMAN** ... [AND] MUST BE **OVERCOME**."

KATE SHEPPARD, WOMEN'S SUFFRAGE CAMPAIGNER, ON HER SENSE OF EQUALITY AND JUSTICE IN SOCIETY

WOMEN FACED MANY barriers when it came to taking part in exploration and travel in the past, but the one that proved most difficult to overcome was the view of women as "the weaker sex". Where in the world a woman could go – and what was deemed appropriate for her to do or see at her destination – was too often dictated by her gender. Historically, women took part in pilgrimages to religious shrines, or accompanied their husbands on military campaigns, but in times of exploration and conquest, often only followed their men to foreign countries after the conquest had been completed.

Adventurers turned writers

During the Age of Discovery (1450–1600) explorers such as Christopher Columbus were unwilling to take women – whom they considered both physically and intellectually unfit for exploration – into the unknown. From the 1700s, however, the growth of empires and trading links meant that the wives of pioneering men had more

◀ **Feminist mountaineer**
American mountaineer Annie Smith Peck was a passionate suffragist. When she reached the summit of Coropuna, Peru, in 1911 at the age of 65, she placed a "Votes for Women" banner on its peak.

▲ **Maverick aviator**
This pair of flying goggles was worn by aviator Amelia Earhart during her 1932 solo transatlantic flight. In a letter to her husband before her final flight in 1937 she said: "Women must try to do things as men have tried."

opportunities to travel than their single (unaccompanied) counterparts. Some women resorted to cross-dressing in order to see the world – such as Louise Séguin, who in 1772–1773 became the first European woman to go to the Antarctic.

On the rare occasions that women were allowed to venture on expeditions, they often proved themselves to be invaluable assets: drawing maps, keeping assiduous records, and generally eliciting a more positive response from locals. These female adventurers also recorded their observations, producing letters, drawings, novels, and travel books that offered insights into other cultures. These narratives have inspired countless other women to follow in their footsteps.

From the mid-19th century, female European traveller-writers, such as Ida Pfeiffer (whose works were translated into seven different languages), began to rove over land and sea in pursuit of new discoveries. Although they were often derided as butterfly-net-wielding eccentrics, many of these travel writers were in fact experts who advanced scientific knowledge – among them biologist and botanical artist Marianne North and naturalist Isabella Bird – the first woman to be elected to the Royal Geographical Society.

THROUGH THE AGES

Adventurers

Despite the prejudices and obstacles that stood in their way, there have been many daring, determined, and courageous women who defied expectations and journeyed into the unknown - as travellers, explorers, mountaineers, aviators, and adventurers.

> ## "There was **never a question** in my mind that **I wanted** to **climb that mountain**, no matter what **other people** said."
>
> **JUNKO TABEI,**
> ON MOUNT EVEREST, 1975

From the late 19th century, new technologies made exploration easier as journeys by train, plane, balloon, motorcycle, and car became possible. Marie Marvingt was a talented athlete who, when refused permission to join the male–only Tour de France in 1908, waited until the race had finished and rode the route. A pioneer too, in 1909 she became the first woman to pilot a balloon across the English Channel. The first black female pilot, Bessie Coleman, was inspired to fly by the stories of World War I pilots. Banned from US flying schools, she learned French and went to Paris in 1921 to gain her pilot's license.

Magazines such as *National Geographic*, film, and television galvanized others. The feats of underwater filmmaker Lotte Hass and Valentina Tereshkova (see pp. 258–259), the first woman in space in 1963, were televised. Today, the world still beckons women to explore. As adventurer Lois Pryce advises: "The only way to get ready for an adventure is to have one."

▶ **Marrying adventure**
Osa and Martin Johnson thrilled the US public with their films and books of exotic adventure in East and Central Africa. This is the poster for the 1940 film based on Osa's autobiography *I Married Adventure*.

PROFILES
INTREPID EXPLORERS

Jeanne Baret (1740–1807) was the first woman to complete a voyage of circumnavigation. She joined Admiral Bougainville's 1766 expedition by cross-dressing and acting as assistant botanist to Philibert Commerçon (women were not allowed on French naval ships at the time and she flattened her chest with tightly bound linen). Her gender was discovered when the expedition reached Tahiti in 1768. When a Tahitian, Ahu-toru, suggested she was a transvestite, Baret then confessed she was a woman to Bougainville but he allowed her to continue to travel as Commerçon's assistant.

Sacagawea (c.1788–1812) was a Lemhi Shoshone tribeswoman who achieved more adventures than most minority women due to her linguistic skills. She acted as a guide, interpreter, mediator, and naturalist on the Lewis and Clark Expedition of the Louisiana Territory – a two-year mapping, scientific, and trading venture. She was the only woman to accompany the expedition.

Nellie Bly (1864–1922) was an American investigative journalist who travelled around the world in 72 days. Her journey was a successful rebut to her *New York World* editor who had argued that she would need a chaperone and many suitcases, and so would not succeed. Travelling by public transport, Bly beat reporter Elizabeth Bisland who *Cosmopolitan* had sent to attempt the same feat in the other direction.

Clärenore Stinnes (1901–1990) was the first woman to circumnavigate the world by automobile, from 1927 to 1929. In an Adler Standard 6, this prize-winning racer and industrialist's daughter drove 47,000 km (29,000 miles) with Carl-Axel Söderström – whom she had met only two days earlier. They had two mechanics and a support truck.

Barbara Hillary (b.1931) is the first African American woman to reach both Poles. She attained the North Pole in 2007, aged 76, and the South Pole in 2011. After surviving cancer twice this retired nurse set herself the goal of becoming the first black person to get to the Arctic and Antarctic extremes, and raised over $25,000 to do so.

THE FIGHT AGAINST
Napoleon

EUROPEAN NATIONALISM

In the aftermath of the French Revolution, Napoleon Bonaparte (national leader from 1799 and emperor from 1804) sought to conquer Europe. To this end he fought a series of wars lasting until 1815 that affected millions. Women became involved in the nationalist movements that sprang up in various European cities, and also in the colonies of the New World (see pp. 154–155).

Queen's influence

Nationalism was particularly important in the German states. Prussia, the largest one, initially attempted to stay neutral under the leadership of its indecisive king – Frederick William III – but his wife, Queen Louise, realized the threat that Napoleon's ambitions

posed to Prussia. She convinced her husband to declare war in 1806, and the Prussian Army paraded through Berlin to cheering crowds as they marched to battle. Later (romanticized) accounts claimed that Louise, who urged men and women in Prussia to resist the French, led the Queen's Dragoons in the procession wearing a crimson and blue colonel's uniform. Louise accompanied Prussian forces to meet Napoleon at the Battle of Jena-Auerstedt, and, despite the bloody defeat, stayed on the battlefield until the bitter end.

After numerous defeats, Prussia was forced to sue for peace in 1807 and Louise, pregnant at the time, personally appealed to Napoleon for clemency at the negotiations. Her pleas were ignored, but Louise nonetheless became

▶ **Held as a heroine**
Belgian soldier Marie Schellinck fought for France, disguised as a man. Paintings glorified her as the first woman to be awarded the Legion of Honour by Napoleon, but there are no records of her having received it.

◄ The Maid of Saragossa
Agustina de Aragón fought the French during the seige of Zaragoza. She was imprisoned when the French seized the city, but escaped and became a guerrilla leader, as well as a symbol of Spanish resistance.

a symbol of national resilience; she rallied her beleaguered people and supported reforms to strengthen the military. She died in 1810, and the Order of Louise (Luisen-Orden) was founded in her honour in 1814 to recognize women's distinguished service to Prussia, regardless of their social class.

Patriotic women

Across Europe, women followed Louise's example and took part in nationalist anti-Napoleonic activism. Societal norms meant they did so primarily along traditional gender lines, separately from men, for example by caring for the wounded, sewing flags, or preparing supplies for soldiers. They also formed women's patriotic associations (there

were over 600 in the German lands alone) to collect money and organize charitable efforts. Women were lauded as heroines for their patriotism during the wars, as long as they expressed this within the boundaries of accepted female behaviour, and did not take up arms, which was regarded as a male activity.

Yet not all women stayed within this docile realm of feminine patriotism. Some of the fiercest responses to Napoleonic rule came from female Spanish guerrillas, such as Agustina of Aragón, who single-handedly manned the defences of Zaragoza in 1808. As in the French Revolutionary Wars (see pp. 130–133) thousands of women joined armies in the battlefield as camp followers, and some served as soldiers, disguising their gender. The most celebrated female soldier was Nadezhda Durova, who joined a Russian cavalry regiment disguised as a boy in 1807 and distinguished herself for her valour in battle. Durova was not dismissed when her gender was discovered; rather Tsar Alexander I gave her a medal and promotion, and she served until 1816. Other women who fought were not so lucky – many were punished while alive and only glorified as national heroines after their deaths.

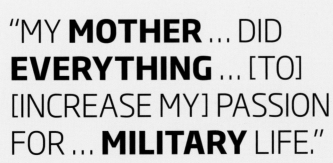

"MY **MOTHER** ... DID **EVERYTHING** ... [TO] [INCREASE MY] PASSION FOR ... **MILITARY** LIFE."

NADEZHDA DUROVA (1783-1866), *THE CAVALRY MAIDEN: JOURNALS OF A RUSSIAN OFFICER IN THE NAPOLEONIC WARS*

WOMEN OF
industry

In **1832, men's wages** in American cotton factories **exceeded women's** wages by
58%

THE INDUSTRIAL REVOLUTION

From the mid-18th to the mid-19th century, economic and industrial production changed dramatically. Termed the Industrial Revolution, it began in the United Kingdom, and other countries in Western Europe and North America soon followed. Many areas of manufacturing, particularly textiles, became mechanized and shifted towards factory-based production. New techniques made iron and steel cheaper and stronger, while steam (fuelled by coal and water) powered machines and engines. Improved farming systems meant that agriculture required less labour, allowing people to move from rural to urban areas. Although the Industrial Revolution would eventually lead to increases in income and life expectancy in the 20th century, it also caused significant social dislocation.

Benefits for women

Historians disagree on how beneficial the Industrial Revolution was to women. Some argue that overall women gained from industrialization, as it boosted their economic independence by increasing their paid labour participation outside of the home. Others are more pessimistic; they point out that before the Industrial Revolution men and women worked together in a family's economic activity, be it running a farm or a "cottage industry" (small-scale, home-based manufacturing, such as spinning or weaving). Once manufacturing

◀ **Weaving revolution**
Patented in 1770, the spinning jenny was a vast improvement upon the spinning wheel. The jenny, which could do the work of eight traditional wheels, could be operated by one person, leading to a huge increase in productivity.

INDUSTRIAL BOOM

Women workers were directly affected by increases in mechanization, which in some cases allowed them to do the same work more efficiently than ever before.

1700

1764 James Hargreaves invents the spinning jenny, which connects multiple spools to process up to eight threads at once.

1769 Richard Arkwright patents the water frame, a device to spin yarn, which can be connected to a water-wheel.

1776 Matthew Boulton and James Watt produce the first version of their steam engine. Unlike earlier devices, it has a sufficiently smooth motion to drive machinery.

1793 Hannah Slater is the first woman to be granted a patent by the US Patent Office for an improved technique of spinning cotton thread.

1800

1828 In the first recorded women's strike in American history, 400 women at a cotton factory in Dover, New Hampshire, walk out in protest against strict new rules.

1832 First strike for equal pay by 1,500 female textile workers at Peep Green in Yorkshire, UK.

1842 Mines and Collieries Act prohibits women in the UK from working underground in mines.

1844 Factories Act in the UK restricts women from working more than 12 hours a day.

1847 Legislation in the UK restricts the working hours of women and young people in textile mills to 10 hours a day.

1888 Clementina Black secures the first resolution for equal pay at the British Trades Union Congress.

1900

1903 Women's Trade Union League founded in the US to campaign nationally for better working conditions for women.

◀ **IN THE SPOOLING ROOM** WOMEN WORKING IN A COTTON MILL IN SPAIN, 1898.

moved to factories, where working-class men earned very low wages, women and children joined the workforce in order to help support their families. Women were largely excluded from burgeoning sectors of the economy such as mining, heavy industry, and transport, notably the railways. The vast majority of female workers were crowded into a small number of occupations, particularly textile and clothing manufacturing, domestic service, and farming.

The 19th century saw the rise in influence of the notion of "separate spheres", according to which the ideal place for women was the "domestic sphere", meaning life as a wife and mother. Middle-class men's wages rose during the Industrial Revolution; this meant that, in some cases, a husband could earn enough that his wife did not need to take on paid work outside the home. Middle-class married women were increasingly expected to oversee the management of the household rather than go out to work. For many women, therefore, the Industrial Revolution actually altered their economic and public roles. However, among the working class – roughly two-thirds of the population – women had little choice but to work outside the home.

▼ **Women's work**
In some European countries, women were employed in the mining industry until the late 19th century. Here, women load coal in Hainaut, Belgium, 1873.

Throughout the 18th and 19th centuries women's pay was generally two-thirds to half that of men doing the same job. In addition to inferior wages, many women faced unsafe or unsanitary working conditions. Many females (and males) entered the workforce while they were children, particularly in textile mills. They were employed because they were cheaper. Before regulations were introduced from the mid-19th century (first in the United Kingdom), children worked long hours, and often suffered injury or death in accidents. One of the worst industrial disasters was the 1911 Triangle Shirtwaist Factory fire in New York, where 123 women and 23 men died in a blaze, trapped in the building partly because one of two exit doors was locked to prevent theft.

Women unite

Spurred on by the Triangle Shirtwaist Factory disaster, women campaigned for improvements in working conditions. There were occasional strikes – for example, the Mill Girls of Lowell, Massachusetts, walked out in 1834 and 1836 in protest against wage cuts and rises in rent for employee housing. In 1844, they organized themselves into the Lowell Female Labour Reform Association, one of the first women's trade unions. Although women formed a minority in the trade union movement, where female membership was often discouraged or prohibited, by the early 20th century, tens of thousands of women had joined trade or

▲ **Toil and drudgery**
In the early 20th century, large numbers of Japanese women - often very young girls from the countryside - worked in the textile industry. They were generally poorly paid.

labour unions. One of the largest groups was the International Ladies' Garment Workers' Union, founded in New York in 1900. In 1909, the Women's Trade Union League (established in 1903) lent legal and financial assistance to a huge strike of mostly Jewish shirtwaist factory workers in a protest known as the "Uprising of 20,000".

The Industrial Revolution transformed Europe from a largely rural and agricultural society to an urban, industrial one. New inventions improved the lives of many people and brought prosperity for some; others, however, were held down by poverty and poor working conditions. Although female labour played a central role in this change, women continued to be socially and economically marginalized.

BIOGRAPHY
MARGARET KNIGHT

Born in 1838 in Maine, as a child Margaret Knight went to work at a cotton mill. Despite a limited education, at the age of 12, she invented a device that made looms safer. In 1867 Knight went to work at the Columbia Paper Bag Company. There she invented a machine to form flat-bottomed shopping bags. Although a co-worker attempted to patent it for himself, Knight was awarded the patent in 1871. She continued to invent until her death in 1914.

"[COMPANIES] SUCK WEALTH OUT OF THE STARVATION OF HELPLESS GIRLS."

ANNIE BESANT, "WHITE SLAVERY IN LONDON", 1888

◀ **Overworked and underpaid**
This 19th-century illustration depicts an exhausted young countrywoman on her train journey back home from her job in town.

DARKNESS AND
immorality

The Romantic movement in art, music, and literature emerged in the late 18th and early 19th centuries as a reaction to the ideals of the Enlightenment. Whereas the earlier movement had been about knowledge, progress, and reason, Romanticism took an opposite approach, exploring themes of darkness, passion, the natural world, and immorality. Women were more present in literature than any other Romantic art form, using their writing to express their sexuality and to criticize the social order. Christina Rossetti's "Goblin Market" (1862), for example, uses forbidden fruit as an allegory for women's sexual temptation, sacrifice, and salvation. It also features and criticizes male sexual violence: when one sister is seduced by the "goblins" in the poem, they abuse her by holding her down and tearing her dress.

A dark genre

The Gothic, which developed as a popular subgenre of Romantic literature, also appealed to female writers. It was characterized by its gloomy settings – abandoned castles or eerie forests – and what was called the "explained supernatural", in which fantastical ideas had pseudo-scientific explanations. An early pioneer was Ann Radcliffe, a British writer whose *Mysteries of Udolpho* (1794), a Gothic romance with a female protagonist, became a literary sensation. Gothic literature allowed women to explore psychological issues – as in the case of American writer Charlotte Perkins Gilman, who wrote *The Yellow Wallpaper* (1892) about a woman's descent into madness. Gothic literature also dealt with religion: Mary Shelley's *Frankenstein* (1818) criticized

◀ **Fairy tales and folk stories**
This book of Grimm tales was published in Berlin in 1865. Their versions, and others by male writers, still form the foundations of many fairy tales today.

the arrogance of man trying to play God, and pioneered the fantasy horror genre.

Folk traditions

Romanticism was spurred by nationalist ideas, as people used art to reinforce their national identity. During Napoleon's empire (see pp. 146–147), resistance movements sprang up in conquered nations to celebrate their own dialects and traditions. Folk music and tales were recorded by artists who collected them; the Brothers Grimm were part of this movement, and collected hundreds of tales to edit for a 19th-century audience. Many came from Dortchen Wild, an aristocratic girl who lived in Hesse-Cassel – taken over by the French in 1806. She eventually married Willhelm Grimm, but received no credit for her stories. In their new forms, the Grimm tales pushed the very moral agendas that female Romantics criticized. *Rotkäppchen* (Little Red Cap), for example, warned girls not to be promiscuous, lest they be eaten (ruined) by the wolf (man).

Tales recorded by men starkly contrasted those written by women. In the 18th century, French salon host Madame d'Aulnoy and her peers wrote stories criticizing monarchy, marriage, and religion, featuring quickwitted heroines and not damsels in distress. Yet their provocative stories fell from favour in the 19th century, while the moralizing tales of the Grimms and Charles Perrault (author of the Mother Goose tales) were celebrated and preserved as archetypes of the fairy tale genre.

◀ **Sexual allegory**
In Christina Rossetti's "Goblin Market", Laura trades locks of her hair to buy fruit from goblin men. Using the imagery of fruit to refer to the biblical Adam and Eve, the poem symbolizes the forbidden nature of female sexuality.

Literature

The first known female writer was Sumerian poet Enheduanna in the 3rd century BCE, but women's works in the English language did not appear until the 14th century. Women have since written prolifically across all genres – from simple recipes to novels, plays, and poems.

ALTHOUGH FEMALE WRITERS played a major role in Chinese, Korean, and Japanese literature from as early as 220 BCE (see pp. 74–75), women's writing did not flourish elsewhere until the advent of the printing press in the 15th century. It prospered further in the 1700s with the evolution of the novel and an increase in female readers, particularly in Europe. Writers such as Germaine de Staël and George Sand, infamous for wearing male clothing, wrote novels that explored the impact of social conventions on women. To reach a wider audience – or to ensure anonymity – some Western female writers resorted to male pseudonyms, even for novels

> " **Everything** in life is **writable** about if you **have the** ... **guts** to do it. "

SYLVIA PLATH, POET AND WRITER, IN HER JOURNAL, 1950-1955

◀ **Baroque girl genius**
Miguel Cabrera's 1750 portrait of poet nun Sor Juana Inés de la Cruz shows her surrounded by books and writing materials.

about the lives of women. Famous examples include Charlotte Brontë's *Jane Eyre* (published under the pseudonym Currer Bell) and her sister Emily Brontë's *Wuthering Heights* (Ellis Bell) in 1847. Another successful novelist, Mary Anne Evans, insisted upon the pseudonym George Eliot for her novels, such as *Middlemarch* (1872), partly to deflect scandal about her living openly with a married man separated from his wife.

Over time it became more acceptable for women to write under their own names. Edith Wharton and Kate Chopin wrote works dissecting the worlds they inhabited in late 19th- and early 20th-century America. Wharton's *The House of Mirth* (1905) and *The Age of Innocence* (1920) explore the lives of high society women in New York. Chopin was from Louisiana, and her stories address the racism affecting the mixed-race milieu of the South due to slavery. Later, *Beloved* (1987) by Toni Morrison was inspired by the true story of African American slave Margaret Garner.

Pushing the boundaries

The 20th-century postcolonial era has seen a significant rise in writing by women from Africa. *Une si Longue Lettre* (*So Long a Letter*) (1979) by Mariama Bâ from Senegal, thought to be the first African feminist novel, explores the experiences of African Muslim women. Modern female writers have also begun to explore new techniques and cover more controversial subjects, from politics to sexuality to mental health. Margaret Atwood exposes women's subjugation within a patriarchal society in *The Handmaid's Tale*, while Janet Frame's autobiography *An Angel at My Table* (1984) discusses her experiences of mental illness and shock therapy in New Zealand

Not all societies enjoy such freedom of expression, however. In China, Ding Ling's work was banned in the Anti-Rightist movement of 1957 and during the Cultural Revolution (1966-1976). It was finally republished in 1978.

▲ **Slave poet**
This portrait of poet Phillis Wheatley shows her writing with a quill pen. Despite living as an African slave, Wheatley was one of the best known poets in pre 19th-century America. She wrote her first published poem at around the age of 13.

TYPEWRITER USED BY MARGARET MITCHELL, GONE WITH THE WIND (1936)

WOMEN WORDSMITHS

Sor Juana Inés de la Cruz (c.1651–1695) chose to become a nun in 1667. The patronage of the viceroy and vicerine of New Spain gave her the freedom to pursue her writing and learning. In 1691 she wrote a defence of all women's right to knowledge–the *Respuesta a Sor Filotea de la Cruz* (Reply to Sister Filotea of the Cross). Her best-known poem is *Primero sueño* (1692).

Annette von Droste-Hülshoff (1797–1848) grew up in Münster in an intellectual circle that included the Brothers Grimm, Adele and Johanna Schopenhauer, and Friedrich Schlegel. One of the foremost women in German literature, her best-known work is the Gothic murder-mystery, *Die Judenbuche* (*The Jew's Beech*, 1842).

Higuchi Ichiyō (1872–1896) was famed in her lifetime in 19th-century Japan, both for her talents and for the novelty of being a successful female writer. She wrote stories and poems in order to support her very poor family. Her main characters are nearly always women and outcasts, such as orphans, divorcees, and prostitutes. Her stories include *Takekurabe* (*Growing Up*, 1895).

Miles Franklin (1879–1954) grew up as Stella Franklin in a pioneer farming family on the edge of the Australian Alps in New South Wales. She wrote her first novel, *My Brilliant Career* (1901), when she was only 16, in just a couple of weeks. She wanted her female identity to remain a secret, so she did not use her real name as a writer. Named in her honour, the Miles Franklin Award is Australia's most prestigious literary prize.

Maya Angelou (1928–2014) wrote a much-loved memoir about her early childhood in America's south, *I Know Why the Caged Bird Sings* (1969), the first of seven "autobiographical fictions" chronicling her extraordinary life experiences as a woman, poet, singer, and civil rights activist. She was also highly respected as a spokesperson for Black Americans.

Margaret Atwood (b. 1939) is the Canadian author of *The Handmaid's Tale* (1985) and the Booker prize-winning *The Blind Assassin* (2000), her best-known novels. Her achievements reach beyond the literary, and she is also well-known and respected for her environmental activism.

SPIES, SOLDIERS, AND
victims

LATIN AMERICAN REVOLUTIONS

Latin America in the early 19th century was characterized by a deeply patriarchal system, but nevertheless women played an important role in the political upheavals, wars, and confrontations that occurred across the area from 1809 to 1825. This series of bloody revolutions against Spanish rule became known collectively as the Wars of Independence.

Heroines of the fight

While most women involved in these conflicts undertook non-combative, supporting positions, some women actively participated in guerrilla campaigns. An early heroine of the independence struggle was Micaela Bastidas, the wife of the rebel Tupac Amaru II. She fought beside her husband in an unsuccessful rebellion against Spanish rule in Peru in 1780. Due to the failure of the uprising, she and her husband were executed, along with Captain Tomasa Condemyata, who had successfully led her female battalion against the Spanish in several clashes.

◀ **Complete commitment**
Juana Azurduy de Padilla joined the Bolivian guerrilla forces to fight the Spanish regime and became a notable military leader. Her commitment to the cause was such that she even fought while she was pregnant.

Many women pushed their male relatives and husbands to fight for independence, as well as taking part themselves. Such female heroines as "Mother of Chile" Javiera Carrera and Policarpa Salavarrieta of Nueva Granada (present-day Colombia) were important underground fighters who spied for revolutionary forces. Often these women, like their male comrades, lost their lives as a result.

Several female revolutionaries became outstanding military leaders – for example, Juana Azurduy de Padilla, who fought for independence in Upper Peru (present-day Bolivia). Azurduy engaged in guerrilla warfare and fought in major

"I AM **GOING** … **TO ATTACK** THEM [THE ENEMY], **EVEN IF IT COSTS** ME **MY LIFE**."

MICAELA BASTIDAS, IN A LETTER TO TUPAC AMARU II, 1780

*Policarpa Sala
Sacrificada p.
ñoles en esta p
el 14 de Nov. d
su memoria
entre nozotro
fama rresuen
á polo*

actions wearing the uniform of a cavalryman. Famously, in 1816 she led her forces to capture the Cerro Rico of Potosí, which was the main source of Spanish silver. In 2015, Argentine president Cristina Fernández de Kirchner granted Azurduy a posthumous promotion to the rank of general in recognition of her role in Latin America's struggle for independence.

Indigenous participants

Women also participated in the Wars of Independence as ordinary soldiers. In the 1821 Battle of Carabobo, dozens of women on both sides were killed fighting. In addition to those of Spanish descent, thousands of indigenous women took part in the wars, notably in 1819–1820 in the Peruvian Andes.

Another way in which women became involved in the struggle was by providing meeting places for the rebels. Manuela Cañizares hosted the gathering of the Quito revolutionaries during which they issued the first Proclamation of Independence in 1809. Many female insurgents who organized networks of rebels courageously refused to betray them even under torture.

Although women played a significant role in the struggles that led to the countries of Latin America gaining their independence, "liberty" was not granted to women in the new nations. They continued to be denied political privileges and to fight for their rights, well into the 20th century.

BIOGRAPHY
MANUELA SÁENZ

A young married woman with elite connections in Peru, Manuela Sáenz (1797–1856) defied her husband to join the rebels fighting to liberate Peru from Spain. She became the mistress of Simón Bolívar, credited as the liberator of South America. Sáenz gathered important information, distributed leaflets, organized troops, and rescued the injured. She campaigned for women's rights and was a significant posthumous influence on the 20th-century feminist movement in Latin America.

◀ **Tried and convicted**
Policarpa Salavarrieta (c. 1795–1817) joined the rebel cause in what is now Colombia. In 1817 she was tried for treason, convicted, and executed by firing squad along with her lover.

UNDER THE
British Raj

COLONIAL INDIA

In 1857–1858, the people of India rose up against the rule of the British East India Company in what was known as the "Mutiny" or India's First War of Independence. Although the Mutiny failed to win back the subcontinent, it ended Company rule, and marked the dawn of the "Raj" – an era of direct rule by the British government.

During Company rule, life for the British in India had been culturally and racially mixed. Company employees were encouraged, in the absence of British women, to marry high-class Indian women. Known as *begums,* these were often Muslims from courtly families whose Anglo-Indian children then went on to be reared and educated in Britain. About 90 per cent of British men in India had Indian wives by the mid-18th century. This practice had reduced greatly by the 19th century, but it was still common to keep a *bibi,* or mistress. One army colonel even agreed to circumcision so that a Muslim woman would become his mistress.

The Mutiny and the forging of the empire sharpened racial divisions. In the uprising, British women had been attacked and killed, and this was used to bolster ideas of white superiority. The "native rapist" was juxtaposed with the white man – the gallant protector of the pure, white woman. By the second-half of the 19th century, relations between British men and Indian women had practically ceased, existing only between lower-class British men and Indian prostitutes or servants. Eurasians, the offspring of Anglo-Indian liaisons, were perceived as a threat to white superiority. British interactions with Indians in general were much less, too, and the British began to create a "home away from home" on Indian soil. They built towns at high elevations – creating greater physical distance between themselves and the

▶ **Agency on the stage**
In India, the performing arts gave women, especially those from lower classes and castes (the Indian social hierarchy), the opportunity to shine in a career, perhaps more than any other profession of that era.

"YOU HAVE **NEVER GIVEN** A **WOMAN** THE **CHANCE TO MAKE** HER **VOICE STRONG**!"

PANDITA RAMABAI, ANNUAL CONGRESS MEETING, DECEMBER 1889

"natives" – with British plants and European architecture. Once the Suez Canal opened in 1869, they had even less need for Indian women because British women could then travel to India much more easily.

Writers and freedom fighters

After the Mutiny, a "New Indian Woman" emerged, who challenged male and colonial superiority, and sought political equality. Poised between tradition and modernity, these privileged and educated women were writers and activists. Among their ranks were Cornelia Sorabji, the first female graduate of Bombay University, and the first woman to study law at Oxford University and practise in Britain and India; Pandita Ramabai, a champion of women's rights; and Sarojini Naidu, a poet, freedom fighter, and President of the Indian National Congress. Along with many others, these women actively participated in debates, lectures, and other cultural exchanges between India and Britain after 1857, which outspokenly criticized both male and colonial dominance.

▲ **Braveheart rebel**
This postage stamp commemorates feisty female ruler Kittur Chennamma, who, sword in hand, led a rebellion against the British East India Company in 1824.

BIOGRAPHY
KHAIR-UN-NISSA

When British imperialist Colonel James Achilles Kirkpatrick stepped off the boat in Hyderabad, India, in 1795, he was eager to conquer the subcontinent. Yet, he found himself beguiled by Indo-Persian culture. He mingled with the local elite, where he met his future bride, 14-year-old Khair-un-Nissa, a wealthy noblewoman. Their union caused a scandal, but she bore him two children. Their story is the focus of William Dalrymple's social history *White Mughals* (2002).

KEEPING UP
appearances

REGENCY AND VICTORIAN BRITAIN

Succeeding socially in Georgian Britain (1714–1837) relied on the skilful negotiation of many conventions governing behaviour and relationships. This was especially important for women, whose reputation was usually their ticket to marriage and its associated financial security. To attract a husband, middle- and upper-class women were expected to be fashionable in both dress and lifestyle, to boast impeccable manners, and to have an intricate knowledge of etiquette. Connections were fostered through "morning" visits to other homes, following a strict protocol. In London, for example, a woman could visit her social equals or inferiors, but she had to wait for higher-ranked women to call on her. Good form was so prized that British high society was dubbed "the Ton", from the French word *bon ton* for good manners or style. Such conventions played a key role in the works of British writer Jane Austen, whose novels provided an often damning social commentary on the upper class.

In the Regency period of the early 19th century, women changed clothes around six times a day for different occasions: breakfast, morning visits, afternoon promenades, evenings at home, dinners out, and balls. They were expected to be well read on the politics and prevailing tastes of the time, but any sign of ostentatiousness was frowned

▶ **Fan flirtation**
Decorative fans were significant in the elaborate rituals of flirtation at European balls. They allowed women to communicate their feelings towards suitors in a socially acceptable manner despite restrictive social customs.

▶ **False advertising**
Cornelius Bennett Harness made "electric" corsets (really magnetic) that he claimed were not only comfortable but would solve all manner of health problems. Many women asked for their money back after doctors proved him a fraud.

▲ **Caged in**
A woman is helped into an oppressive crinoline cage, which was used to achieve the fashionable Victorian silhouette of the mid-19th century. They dramatically reshaped the female form, and were covered in heavy fabrics to fit the conservative mood.

upon. Regency women had to tread a fine line between appearing superficial and sincere.

A conservative shift

When Queen Victoria came to the throne in 1837, the moral tone of society changed. This partly reflected the differing approaches of the two monarchs. The court of Victoria's predecessor George IV, the Prince Regent, was perceived as extravagant and morally fluid, whereas Victoria's reign was marked by strict morality and a greater focus on the private realm of the family. In the Victorian era, transgressions by women who broke sexual norms were taken particularly seriously. "Fallen women", who could be prostitutes or simply those caught having sex out of wedlock, were the subject of pamphlets by social reformers who felt it their duty to rescue them. In high society, once a woman was deemed to be "ruined" by premarital sex, she had little hope of social acceptance or marriage.

The lower classes

In the 18th and 19th centuries, the majority of working class women were employed in domestic service (see pp. 192–193), which provided them with a steady income and a place to live. Female servants were cheaper than male servants, and by 1891, as many as one in three women between the ages of 15 and 20 worked in domestic service. They were often overworked and poorly treated, as well as subjected to sexual violence from men working in, living in, or visiting the house. While premarital sex was common for these women, both laws and social stigma punished those who bore illegitimate children.

"HAPPINESS IN MARRIAGE IS ENTIRELY A MATTER OF CHANCE."

JANE AUSTEN, *PRIDE AND PREJUDICE*, 1813

> " ... systematic **low wages** ... force women to **sell sex** to **survive**. "
>
> **ANDREA DWORKIN**, FEMINIST, 1983

THROUGHOUT HISTORY, women and girls have often entered into prostitution out of economic desperation or force, and continue to do so today. However in many societies, prostitution was linked to religion too. Sacred prostitution and sacred sex (in which money is not involved) are practices that date back to the ancient world. In ancient Greece and Rome, sacred prostitution and sex was practised at temples dedicated to Aphrodite and Venus. There is evidence that prostitution was regulated in ancient Rome and that the state may have owned large brothels in the 4th century BCE. In Aztec society, women (and some men), were allowed to work as prostitutes at the *Cihuacalli*, or "House of

◄ **English "man trap"**
This engraving of an English prostitute c. 1780 was published in German Marxist scholar Eduard Fuchs's *Sittengeschichte* (1911-1912), art and caricatures on the theme of morality.

THROUGH THE AGES

Prostitution

Women and girls—and boys and men of lesser social status—have been providing sex for money since ancient times. Governments have long faced the challenge of how to legislate the practice, choosing variously to ban it outright or to attempt to regulate it.

Women". They did so under a statue of Tlazolteotl, who was the goddess of vice and disease but also of purification.

Non-sacred prostitution was also common. As well as purely sexual encounters, there were several types of companionship women could be employed in. Courtesans might act as companions to wealthy men, and entertain them through dancing, reciting poetry, or conversation; in some societies, although these women could engage in sexual activity with patrons, such services were not always assumed.

Prostitution and the Law

Modern societies have taken a range of approaches to prostitution legislation – from outright bans, to partial criminalization, to full legalization and government regulation, as in Amsterdam, where a prostitution ban was lifted in 1811. Those working in the "red-light" (pleasure) district were made to have health checks as the Dutch government regulated the industry. Early feminists such as Josephine Butler fought against these compulsory checks, seeing them as violations of women's bodies.

In the late 20th century, legislation moved towards protecting women, rather than simply banning solicitation. In 1978, activist Carol Leigh used the term "sex work" to emphasize that, as workers, prostitutes are workers, and deserve better pay, working conditions, and health care, and in the 20th century, the Scandinavian countries introduced the "Nordic Model", which made it illegal to buy sex but not to sell it.

Since the early 20th century, laws have distinguished between prostitution and sex trafficking, in which women are coerced into sex work. The League of Nations sought to address trafficking in 1921, and it is now illegal under international law, whereas legislation against prostitution is much more varied.

▲ **Ancient priestess**
This Assyrian ivory carving, from the 8th century BCE, shows a sacred prostitute– a priestess of Inanna (see pp. 18-19), who would have ritual sex with male visitors to the temple to release divine energy.

COURTESANS IN A SALON OF RUE DES MOULINS, PARIS, 1894

PROFILES
WORKERS AND REFORMERS

Su Xiaoxiao (d. 501 CE), also known as Su Xiaojun and "Little Su," was a courtesan and poet during the Southern Qi Dynasty in ancient China. There are almost no historical records of her life, but some accounts say she was forced into prostitution at fifteen to help her family.

Jeanne Bécu, Comtesse Du Barry
(1743-1793) was the *Maîtresse-en-titre*, or chief mistress, of King Louis XV of France. When she was 20, Bécu's great beauty caught the eye of pimp Jean-Baptiste Du Barry, who facilitated her career as a courtesan to aristocratic men before she caught the eye of the king. She was beheaded during the French Revolution.

Josephine Butler (1828-1906) was a 19th-century English feminist and social reformer. In 1869, she began campaigning to repeal the Contagious Diseases Act, which forced prostitutes to submit to medical exams. The Act was finally repealed in 1886. Butler fought for similar reforms in other parts of Europe through her organization the International Abolitionist Federation.

Tilly Devine (1900-1970) engaged in prostitution as a young woman before moving to Australia with her husband and becoming a prominent crime boss and madam. She acquired dozens of criminal convictions for prostitution and spent time in prison for slashing a man in a barbershop with a razor. Devine was called the "Worst Woman in Sydney" and "The Queen of the Night" in the press. She ran her brothel in Sydney until 1968.

Margo St James (b. 1937) is the founder of COYOTE (Call Off Your Old Tired Ethics), an organization that calls for the decriminalization of sex work. In 1999, COYOTE helped to create the St James Infirmary Clinic, a free health and safety clinic run by and for sex workers in San Francisco. St James is herself a former sex worker.

Somaly Mam (b. 1970) is a Cambodian anti-trafficking activist who focuses on sex trafficking. In 1996, Mam founded the organization *Agir pour les Femmes en Situation Précaire* (Acting for Women in Distressing Situations,) which rescues and rehabilitates women and children trafficked in Cambodia, Laos, and Vietnam.

SERVANTS AND
suburbia

SOCIAL CLASS IN THE WEST

By the mid-19th century, the middle class (or *bourgeoisie*) was expanding rapidly as a result of the increasing trade and wealth created by the Industrial Revolution, and was becoming more and more separated from the working class. The expanding middle class was most evident in Britain, northwestern Europe, and the US. The bourgeoisie ranged from the *haute* (upper) including factory owners and bankers, to the *petite* (petty) – clerks, teachers, and shopkeepers. What distinguished them all from the working class was that they did not work with their hands. The middle class viewed themselves as the respectable, thrifty, and sober bedrock of society, and distanced themselves from what they saw as the feckless working class and indolent aristocracy.

The housewife

Due to rising real wages most middle-class families – and some working-class ones – could live on one salary: the husband's. This led to the "male breadwinner" model and the notion that a woman's place was in the home. A wife's duty was to be meek, obedient, and run the household. Managing domestic servants was a key skill and being able to afford at least one maid was an important mark of the bourgeois household. Numerous books were published to guide wives with advice on cooking, entertaining, and childcare. These ideas about a wife's role were to persist for some time – in Ireland, with the exception of teachers, wives could not work until 1973.

The working class mostly lived in urban areas, worked in factories and mines, and their only possession of any significant value was their labour. The middle classes, on the other hand, as a result of the introduction of mass-transit commuter systems, were able to move

▼ Life below stairs
These two women posing with household utensils are Victorian servants from around 1880. By 1891, 1.3 million girls and women worked as domestic servants in Victorian England.

▶ Picture perfect
This photograph of an American middle-class family at home in 1910 shows the women sewing and reading surrounded by material possessions – indicating the affluence of the head of the house.

"NEATNESS SHOULD BE STUDIED BY ALL ENGAGED IN **DOMESTIC WORK**."

ISABELLA BEETON, *BOOK OF HOUSEHOLD MANAGEMENT*, 1861

to suburbs on the outskirts of towns, far away from working-class areas, and live in single-family homes that were scaled-down versions of those inhabited by the nobility. For many middle-class women, such a lifestyle often brought with it isolation, which they often combated by taking on voluntary charitable work outside the home. In contrast, working-class households, while often densely packed and unhygienic, fostered more of a communal spirit.

◀ **Luxury for the masses**
Despite its luxurious debut in British society, tea became widely accessible to both the middle and working classes when prices fell during the 19th century. By this time, serving tea had become a woman's duty.

Time to spend money

Consumer behaviour was transformed during this period. Falling transport costs meant imported goods such as tea, coffee, and sugar became affordable, even for the working class. Mass-production techniques also lowered the cost of many commodities: after British ceramic firm Wedgwood used steam power to mass produce china, it went from being a luxury item to an everyday one. Shopping became a leisure activity for middle-class women who travelled to urban centres to view the latest merchandise; stores adopted colourful display windows and signs to attract them. Mail-order catalogues offering a range of goods – distributed by the railways and a reliable postal system – became popular, particularly for women in rural areas and African American women, who could order goods that they could not purchase in person from prejudiced store owners. Eventually, the working classes, too, were to take advantage of these new consumer methods.

"Organize, agitate, educate, must be **our war cry**."

SUSAN B. ANTHONY, 1850

▲ **Women unite**
The National Council of Women in the US meet in 1895.

▶ **Crusader for women's rights**
Susan B. Anthony, born in 1820, was an influential social reformer. In the 1850s, she joined with Elizabeth Cady Stanton to become a leading figure in the fight for women's rights. Anthony travelled across the world, writing and giving speeches.

RALLYING FOR
reform

FIRST-WAVE FEMINISM

From the mid-19th century onwards there was a growing demand for women's rights. The Enlightenment and subsequent revolutions (see pp.130–133) had brought sweeping changes to Western society, yet the traditional role of women remained mostly unaltered. This changed as activists came together in the first wave of feminism, so called to distinguish it from the second wave of the 1960s.

Earlier women had played a vital role in campaigning for change across a number of issues, ranging from the abolition of slavery to prison reform. However, many now turned their attention to the growing women's rights cause, which was being championed by women such as Mary Wollstonecraft, an English advocate for women's education. A founding event in first-wave feminism was the Seneca Falls Convention, held in July 1848 in upstate New York, an area home to many radical Quakers. The main organizers were the abolitionists Lucretia Coffin Mott and Elizabeth Cady Stanton. Together they wrote the Declaration of Sentiments and Grievances, which called for equal rights for women. Although only around 300 people, including men, attended the convention, it served as a catalyst for later campaigning in the US.

An expanding movement

In the UK, the Langham Place Circle, named after the location of the *English Woman's Journal*, provided a forum for the exchange of ideas by women. In 1855, they founded the Married Women's Property Committee to demand reform of the British laws of coverture. These laws stated that after a woman married, all of her money, property, and earnings were transferred to her spouse. The committee's work led Parliament to pass the Married Women's Property Act in 1870, which made a woman's wages and property separate from those of her husband.

The drive for greater rights for women began to spread further afield. A few weeks before Seneca Falls, a conference was held in Badasht, Persia (modern Iran), where women discussed gender equality in the Bábís religion. In Europe, several national groups were founded including the General German Women's Association in 1865, the French Society for the Demand for Women's Rights in 1866, and the Danish Women's Society in 1871. In early 1888, the first meeting of the International Council of Women took place in Washington, D.C. Its members publicized the women's movement, laying the foundations for the later campaigns for suffrage.

▶ **In search of equality**
The US National Woman Suffrage Association was founded by Susan B. Anthony and Elizabeth Cady Stanton in 1869. Satirized here, it spoke out on issues such as inequality in jobs and pay.

THE AGE OF
discovery

SCIENCE AND PROGRESS

The 19th century was a time of immense change. In 1800, most people travelled by foot, and communication was by letter. Yet in the hundred years that followed, new scientific discoveries came one after another, and by the 1900s, large swathes of the world were linked together by railroads and telegraph wires. Internal combustion engines powered vehicles, microbes were proved to cause diseases, electricity was harnessed and utilized, and the theory of evolution was proposed. In 1833, the term "scientist" was coined to describe the researchers who were changing the world – a growing number of whom were women.

One of the first female scientists of the age was Scottish polymath Mary Somerville, who studied math and astronomy. Another pioneer was Ada Lovelace, who worked with Charles Babbage on his Analytical Engine, an early version of the computer. She became an expert in sequencing instructions on the punched cards that it used, and wrote the earliest machine algorithm, becoming the world's first computer programmer. Perhaps the most famous female scientist of the age, however, was Polish chemist and physicist Marie Curie (see right), who studied radioactivity.

Outside of the laboratory, in the 19th century naturalists revolutionized the study of living things. Breaking with religious teachings about creation, palaeontologists such as Mary Anning and Elizabeth Philpot dug fossils out of the earth and used them to piece together a picture of prehistoric life. Biologists such as Jeanne Villepreux-Power, who invented the aquarium, studied living animals. The botanist Anna Atkins merged the study of the natural world with cutting-edge technology, using the new invention of photography to make images of algae and plants. In the medical world, Elizabeth Blackwell and Elizabeth Garrett Anderson fought for, and won, the right to train and qualify as doctors in the US and Britain respectively.

Making the modern world

Women were also involved in engineering and inventing. When her engineer husband became incapacitated, Emily Warren Roebling took over the management of the construction of the Brooklyn Bridge. In Britain, inventor Hertha Marks Ayrton became the first female fellow of the Royal Society for her work to improve the design of the electric arc lamps that were starting to light up the world's cities.

The female scientists, engineers, inventors, and doctors of the 19th century helped to start a revolution. By campaigning for women's education and the opening up of careers in all fields to females, they paved the way for the increased rights women would attain in the 20th century, including the right to vote (see pp. 206–209).

"THAT **BRAIN** OF MINE IS **SOMETHING MORE** THAN **MERELY MORTAL**."

ADA LOVELACE, ENGLISH MATHEMATICIAN AND WRITER, 1843

BIOGRAPHY
MARIE CURIE

Born in Poland in 1867, Maria Sklodowska moved to Paris as a young woman to study physics. There, she met Pierre Curie, who would become her husband as well as her scientific partner. They discovered the radioactive elements polonium (which Marie named after her home country) and radium. After Pierre's death, Marie worked with their daughter Irène to pioneer the use of X-rays in medicine. In 1903 she became the first woman to win a Nobel Prize, and she is still the only woman to win it twice, in two different fields — firstly in physics and then in chemistry in 1911.

◀ In the lab
Marie Curie surveys her laboratory at the Radium Institute in France in 1921. She trained around 150 women as radiological assistants during her time at the Institute.

Science

For centuries, brilliant women have worked tirelessly to discover and analyze the unknown processes of the universe. Nonetheless, women in science and mathematics have had to fight for their work to be recognized by the academic community.

SINCE ANTIQUITY, trailblazing women have pursued the studies of science and mathematics. Hypatia of Alexandria was the first documented female mathematician in 4th-century ancient Greece, where she taught philosophy and astronomy as head of the Neoplatonic School. Women worked as healers in ancient Egypt and, across diverse cultures, women have a long history of experimenting with herbs and other natural remedies. They practised as midwives and nurses, and passed down their skills and knowledge from one generation to the next. In the Middle Ages, convents in Europe provided education for women – a crucial resource, as most of the world's earliest universities did not accept women students.

As the centuries passed, upper-class women pursued science and mathematics as a hobby. Some assisted their husband's research, while others struck out on their own. However, these pioneers were usually denied formal qualifications, and their work was often ignored. There were notable exceptions: in 1732 the Italian physicist Laura Bassi became the first woman to be admitted to the Bologna Academy of Sciences. She was awarded a doctorate and a chair (the first physics professor at a European university) but

▼ **Flair for numbers**
Émilie du Châtelet was a French scientist in the 18th century. She applied her talent at math to win at gambling, using the proceeds to buy books and laboratory equipment. She was Voltaire's mistress, and together they made Newton's work accessible for the rest of France.

> "Nothing worthwhile comes **easily** ... In my day I was told **women** didn't go into **chemistry**."
>
> **GERTRUDE ELION**, NOBEL PRIZE WINNER, 1988

due to her gender she was not allowed to teach at the university, and had to give lectures at her home. Maria Agnesi was appointed as the first woman mathematics professor, also at Bologna, in 1750, but it is doubtful that she actually took up the post.

In the 19th century, more women began to work as scientists (see pp. 166–167). Mary Anning made discoveries in Jurassic marine fossil beds on the south coast of England that changed our understanding of prehistory and Earth's history. Astronomers such as Caroline Herschel and Maria Mitchell used telescopes to see beyond our own planet and reveal the mysteries of the galaxy. Yet, as late as 1882, even eminent scientist Charles Darwin wrote: "I certainly think that women, though generally superior to men [in] moral qualities, are inferior intellectually." Prestigious universities such as Oxford and Cambridge established women's colleges around 1870, but although female students could attend lectures and take exams, they were not awarded degrees until 1920 at Oxford – and 1948 at Cambridge.

Scientific revolution

In the 20th century, the number of women in science exploded. From Gerty Cori, whose work in biochemistry led to discoveries about human metabolism, to Chien-Shiung Wu and Lise Meitner, who made breakthroughs in nuclear fission in the 1930s and 1940s, women were behind some of the century's key innovations. Despite these advances, women often saw the credit for their work go to male scientists. Meitner, along with chemist Isabella Karle, and astrophysicist Jocelyn Bell Burnell were overlooked for Nobel Prizes, while their male team members were honoured.

Nowadays, the story is very different. Women work as engineers, researchers, nuclear physicists, and more. Today's female science and mathematics students will continue to change the world, but they owe a huge debt to the brave women who led the way.

JANE GOODALL CHIMP CHAMP IN TANZANIA 1995

▼ **Scary Sue**
The world's largest complete *Tyrannosaurus rex* skeleton is named Sue after the paleontologist Sue Hendrickson, who discovered the fossil in South Dakota in 1990.

STEM SCHOLARS

Hypatia of Alexandria (c. 355–415) studied under her father, a noted mathematician and astronomer. Although Alexandria was under Roman rule, Hypatia worked to preserve the works of Greek mathematicians and astronomers. She produced works on astronomy and geometry and, but they have been lost. During her life she taught widely and gave popular lectures on many topics.

Wang Zhenyi (1768–1797) was taught astronomy, medicine, and mathematics by her older relatives, as well as poetry. An avid reader, Wang wrote a simplified version of the famous mathematics book *Principles of Calculation*, intending it for female and male students. Her astronomical work included calculating the movement of stars and planets, and explaining the causes of a lunar eclipse.

Caroline Herschel (1750–1848) trained as a singer but she eventually gave up her musical career to help her brother William with his astronomical research. She ground mirrors for his telescopes and performed the calculations needed for observing the skies. Once she got her own telescope she scanned the skies, discovering three nebulae and eight comets.

Sofia Kovalevskaya (1850–1891) was refused a place at a Berlin university because she was a woman, so she studied privately instead. Her work on differential equations won her recognition in mathematics, and she later taught at the University of Stockholm. She was the first woman in modern Europe to earn a doctorate in mathematics and the first to be given a full professorship.

Rosalind Franklin (1920–1958) was a pioneer in the use of X-ray diffraction technology. She used it to study DNA at a time when the chemical makeup and structure of DNA was still unknown. She showed that it had a helical shape, producing X-ray patterns of the complicated molecule that allowed Nobel Prize winners Watson and Crick to confirm its structure.

Katherine Johnson (b. 1918) began her career as a teacher, at a time when few professions were open to African American women. She got a job analyzing data and performing computations for the space programme. Her work helped calculate the flight paths of spacecraft, including the Apollo 11 mission to the moon. Her story featured in the acclaimed 2016 movie *Hidden Figures*.

THE FIGHT FOR
freedom

From the 1400s to the end of the 1800s, European powers captured, bought, and sold people of African descent as commodities in what was known as the transatlantic slave trade. African slaves, who survived horrific conditions on overcrowded slave ships, were forced to labour without pay in European colonies across the Atlantic. About 12.5 million slaves were shipped to North America, South America (Brazil was the world's biggest importer), and the Caribbean, but only 10.7 million survived the passage. More than half of the slaves were transported during the 18th century, when demand for labour rose with the growth of plantations for cash crops such as tobacco and sugar.

Slavery affected African women in a distinct way: they faced sexism and racism, and were vulnerable to sexual violence and coercion. Despite crushing oppression, enslaved women resisted their condition by various means including escape, infanticide, suicide, and feigning sickness or pregnancy.

Working the fields

Although Western cultural norms considered women unsuited to manual labour, enslaved African men and women often did the same work. They toiled side by side in tobacco fields in Virginia, under an overseer who was usually armed with a whip or a pistol. On Caribbean sugar plantations, women worked in the cane fields in the gruelling heat, and risked physical harm in the sugar mills. To justify women doing the field labour that white women were not believed capable of performing, slave-owning European colonialists characterized black women as subhuman. Some slaveholders even

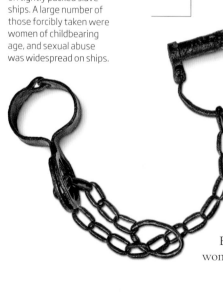

▼ **Slave shackles**
These iron ankle shackles chained captives together on tightly packed slave ships. A large number of those forcibly taken were women of childbearing age, and sexual abuse was widespread on ships.

BONDAGE TO FREEDOM

Up to 12 million African slaves were transported to the Americas from the 16th century onwards. Many were women, who were later pivotal in the abolition of slavery.

BEFORE 1700

1619 The first African slaves, including at least one woman, land at the British colony of Jamestown in what is now Virginia, US.

1621 The Dutch West India Company is formed, a principal mover in the transatlantic slave trade.

1656 Elizabeth Key successfully sues for her freedom on the grounds that her father was an English settler; the Virginia House of Burgesses then rules that a child born to an enslaved mother is a slave, regardless of the status of the father.

1700

1716 A slave known only as Maria leads a slave rebellion in Curacao, in the Dutch West Indies.

1781 Philadelphian slave Elizabeth Freeman sues her owner for her freedom and wins.

1791 A slave insurrection in the French colony of St Domingue sparks the Haitian Revolution; in 1802, freed woman Sanité Bélair is executed at the age of 21 for her part in the rebellion.

1800

1831 Nat Turner incites a slave revolt in Virginia; one woman is tried for her involvement.

1833 The Philadelphia Female Anti-Slavery Society is founded by 18 women, in response to the fact that the American Anti-Slavery Society only admits male members.

1843 A woman, Carlota, is one of three slaves to lead a rebellion in Cuba known as the Year of the Lash.

1863 During the US Civil War Harriet Tubman leads the Combahee River Raid, destroying confederate provisions and freeing c. 750 slaves.

1865 The 13th amendment abolishes slavery (except in the case of imprisonment) in the US.

◄ **WOMEN PICK COTTON** UNDER THE EYE OF AN OVERSEER IN GEORGIA, US, c. 1900

suggested that black women did not feel pain, needed no assistance in childbirth, and did not suffer when separated from their children.

Children born of enslaved women were legally slaveholders' property, so female slaves, known as "increasers" for their ability to reproduce, were seen as an investment. Slaves were encouraged to have families, but not allowed to legally marry, and families could be separated by sale at any time without warning. It was common for slave owners to have children with their slaves, who did not possess the legal, cultural, or physical power to resist their owner's advances. Hypersexualized stereotypes of black women also made them more vulnerable to sexual violence. The abolitionist speaker and reformer Harriet Jacobs, who escaped from slavery and gave an account of her experiences in *Incidents in the Life of Slave Girl* (1861), wrote that sexual harassment and abuse was widespread, and began for her when she was only 14 years old.

Resistance and abolitionism

Although enslaved women had very little control over their lives, they still fought their slavery. Refusing to work, or working slowly, were common methods of resistance. Some women broke the law and ran for freedom. Oney "Ona" Maria Judge, the enslaved maid of First Lady Martha Washington, evaded capture for over 30 years after her escape from the presidential house in 1796. Others rebelled on a larger scale; former slave Luiza Mahin reportedly made her home the headquarters of the Malê slave revolt of 1835, the biggest slave rebellion in Brazil. In August 1791, Cécile Fatiman, a Haitian voodoo practitioner, performed a religious ceremony at a slave meeting that helped to incite the Haitian Revolution, a successful anti-slavery revolt against French colonial rule.

From the late 17th century onwards, philosophers had argued that slavery was incompatible with a progressive, liberal society. The political battle to end

60%
of field labourers in the British colonies in 1838 were enslaved women

slavery began in the late 1700s with abolitionist societies such as the French *Société des Amis des Noirs* and the English Society for Effecting the Abolition of the Slave Trade, founded in 1787. More countries banned slavery in the decades that followed the American Revolution (see pp. 130–133), but the cotton-producing states of the Deep South held on to protect its plantation economy.

BIOGRAPHY
HARRIET TUBMAN

Born into slavery c. 1820 on a Maryland plantation, Harriet Tubman dedicated her life to freeing enslaved people as a "conductor" on the Underground Railroad – a secret network of routes whereby slaves escaped to free states. Tubman herself escaped slavery in 1849, using the railroad to flee to Philadelphia. From 1851 to 1857, she made two trips a year back to the South to help her family and many others escape. Tubman died of pneumonia in 1913.

◀ **Free at last**
A former slave poses with two men of the so-called Abolition Regiment who have escorted her to freedom, via the Underground Railroad. For women, escaping was particularly difficult as they had fewer opportunities and often had children to take care of.

As the abolitionist movement gained momentum, women played a prominent role. Black women such as Sojourner Truth (see pp. 174–175), Harriet Tubman, and Mary Ann Shadd Cary toured the US giving impassioned speeches that described the horrors and hypocrisy of slavery. Learning of the struggles of black mothers searching for their families inspired empathy in some white Americans, and convinced women such as novelist Harriet Beecher Stowe to take up the cause. Still, full emancipation in the US did not come until 1865, after a bloody Civil War (see pp. 176–177). In 1888, Brazil made slavery illegal, which many regard as the end of the transatlantic slave trade.

▲ **Into the light**
This quilted mural, entitled "Into the Light" depicts Harriet Tubman leading escaped slaves to freedom on the Underground Railroad (see left).

"SELF-RELIANCE IS THE TRUE ROAD TO INDEPENDENCE."

MARY ANN SHADD CARY, MOTTO OF HER NEWSPAPER, *PROVINCIAL FREEMAN*, FOUNDED IN 1853

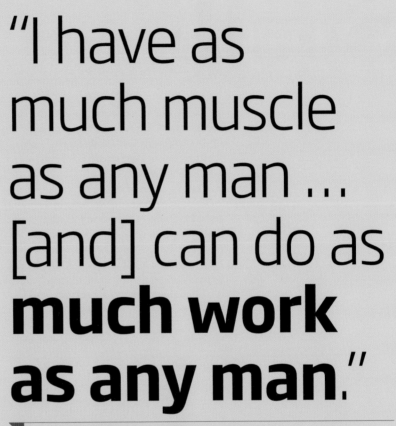

"I have as much muscle as any man ... [and] can do as **much work as any man.**"

SOJOURNER TRUTH, AT THE WOMEN'S RIGHTS CONVENTION IN AKRON, OHIO, MAY 1851

SPEAKING OUT

Feminist and abolitionist activist Sojourner Truth was born Isabella Baumfree in c.1797 to slave parents. After escaping and gaining freedom in 1826, Truth became one of the few African American women to speak publicly against slavery and for women's rights. In May 1851, she gave a rousing speech – later known as "Ain't I a Woman" – at the Ohio Women's Rights Convention in response to male ministers' claims of female inferiority. Truth supposedly pointed to her own muscles, gained in years of slave labour, to demonstrate a woman's strength. One common task for both male and female slaves in the South was picking cotton (left), which African American men and women continued to do for a living even after slavery was abolished.

NORTH VERSUS
South

THE US CIVIL WAR

By 1850, abolitionists (see pp 170–173) in the Northern US had grown more aggressive in their fight for universal liberty. The serialization of Harriet Beecher Stowe's novel *Uncle Tom's Cabin* in 1851, followed by its edition in book form in two volumes in 1852, inflamed existing opinion by bringing attention to the realities and immorality of slavery. The views of the Southern states, however, starkly contrasted those in the North. South Carolina, followed by the rest of the Southern states, chose to secede from the Union rather than end slavery, sparking a bloody civil war. Fighting began on 12 April, 1861, with the bombardment of Fort Sumter by Southern "Confederate" states.

War work

The war was one of the most significant events in US history, and women played an important role on the battlefield, in hospitals, and at home. About 20,000 females on both sides of the conflict became nurses in military hospitals. Dorothea Dix, a white educated woman from Maine, became the Union's "superintendent of female nurses" in 1861 and improved conditions for nurses and wounded soldiers. As the war progressed, formerly enslaved black women volunteered to assist as nurses, cooks, and laundresses. Some of the so-called "camp followers" who followed the troops were married to soldiers; others

▼ **Female partisans**
This flag designed for the Confederate States of America was allegedly made by the "secessionist ladies" of Washington, D.C., in around 1861. The women presented it to the 6th Virginia Cavalry who carried it during the war.

▶ **Camping out**
A Union soldier's wife stands with her husband and children in the 31st Pennsylvania Infantry camp. In addition to taking care of her family, she may have worked as a camp laundress, cook, or nurse.

"**NO CREATURE** ON GOD'S EARTH IS LEFT MORE … **DESOLATE** THAN THE **SLAVE**."

HARRIET BEECHER STOWE, *UNCLE TOM'S CABIN*, 1852

were prostitutes. Between 400–750 women disguised themselves as men and enlisted to fight as soldiers; Canadian Sarah Edmonds, for example, fought for the Union Army in the Battle of Blackburn's Ford and the first Battle of Bull Run under the name Franklin Thompson. Former slave Mary Elizabeth Bowser acted as a spy for the Union, while working as a maid in the home of the Confederate president, Jefferson Davis, in Richmond, Virginia. She allegedly had a photographic memory and could recite nearly every document she saw on Davis's desk to her spymaster.

Closer to the fighting, women in the South witnessed the violence of the war first-hand. The economy in the South, which relied on close to 4 million slaves, suffered greatly, and views of the war were often linked to class or financial status. The diaries of Mary Boykin Chesnut, the wife of a southern politician, show that some wealthy women personally supported the Confederacy. However, poor white women tended to see the war as a rich man's fight; in 1863, a mob of 65 armed women looted the city of Columbus, Georgia, for food.

President Abraham Lincoln issued the Emancipation Proclamation on 1 January 1863, effectively bringing the Southern slave economy to an end. The Civil War ended with a Northern victory in 1865. Although 620,000 lives were lost in the conflict, it won the freedom of millions of enslaved women and men alike.

BIOGRAPHY
CLARA BARTON

A well-educated woman from Massachussetts, Clara Barton (1821-1912) became a nurse when civil war broke out. She was initially a teacher but volunteered as a hospital nurse to Union soldiers from 1861. Soldiers dubbed the self-taught nurse the "Angel of the Battlefield". On one occasion while nursing at the front, a bullet tore through the sleeve of her dress and killed the man she was tending. In 1881, she founded the American Red Cross.

THE FIGHT AGAINST
imperialism

China's first peasant revolution, the Taiping rebellion of 1850 to 1864, exacted an enormous death toll: between 20 and 30 million people. Beginning in Guangxi Province, the rebellion was a morphing of theology and political activism that criticized the cultural dynamics of the ruling Manchu-led Qing Dynasty (see pp. 124–125) and the doctrines of Confucianism. By challenging tradition and imperialism, it was also the first movement to address women's rights in China. The Taipings were inspired by the Christian beliefs of European missionaries. Fighting with religious conviction, the rebels based ideas of equality on divine theology: as men and women were both children of God, they were entitled to the same treatment. Led by Hong Xiuquan, the Taipings successfully ruled a significant part of southern China during the middle of the 19th century.

Oppressions lifted

In the aftermath of the rebellion, women's lives under the Taipings improved in several ways. For example, attitudes towards concubinage and prostitution changed. Hong emphasized the importance of virtue in keeping with Biblical teachings on marriage; this led to polygamy and prostitution being banned. Hong's initial intentions regarding equality impacted on Chinese society positively too. British missionary Augustus Lindley noted that there was a distinct decline in the practice of female foot binding under Taiping rule. The Taipings were Hakka Chinese, an ethnic group who originate from provincial areas including Guangxi,

and their societal norms differed from Qing convention. Hakka women did not bind their feet, and the rebels discouraged what they considered to be as an oppressive practice. When the rebellion ended, Christian missionaries and Chinese Protestants continued to lobby against foot binding, leading to the practice being outlawed in the 20th century (see pp. 196-197).

The Taipings also provided women with new employment opportunities. In stark contrast to the domestic roles assigned in the

▼ **Material privileges**
The luxurious silk and satin house robe shown here suggests that the women of the Manchu elite had lives of material privilege, although the Qing system curtailed their social and civil rights.

Qing Dynasty, the rebels employed women in farming and construction. Women's work even extended to politics and education. Females were permitted to sit examinations and scrutinize Confucian texts for the first time.

However, although new opportunities materialized, the gap between reality and rhetoric was greater than first appeared. While the rebellion promised equality and liberation, newly independent women were often considered promiscuous and unprincipled. Furthermore, women's work groups were separate from men's, and those women who achieved any political authority were unable to exert influence over men, suggesting that segregation had simply been dressed up as egalitarianism. Chastity remained a focus in Taiping principalities, and some Qing traditionalism was ingrained, meaning that the promise of real gender equality was never fulfilled.

▲ **The ruling elite**
This 19th-century lithograph depicts upper-class Manchu women of the Qing Dynasty. After capturing Nanjing, the Taiping rebels killed all Manchu men, and then burned the Manchu women to death.

▼ **Taking Anqing**
Qing soldiers laid siege to the Taiping city of Anqing for a year. When it fell, the Qing killed the Taiping men and took more than 10,000 women for their own pleasure.

◀ **Native medicine**
Samoan women here prepare kawakawa, one of the key healing herbs in *rongoā* - traditional Māori medicine. Women all over the world have practised herbal medicine since antiquity.

Being a female physician was risky; if a patient failed to get better or died she could be accused of witchcraft (see pp. 122–123). By the 18th century traditional cures tended to be dismissed as folklore by male doctors, anxious to protect their professional status. Increasingly, the wealthy chose male obstetrics over midwives as their techniques were deemed more "scientific".

THROUGH THE AGES

Medicine

Women have always worked as healers, herbalists, nurses, and midwives, but they were largely excluded from the male-dominated medical profession. However, since the mid-19th century, increasing numbers of women have trained to become physicians and surgeons.

THE FIRST RECORDED FEMALE PHYSICIAN in history was Merit–Ptah, who held a senior position at the pharaoh's court in Egypt in c. 2700 BCE, but before the 19th century such a role was very rare. Even when women were allowed to practise medicine, they focused mostly on gynaecological and obstetrical health, and worked as midwives. Women were also herbalists who used plants to treat illnesses. Denied access to trade guilds and universities, most females were trained informally. An exception was in convents, where women such as 12th-century German abbess Hildegard of Bingen wrote texts in order to train nuns to perform medicine.

In the 19th century women campaigned for the right to formally train as doctors. Pioneering figures such as Elizabeth Garrett Anderson found ways around the sexist attitudes of the mainstream medical profession. Born in London, Garrett Anderson was inspired to become a doctor after meeting Elizabeth Blackwell, the first female doctor to

HILDEGARD OF BINGEN 12TH-CENTURY PORTRAIT

> " It is ... the **instinct of** ... **women** to appear as **physicians** ... "
>
> **ANN PRESTON**, FIRST FEMALE DEAN OF A MEDICAL COLLEGE

graduate in the US. When Garrett Anderson was denied access to medical school on account of her gender, she was undeterred. She discovered a loophole; a London guild called the Worshipful Society of Apothecaries could still license physicians, and its charter did not permit them to bar women. In 1865, she passed their examinations and earned the right to practise medicine. Garrett Anderson went on to have a distinguished medical career, and paved the way for countless other women.

As many medical colleges would only accept men, specialist institutions for women began to be set up, such as the New England Female Medical College, established in Boston in 1848. This, and similar institutions such as the London School of Medicine for Women (founded in 1874), allowed women to earn medical degrees. Around the same time, the training of nurses was modernized and professionalized. An influential pioneer in this endeavour was the English nurse Florence Nightingale who, after serving in the Crimean War (1854–1856), established a nursing school at St. Thomas' Hospital, London, in 1860.

Women break through

Despite these advances, the barriers faced by women in medicine were numerous, and numbers in the field remained low. Even those who had completed training were rejected by the male medical establishment, and consequently, many female physicians set up their own clinics. World War I proved to be a watershed; the need for doctors and the death of so many men led to more universities opening their doors to women to train in medicine. As a result women became more active in medical research; in 1947 the Czech-American scientist Gerty Cori became the first woman to win the Nobel Prize in Physiology or Medicine. The 1970s saw another profound change as anti-discrimination laws in many countries led to more women enrolling at medical colleges. In most Western countries in the world, there are now roughly equal numbers of men and women training to be doctors.

▲ **Lady with the lamp**
This Turkish lantern was used by Crimean war nurses and possibly by Florence Nightingale herself in the 1850s. The nurses' workload was huge; at one point less than 100 nurses had 10,000 men under their care.

PRACTITIONERS

Jacqueline Felice de Almania (c. 1322) highlights the suspicion that women practicing medicine faced. Born to a Jewish family in Florence, she moved to Paris where she worked as a physician and performed surgery. In 1322 she was tried for practising unlawfully. In spite of the court hearing testimonials of her ability as a doctor, she and three other female doctors were banned from medicine.

Tan Yunxian (1461-1554) was a Chinese physician who learned her skills from her grandparents. Chinese women at the time could not serve apprenticeships with doctors, but Tan passed the jinshi exam despite being humiliated and insulted by her examiners. Tan treated women from the humble to the elite. In 1511, Tan wrote a book, *Sayings of a Female Doctor*, describing her career as a physician.

James Barry (c.1789-1865) was born Margaret Bulkley in Ireland but, disguised as a man, she enrolled at Edinburgh University to study medicine. She qualified as a surgeon in 1813, then joined the British Army, serving overseas. Barry was a skilled surgeon and promoter of sanitation, who rose to the rank of Inspector General of Hospitals. Barry retired in 1859, having spent her entire medical career living and working as a man.

Elizabeth Blackwell (1821-1910) was born in England but emigrated to the US in 1832. In 1849, she graduated top of her class at medical college - the first woman in America to earn a degree in medicine. In 1853, she opened a dispensary in New York, and during the American Civil War trained nurses. She returned to England in 1869, where she had her own practice and taught medicine.

Rebecca Lee Crumpler (1831-1895) worked as a nurse for eight years before enrolling in medical college in Boston in 1860. Four years later, she was the first African American woman to receive a medical degree. She moved to Virginia in 1865, where she provided medical care to freed slaves. Four years later she returned to Boston where she continued to practise medicine.

Kadambini Ganguly (1861-1923) was born in Bhagalpur, northern India. In 1883, she became the first of two Indian women to gain a university degree. In 1886, she graduated from medical college in Kolkata - the same year another Indian woman, Anandi Gopal Joshi, graduated with a medical degree in the US.

"I thought it my duty to ride up to the hut ... and do **my woman's work**."

MARY SEACOLE, EMBARKING ON THE SHIP
TO BALACLAVA, 1854

NURSING ON THE FRONT

Mary Seacole, a Jamaican-born nurse, played a pioneering role in caring for British soldiers in the Crimean War (1853-1856). When Seacole offered her services as a nurse, she was rejected by various British government offices due to racial discrimination. In contrast to Seacole's experiences, white women were warmly welcomed. Undaunted, Seacole travelled to the Crimean Peninsula using her own resources. She arrived in Balaclava in 1854 where, at her own expense, she tended to the wounded and established a "British Hotel", which provided food, drinks, and supplies for soldiers. Although Seacole's contribution faded from memory after her death, in the late 20th century she received wide recognition and was awarded the Jamaican Order of Merit in 1991.

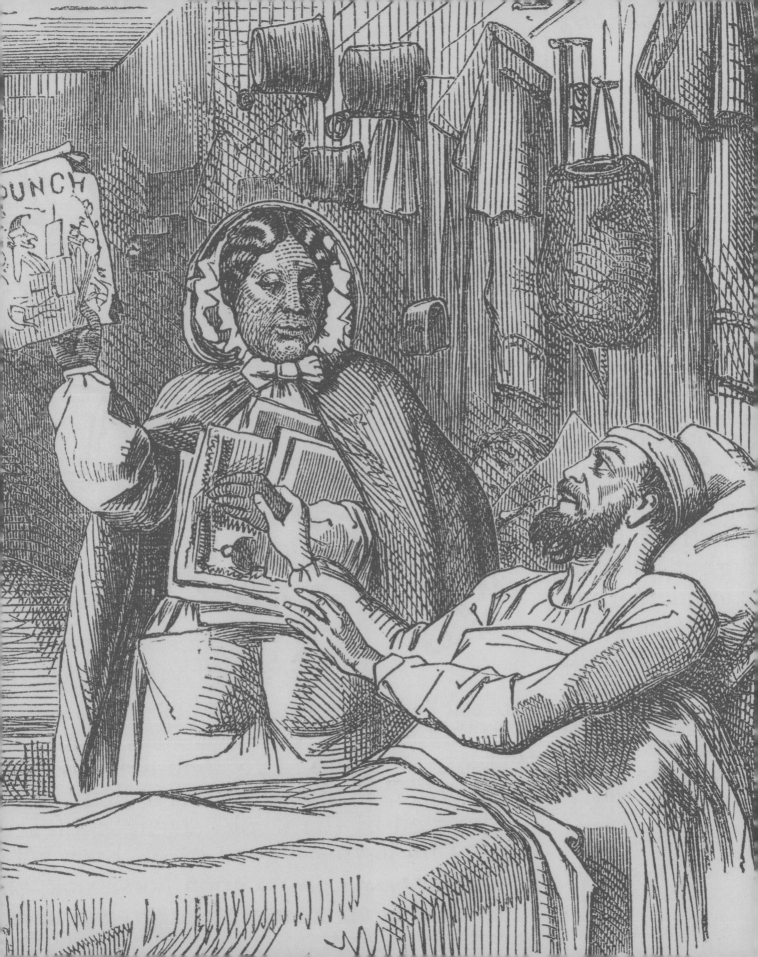

LIFE ON
the frontier

The settlement of the American West is a much-romanticized period, but undeniably one during which female pioneers were granted unprecedented opportunities for independence. However, westward expansion took place at the expense of America's indigenous peoples; the opportunities created for white women were often founded on the destruction of Native women's traditional homelands and their way of life.

In the years after the founding of the US, its citizens explored land farther and farther west. As early as 1787, Congress adopted the Northwest Ordinance, which allowed US citizens to settle and govern Native American lands. Tribal nations protested the invasions of territories that their people had occupied for millennia, but the government saw westward expansion as the country's destiny and pushed Native people to join US society. In 1862, Congress passed the Homestead Act, which offered settlers 160 acres of land, free of charge, which they could claim if they agreed to live on and farm ("improve") the land for five years. The Act provided a unique opportunity for single and widowed women to provide for themselves, as women could claim the title under their own names. However, married women could not file a claim. Between 1863–1930, homesteaders claimed at least 3 million acres a year.

◀ **Native doll**
Dolls were often made by grandmothers for their grandchildren. This one shows a Sioux woman in riding attire, typical of the nomadic Plains people, and a dress style worn by adult women.

WOMEN OF THE WEST

While the Homestead Act and associated laws gave women in the US opportunities, western expansion forced Native Americans off their lands and onto reserves.

1800

1830 Andrew Jackson passes the Indian Removal Act, removing eastern Native American nations to lands west of the Mississippi River.

1841 The Prevention Act allows settlers to claim land before purchasing it.

1848 The gold rush occurs in California, leading to the removal of Native American nations living in the lands needed for mining towns.

1849 Andrew Johnson introduces a homestead bill to provide 160 acres of free land to any man who proved he could "improve it".

1850 The Donation Land Claim Act gives 640 acres to couples and 320 acres to individuals provided that they are over 18, white citizens, and promise to live on it for four years.

1862 President Lincoln passes the Homestead Act; women applying for land under their own name are eligible.

1863 Mary Meyer, who had been living on her land in Nebraska since 1860, becomes the first woman to file a homestead claim – less than three weeks after the first male claim.

1864 The US cavalry murders at least 150 Cheyenne and Arapaho people – mostly women, children, and the elderly – in the Sand Creek Massacre, Colorado.

1871 A total of 144 Apache people, mostly women and children, are slaughtered by the Committee of Public Safety outside Camp Grant Arizona where they have been granted asylum.

1890 Considered the last battle of the Plains Wars, US troops kill at least 150 unarmed men, women, and children in the Wounded Knee Massacre, South Dakota.

◄ **A MORMON AND HIS WIVES** STAND IN FRONT OF THEIR HOMESTEAD IN GREAT SALT LAKE VALLEY, 1869.

»

Life out west was dangerous for settlers for a variety of reasons. Although newspapers emphasized the potential danger of Native American warfare, most settler fatalities came from sickness and deprivation.

The Donner Party, a group of 87 western migrants trapped in California's Sierra Nevada mountains in the winter of 1846, famously cannibalized members of their own party in order to survive in the face of starvation and hypothermia. Forty people died, and the incident became a symbol of the dangers of western settlement. Within the party, more men died than women – this is sometimes attributed to the fact that women stayed inside the wagons to look after children, whereas young, single men were more active and so the most at risk. Women also have lower daily caloric needs and maintain a higher ratio of body fat, which is thought to have aided their survival.

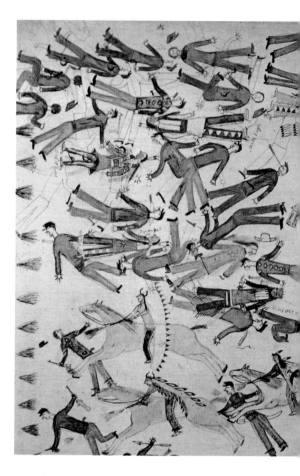

Pioneers

The Homestead Act was especially popular with single, widowed, or divorced women, and later, immigrants. Although these women made singular claims, they were not alone in the west but became part of the new communities that built up. Lucy Goldthorpe, for example, was a young, single woman who claimed a homestead in Williams County, North Dakota, in 1905. There, she continued her previous career as a teacher, and even hosted Christmas dinner for other single women and young men from nearby homesteads. Success stories like Goldthorpe's were not limited to white women. Former slaves were granted the right to make homesteading claims in 1866, and many took up the offer of a new life. An African American woman named Agnes Morgan moved west around 1880 as a domestic servant to a white family, but in time was able to claim her own property in Granite County, Montana, and create an independent life for herself.

Gambling was a problem in the so-called "Wild West" and some pioneer women contributed to it. Eleanor Dumont, a gambler, opened a number of saloons in Nevada City, California, before losing everything and taking her own life in 1879. Alice Ivers opened her own saloon in Dakota territory in the 1870s, but was arrested after killing a violent patron.

◀ **Sharp shooter**
Annie Oakley was one of a few women who made a living as an entertainer, dazzling viewers at Buffalo Bill Cody's Wild West show with her marksmanship.

◄ **Custer's last stand**
The Battle of Little Bighorn was fought between Plains Indians and US troops in June 1876. This artwork celebrates the Native victory and the death of US General Custer. Women (right) prepare a ceremony for the returning warriors.

Worse were the female outlaws. Bandit queen Belle Starr married a string of outlaw men, acting as their partner in crime to steal horses, cattle, and cash.

War for the Plains

In 1830, President Jackson signed the Indian Removal Act, calling for the relocation of the Cherokee, Choctaw, Creek, Chickasaw, and Seminole Indians to land west of the Mississippi River. These forced relocations from Southeastern states became known as the "Trail of Tears" because the tribes had to march in bad weather, and were also subject to disease and starvation. Cherokee woman Chin Deenawash, the only member of her family to survive relocation, even had to dig a trail-side grave for her youngest child with only a broken knife case. As Americans began to settle land farther beyond the Mississippi, the tribes of the Plains (notably the Lakota Sioux and their allies) fought back. From the 1850s until the bloody massacre of the Lakota at Wounded Knee in 1890, warfare broke out regularly. Native women both fought in the skirmishes and suffered as casualties of attacks. The Plains people were ultimately defeated and forced onto reservations – small parcels of land – on which they were pressured to embrace American culture.

90
Shoshone women were killed by US troops in the Bear River Massacre in January 1863.

BIOGRAPHY
BUFFALO CALF ROAD WOMAN

Probably born in the 1850s, Buffalo Calf Road Woman was part of the Northern Cheyenne nation and lived on the northern plains. As the only Cheyenne woman fighting in the Battle of the Rosebud in June 1876, she gained some renown for riding her horse directly into the fray to rescue her brother. The Cheyenne referred to the conflict as the "Battle Where the Girl Saved her Brother", and she was granted the name "Brave Woman" by Cheyenne chief Box Elder for her actions. She went on to fight alongside her husband in the Battle of Little Bighorn. Buffalo Calf Road Woman died in 1879.

THE SCRAMBLE FOR
Africa

The phrase "Scramble for Africa" refers to the rapid colonization of the continent by European powers during the 19th and 20th centuries. An often-cited justification for the so-called "scramble" was to end the African slave trade, but European explorers also took the opportunity to exploit Africa's natural resources. Missionary-explorer David Livingstone claimed that the only way to "liberate" the people of the African continent was to introduce the "three C's" – commerce, civilization, and Christianity.

European missionaries, many of whom were nuns and lay women, played an ambiguous role in this endeavour. They were driven by a genuine desire to improve the

▶ **Enslaving the continent**
Women, who traditionally perform horticultural work in many African countries, labour on a state banana plantation in Irebu Camp in the Belgian Congo, c.1900-1910.

quality of life in Africa by establishing schools and hospitals; however, missionary workers also inflicted their white imperialist values on the indigenous population, so destroying local traditions. Education is probably the area where female missionaries had the most positive impact. Ironically, most of the people who later fought for African independence were educated by missionaries.

The colonization of Africa came at huge human cost. Those Africans who were unwilling to labour for colonizers were sometimes violently coerced. In the Belgian Congo, methods were especially brutal: for example, the hands of women, men, and children who failed to meet rubber-harvesting quotas were routinely chopped off, and

women were sometimes held hostage to force the men to work. In addition, imperial appropriation of communally held land, in the Belgian Congo and elsewhere on the continent, impacted women's traditional role in agriculture. As communal land was reduced and the different types of crops were restricted in order to maximize cash crops for export, women's traditional status as the cultivators of land was undermined. At the same time, as men began to travel to work in mines and factories, women had less help at home, so increasing their labour but not their status.

▲ **Lady Sharpshooter**
British settler Mrs Davies fires on Boer positions during the 217-day siege of Mafeking in 1900. Tales of the plucky woman were widely published in British newspapers.

Casualties and combatants

The jockeying for control and resources on the continent also led to colonial clashes, such as the Boer Wars, between the British, who were expanding into southern Africa, and the Transvaal Republic, an independent country founded in 1852 by Dutch-speaking farmers of the eastern Cape (the Boers). During the Second Boer War (1900–1902), the British, unable to counter the guerrilla-style tactics of the Boers, removed the Boers' support base by rounding up all non-combatants, including women and children, and placing them in concentration camps. These camps were poorly administered and overcrowded and many of the incarcerated died from hunger and disease.

Yet women were not simply passive victims of the conflict in South Africa – some determined individuals fought alongside male fighters. Patriotic Boer Sarah Raal, for example, escaped from a camp and joined her brothers in a commando unit. On the British side, Lady Sarah Wilson, an aunt of Winston Churchill, became the first female war correspondent after writing about the Siege of Mafeking, and Emily Hobhouse, an English philanthropist and social worker, reported on abhorrent conditions in the British camps. After reading Hobhouse's report, suffragette Millicent Fawcett (see pp. 206–209) spent five months visiting the camps as part of an official enquiry that led to substantial improvements, although thousands still perished.

4,000
of the 28,000 who died in Boer concentration camps were women

> "Come, my **beloved**, let us **go forth** into the **field** … Let us **get up early** to the **vineyards** … there will I **give thee my loves**.

THE BIBLE, SONG OF SONGS 7:12

EXPERIENCES OF SEXUALITY

Sex and sexuality

In many societies, female sexuality was - and still is - a taboo subject. A woman's virginity was prized above all else, and her sexual behaviour was a subject of intense scrutiny, while double standards meant that men enjoyed far greater freedoms.

THROUGH THE AGES, a woman's worth has been tied to her virginity. Sexual intercourse, for women, was not about pleasure, but rather about conceiving children and pleasing their husbands. Historically, and today in societies where female sexuality remains suppressed, women have been punished for being promiscuous, or for simply being perceived to have committed a sin, such as having sex outside of marriage. Women's partners, however, were likely to receive little or no censure for such actions.

In 1900 BCE, women's sexual urges were characterized as a medical condition. The ancient Greek philosopher Plato described such urges as a "wandering womb", which likely led to the term "hysteria" ("womb disease") – a diagnosis that became common 4,000 years later, during the Victorian era.

The medicalization of women's sexuality led to extreme methods of treatment. Mentions of chastity belts dating to the 6th century CE in Europe suggest that some societies went to great physical lengths to prevent women from giving in to sexual temptation – although evidence suggests that such devices were mainly used to protect women from rape by invaders during times of war. During the Victorian era, "hysterical" women were placed in mental asylums, where a common treatment was to induce orgasms or "hysterical paroxysms". Today, the practice of female genital cutting in parts of Africa, Asia, and the Middle East also discourages women from sex by making the act a painful prospect.

While women were not expected to have strong sexual urges, they were expected to have enough knowledge and enjoyment of the act to please their husbands. According to legend, Helen of Troy's maid Astyanassa wrote the first book on sexual positions, suggesting

> "[She] **preferred** her **pleasure** to **all the honour** in the world … and **carried** her **head high**.

MARGUERITE OF NAVARRE, 1558

▲ Locked down
Chastity belts were iron locking devices supposedly worn by medieval women to prevent them from intercourse. Some historians now consider their widespread use a 19th-century myth.

> ❝ Women are **not like men** in sensual matters. They … do **not love lust for lust's sake**. **Passion must come** to them **accompanied** not only **with love**, but with … **kindness** … ❞

ELIZA BISBEE DUFFEY, *THE RELATIONS OF THE SEXES*, 1889

that sex advice was privately passed on among women long before modern women's magazines such as *Cosmopolitan* began to publish tips for the average reader. Some women went against social taboos to write treatises and pamphlets to teach their peers about sex. One such writer was Ida Craddock of Philadelphia, who distributed a pamphlet called "The Wedding Night" in 1902, and took her own life to avoid the jail sentence that would have followed.

Erotic art and poetry have also always existed, created by women as well as men. In ancient China, erotic poems were written by both sexes, and female bhakti poets (see pp. 74–75) in India wrote sexual odes to their gods. In the 20th century, female writers pushed boundaries to write about female desires and experiences. Anaïs Nin's 1940s' collection of erotic short stories *Delta of Venus*, published posthumously in 1977, were unflinchingly explicit.

Sexual revolution

The more liberal climate of the postwar years encouraged scientific studies of sexuality that attempted to pinpoint the source of the female orgasm, opening up the topic for debate. In 1948 and 1953, American sociologist Alfred Kinsey shocked readers with his studies, known as the Kinsey Reports, about both male and female sexuality; this contributed to a change in public opinion about sexuality, and helped to lay the groundwork for the "Sexual Revolution" of the 1960s. The Hite Report (1976), a collection of first-hand accounts from women, also drew attention to the subject.

Changing attitudes, plus the availability of birth control (see pp. 278–279) from the '60s onwards, have given women in the West

increased freedom to explore both sex and sexual identity (see pp. 302–303) outside the confines of marriage and heterosexuality. In the 1980s, a "sex positive" movement sprang up among some feminists, who embraced all forms of consensual sexual activity, including pornography. This alienated other feminists who viewed pornography as a form of male oppression.

▶ **Guided pleasures**
A 19th-century illumination from the *Kama Sutra* depicts lovers in an embrace. Written in the 3rd century CE, this manual of sexual pleasure was intended to be read by both men and women alike.

> ❝ I am a **winged creature** who is **too rarely allowed** to use its **wings**. **Ecstasies** do not occur **often enough**. ❞

ANAÏS NIN, *DELTA OF VENUS*, 1977

MISTRESSES, MAIDS, AND
governesses

19TH-CENTURY AUSTRALIA

In the early 1800s there was a significant gender imbalance in the colony of New South Wales and in the new settlements of Port Philip and Adelaide. Male convicts, soldiers, and free settlers greatly outnumbered women in these regions. Good female servants were highly sought after, and English women in Australia who wrote to their relatives often expressed their concerns over finding suitable

servants and governesses for their children. Except for those who had been convicted of violent crimes, female convicts were placed as soon as they arrived as cooks and housemaids. Former convicts, known as emancipists, who were literate were considered unsuitable as governesses, because if they could read it was often the case that they had been convicted of forgery or political crimes. For those lucky

▶ **Colonizing a continent**
A white couple pose with their Aboriginal employees in 1855. Aboriginal staff earned a tiny fraction of the wages paid to white domestic workers, leading to accusations of slavery.

enough to find a female emigrant to employ, the likelihood was that she would find a husband almost immediately and leave her position.

Servitude or slavery?

The lack of female workers led to initiatives to bring more working-class emigrants to Australia. In Britain, the government decided to provide incentives to encourage single, working-class women to emigrate. They offered women not only free passage but also money to get them started in their new lives abroad. Meanwhile, in famine-struck Ireland young women began to emigrate directly from the foundling hospitals and workhouses; some of these girls were as young as 15. At first, there was no infrastructure in place to help females find positions when they arrived, but in the 1840s, Caroline Chisholm began meeting every migrant ship that arrived in Sydney. She found domestic positions for many single girls, and in 1842 published her report *Female Immigration, Considered in a Brief Account of the Sydney Immigrants' Home* – the longest work published by any Australian woman up to that time.

In the 19th century, domestic service was the most common form of employment for Aboriginal women, and the government came to believe that this was the only suitable employment for them. Aboriginal servants were in great demand by European colonists. As a result girls who had been removed from their families were sent out from missions (see pp. 138–139) to work in households and look after children who were not much younger than themselves. Some historians regard this practice as akin to slavery: the youngest recorded Aboriginal servant girl in Queensland was only three years old. Aboriginal women and girls were expected to work incredibly hard, but were treated very poorly in return.

In the 20th century, domestic service in Australia became increasingly linked to the Aboriginal civil rights movement. In 1934, for example, a group of Aboriginal women who worked as domestics for white people petitioned the Royal Commission into Aboriginal Status and Conditions in Western Australia, asking that the commission "give us our Freedom and release us from the stigma of a native and make us happy Subjects of this our country." However, even as late as the 1970s, young Aboriginal girls were separated from their families and forced into domestic work, and so were denied both the wages and education that might bring them freedom.

▲ **Servitude**
Two wealthy European women travel from England to Australia with their young Aboriginal servant seated on the ground beside them in this 19th-century illustration.

▼ **Helping hand**
The philanthropist Caroline Chisholm greets a newly arrived immigrant travelling with her child. Chisholm helped such women find work in Australia and established homes where they could stay.

"THE **BEST THING** ... IS TO **SELECT** SOME **OLD CRONE, NOT PAST WORK,** WHO IS **VERY UGLY**."

CHARLES ROWCROFT, *TALES OF THE COLONIES*, 1843

"In small matters [foreigners] oppress ... people; in large matters they **insult what is divine**."

EMPRESS DOWAGER CIXI, IN SUPPORT OF THE BOXER UPRISINGS, 1900

THE BOXER REBELLION

Empress Dowager Cixi was the de facto ruler of China's Manchu Qing Dynasty from 1861–1908. In 1899, she gave her support to the Boxer rebels, who wanted to rid China of Western influence. Much of their hatred of foreigners was directed at Western missionaries and Chinese converts to Christianity, whom they saw as betraying their culture. In June 1900, over 100,000 people – mainly Chinese Christians, but also 200 foreigners – were murdered at the empress's command. Although the Boxer rebellion ultimately failed, Cixi continued to rule until her death in 1908.

THE END OF
foot binding

20TH-CENTURY CHINA

The spread of feminist ideas in early 20th-century China was due in part to the activities of foreign Christian missionaries, but it also sprang from a new emerging Chinese intelligentsia. Wealthy families sent their children to be educated in Europe or the US, hoping that on their return they would take up prominent positions in society. Inspired by concepts such individual freedom, this young group began to disseminate Western ideas in China. As a result, the Chinese Nationalist Party, known as the Kuomintang, was set up in 1912 by Sun Yat-sen, the founding father of the Republic of China. This opened the way for modernization along Western lines, with a radical transformation of the state system.

Era of reform

Reform-minded intellectuals addressed women's issues such as the centuries-old custom of foot binding. Traditionally, in China small feet represented the pinnacle of female beauty: however, foot binding was a practice that was inextricably linked to suffering and disability. Founded in 1883,

the Anti-foot binding Society campaigned throughout China to end the painful but popular practice, and soon reached 300,000 members. Under pressure from these campaigners, the Empress Dowager Cixi issued an edict against foot binding in 1902. Although the ban was annulled in 1912, with the fall of the Qing Dynasty, the practice was finally ended by the Republic of China in 1949. Thereafter foot binding was seen as an outmoded symbol of China's past.

Chinese reformers also sought fundamental changes in education. Philosopher Liang Qichao, for example, argued that in order to build a strong nation, women needed to be educated and financially independent. Prior to the late Qing period, Chinese

◀ **Footloose, finally**
This watercolour depicts female cyclists on a street in China c.1900. Across the world women on bicycles represented that the times were changing, not least for women's clothing.

"I HOPE WE CAN **LEAVE** THE **PAST BEHIND** US AND **FOCUS ON** OUR **FUTURE**".

QIU JIN, *AN ADDRESS TO HER 200 MILLION FELLOW COUNTRYWOMEN*, 1904

▲ **Aesthetics of cruelty**
A pair of lotus shoes for bound feet, which were seen as highly erotic in Chinese culture. Women had to take tiny steps, adopting a swaying "lotus gait".

education emphasized the importance of being a virtuous wife and good mother. With reforms in the early 20th century and the establishment of new girls' schools, the education system began to extol gender equality. Books and periodicals urged women to participate in actively changing society. The most influential work on women's liberation during this period was the male writer Jin Yi's *Nüjie zhong* (*The Women's Bell*) (1903), which stressed that there was no distinction in moral conscience and intellectual ability between men and women.

Many Chinese intellectuals also advocated for the idea of women's full emancipation in marriage. Confucian scholar Kang Youwei looked forward to traditional marriage being replaced with a series of one-year contracts. The May Fourth Movement of 1919 raised awareness of sexual equality; during the protest men and women interacted with each other in public and advocated making marriage a free choice – a right finally granted in 1950.

◀ **Bound by beauty**
Foot binding began when a girl was around 4 years old. To create "golden lily" feet, the four smaller toes were crushed under the sole and the rear of the anklebone was flattened.

BIOGRAPHY
QIU JIN

A revolutionary Chinese feminist, Qiu Jin was born into a well-to-do liberal family in 1875. In 1903, she left her husband and children to pursue an education in Japan. Upon her return to China in 1906, Qiu cofounded the *Chinese Women's Journal*, which promoted women's emancipation. She argued that liberated women were crucial for a strong Chinese nation. In 1907, however, Qiu was executed for her part in an unsuccessful plot to overthrow the government.

The Age of Empowerment

1914–1960

Women's contributions to the war efforts of the 20th century helped to transform their role. The absence of men forced many women into the workplace, making armaments, producing food, and upholding the home front, while other women took to the battlefields as nurses and soldiers. Women joined forces not only in national efforts, but also in the fight for their own rights. In the first wave of feminism, women mobilized to change unequal laws and to gain the right to vote. Resistance to colonial and oppressive powers also saw women in the developing world unite in protest. By the 1960s, with a new, second wave of feminism just beginning, women were on the brink of a period of great change.

FROM HOME FRONT TO
front lines

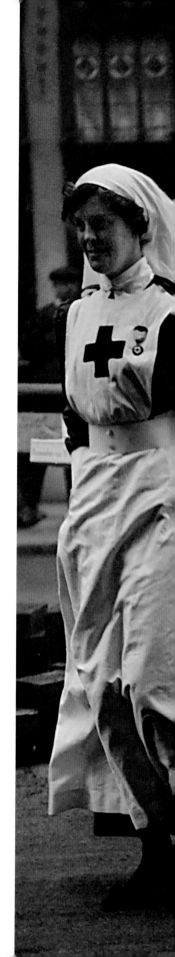

In summer 1917, the Russian Army was in trouble. Beset by desertions and close to defeat, they took the extreme measure of forming several all-female battalions in an attempt to inspire their male soldiers. Around 5,000 women eagerly took up arms, with two of the battalions seeing action on the front line. The most famous was Petrograd's so-called Battalion of Death, led by a peasant women named Maria Bochkareva.

In July 1917, in the Kerensky Offensive, Bochkareva's battalion was placed alongside a male force, and reportedly had to fend off attacks from their own countrymen. When the time came to go over the trenches, the men hesitated, but the Battalion of Death stormed out, pushing into German territory and smashing bottles of vodka they found in the Russian men's trenches. Without reinforcements, they were forced to retreat. Eventually, due to hostility from male units, the women's battalions were disbanded.

Women, including Romanian war hero Ecaterina Teodoroiu, also fought for Serbia and Romania. Initially serving as a nurse, she was allowed to join an infantry regiment but was later killed in battle during a counterattack against German troops.

The fighting women of the Eastern Front were something of an exception. During the war, the women who ventured closest to the fighting were usually nurses. When the war broke out, Dr Elsie Inglis, a British suffragette, offered the War Office her expertise in training nurses but was told to

◄ **"All for the soldiers"**
Propaganda called on Russian women to work to support the war effort. However, it could not stop the women's rebellions that broke out over food shortages in Russia and elsewhere.

WORLD WAR I

Women's contributions to the war effort were varied. Amid the large-scale movements, some singular heroines emerged and many died for their country.

1914

Pamphlets encourage women to contribute on the home front. German women are later asked to donate their hair due to textile shortages.

1915

June English reporter Dorothy Lawrence travels to France and visits the front line disguised as a male soldier.

12 October British nurse Edith Cavell is executed by the Germans in Belgium for helping Allied troops.

1916

French women privately create auxiliary military service organizations within the French War Office; 70,000 women enrol.

December The Prussian War Office creates the Women's Central Work Office, headed by the social worker Dr Marie-Elisabeth Lüders, to help bring female workers into factories.

1917

March Women known as "Yeomanettes" enlist in the US Navy; 600 are on duty by May.

March 31 The British Women's Army Auxiliary Corps arrives in France and Belgium to fill support roles due to a manpower shortage caused by the bloody Battle of the Somme in 1916.

July The First Russian Women's Battalion of Death is sent to the front line.

October 25 The First Petrograd Women's Battalion is sent to defend the Provisional Government against Russian revolutionaries, but it is overwhelmed by Bolshevik forces.

◀ **BRITISH NURSES COLLECT FUNDS** FOR MEDICAL SUPPLIES IN THE UK IN 1916.

»

▶ **Replacing the men**
A French satirical cartoon published in *La Baïonnette* in 1917 shows women in male jobs. Wives, sisters, and daughter began filling these salaried positions in France in 1915.

1892-1973
MILUNKA SAVIĆ

One of the most decorated female soldiers in history, Serbian Milunka Savić fought under her brother's name in the Balkan Wars of 1912-13, wearing men's clothes and cutting her hair. Because of her ability, she was allowed to fight in World War I even after her true identity was revealed, and in 1916 she single-handedly captured 23 Bulgarian soldiers. After the war, she returned to civilian life and worked as a cleaner before she was imprisoned in a Nazi concentration camp.

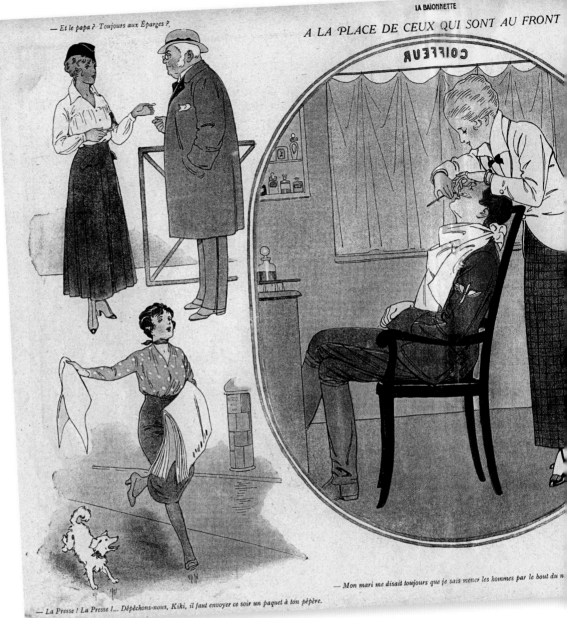

A LA PLACE DE CEUX QUI SONT AU FRONT

— Et le papa ? Toujours aux Éparges ?

— La Presse ! La Presse !... Dépêchons-nous, Kiki, il faut envoyer ce soir un paquet à ton pépère.

— Mon mari me disait toujours que je sais mener les hommes par le bout du n

go home. Undeterred, she went to the French and Serbian governments, who allowed her to set up field hospitals. By the end of the war, her organization operated 14 medical units fully comprised of female volunteers. Similarly, in 1914, Mairi Chisholm and Elsie Knocker set up a dressing station, funded by donations, in some abandoned houses at the front line. The two women ventured into the trenches to retrieve the wounded, wearing nurses' veils so that the Germans would not target them, until they were seriously injured in a gas attack in 1918.

Thousands of women volunteered for auxiliary service, working as cooks, drivers, and secretaries. The US Army employed more than 200 "Hello Girls", who had to be fluent in French and English, to operate their telephone switchboards in France. Many of these auxiliary services were newly established during the war because manpower shortages created a desperate need for additional personnel.

Women were also employed in clandestine activity. The most famous spy of the conflict was Margaretha Geertruida MacLeod, a

— Nous avons la timbale Venizelos...

ED. TOURAINE

— Des canons! Des munitions!... C'est lui qui les leur envoie!...

▼ **Munitionettes**
British women joined munitions factories to make the shells for the guns of World War I. By the end of the war, 80 per cent of them were made by women.

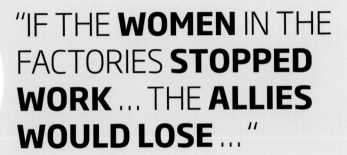

"IF THE **WOMEN** IN THE FACTORIES **STOPPED WORK** ... THE **ALLIES WOULD LOSE** ..."

JOSEPH JOFFRE, FRENCH FIELD MARSHAL, 1914

Dutch dancer known by her stage name, Mata Hari. She was recruited by France to spy for them in Belgium but was later convicted of being a German double agent and was executed by a French firing squad in 1917.

Women go to work

The greatest contribution by the vast majority of women in World War I was made on the home front. The need for women to continue to mobilize led to waves of government propaganda, which encouraged women not to be disillusioned by the war or rising food prices and appealed to their sense of patriotism. With millions of men serving in the armed forces, women went into the workforce to replace them.

The war started in August, so women had to bring in the harvest. In France, 3,200,000 peasant women responded to the call to do the work of the three million farmers sent to the front lines. Even more important to the war effort was the work women did in industry, particularly in munitions factories. By 1918, virtually all women in unoccupied France were in paid employment, and in Germany, over 400,000 women worked in machine shops and 600,000 in ammunition plants, making up 55 per cent of the industrial workforce. Contrary to popular belief, however, the number of working women in France and Germany did not drastically increase between 1914 and 1918 – many women already in the workforce simply moved into more war-focused industries.

3,200
Italian women took over **public transport** jobs to become wartime **tram drivers.**

> **Teach your daughters** how to **wail**; **teach** one another a **lament** … **Death** has **climbed in** through our **windows**.

HEBREW BIBLE, JEREMIAH 9:21

many cases, female spirits heralded death, such as the banshee of Irish mythology, who is said to keen or wail to mark the death of a family member. In Ireland and Scotland the keening woman was a traditional feature of mourning, and professional keeners were often employed.

Women have always played a central role in funerary rituals. For example, among the Cree people of North America, they washed and dressed the body, made moccasins for the deceased's feet, and prepared food. Cree women also took part in the Round Dance ceremony, said to be passed down from female ancestral spirits. Among the Dani people of West Papua, New Guinea, women related to the deceased cut off their fingers to appease the spirits.

EXPERIENCES OF DEATH

Loss and grief

While death is a common thread that links us all, the customs and beliefs surrounding death differ greatly from culture to culture across time. Women, particularly widows, have long played a significant role in burying and mourning their loved ones.

DEATH HAS BEEN personified as a woman in many cultures throughout history. Mexican folk saint Santa Muerte – a skeletal woman not unlike the male personification of the Grim Reaper in medieval Europe – is one such figure, and an Arabic proverb from the Maghreb in Africa declares that death is a woman by the name of Moûny. Various cultures worshipped death goddesses – Haiti's Voodoo Maman Brigitte among them – or had mythological queens of the underworld, such as the Mesopotamian Ereshkigal. In

Women even died in funerary rites, in order to follow dead husbands or masters into the afterlife. One well-known example is the now illegal practice of *sati*, once common in the Hindu community in India, in which a widow immolated herself on her husband's funeral pyre.

> [The] **wailing** and laceration of women in **mourning**, like a **wave** of the **sea**, go on **unceasingly**.

MĀORI PROVERB

◀ **Adorned for death**
This female mummy (c. 200 BCE) is from the Paracas Necropolis in Peru. This woman was buried with textiles, gold, and bone jewellery, indicating that she was royal.

> **"** If a woman has had **more than one** husband in this **life**, she will be **free to choose** the one whose **character** she found **worthiest** to be her **husband in the afterlife**. **"**

LEBANESE PROVERB

Burial practices were – and still are – informed by customs and religious beliefs, and therefore differed for men and women. For example, Muslim ritual specifies that women are wrapped in five *kafans* (plain cloths) for burial, whereas men are wrapped in three (as a living woman is covered more than a man). Such differences in grave goods, burial positions, and inscriptions help archaeologists determine the gender of the dead and hypothesize about women's lives, but this method is now used with caution, as it is not consistently accurate.

Marking mourning

In Western societies during the 19th century, the period of mourning was governed by a rigid dress code. This reached its peak with the "widow's weeds" – all-black clothing – popularized by British Queen Victoria after the death of her husband in 1861. Women wore full mourning dress for a year, then half-mourning for another two. The colour women wore lightened during half-mourning, changing through grey, mauve, and white. Female mourning dress symbolized a family's status and respectability; being able to afford the jet black silk of widow's weeds, black accessories, and the various changes of coloured clothing was an indication of wealth.

In other cultures and times different colours have been used to signify mourning. White was a popular choice, worn by French queens in the 16th century (known as the *deuil blanc*) and is still worn today by Cambodians, who regard it as a colour of rebirth. Colour remains important in today's practices. For example, Aboriginal Australian widows wear white plaster caps to signify their mourning, with the thickness showing the level of grief. In Papua New Guinea, widows paint themselves with grey clay and don layers of necklaces that they remove as the mourning period progresses.

Attitudes to mourning vary worldwide, depending on cultural beliefs. For as many as 3,000 years, Mexicans have celebrated the lives of their ancestors in rituals that became the three-day Day of the Dead festival from 31 October to 2 November, when family and friends gather to remember the deceased. Many women dress as La Catrina – a modern incarnation of the Aztec death goddess – reflecting their comfortable relationship with death.

WOMAN DRESSED AS LA CATRINA, DAY OF THE DEAD CELEBRATION, MEXICO

> **"** **Rain comfort** on the throne! The **Royal Widow**, **strengthen** as **each hour doth roll**; her **mental anguish** cease … **"**

MOURNING SONG FOR PRINCE ALBERT, 1862

SUFFRAGISTS
take action

WOMEN WIN THE VOTE

Women in New Zealand (see pp. 138–142) had won the right to vote in 1893, but the rest of the world proved slow to follow, despite the campaigning of suffragist groups. In Britain, one such group was the National Union of Women's Suffrage Societies (NUWSS), founded in 1897 under the leadership of Millicent Fawcett. She was a suffragist who believed in peaceful campaigning, as only then would women be seen as intelligent and responsible enough to participate in politics.

However, progress was slow and frustrations grew. The suffragists continued their work, but another, more militant kind of activism soon came to overshadow their contributions.

In Finland, women won the right to vote in 1906 as part of a socialist uprising against the Czarist regime, which they pressured with demonstrations and threats of a general strike. As the journal *Palvelijatarlehti* declared, it was not time for compromises. A British group known as the Suffragettes took a similarly

bold approach. Unlike Fawcett's NUWSS, the Suffragettes advocated violence and acts of public disobedience as the only way to draw attention to their cause. Officially, these Suffragettes called themselves the Women's Social and Political Union (WSPU), a group led by Emmeline Pankhurst and her daughters Sylvia, Christabel, and Adela. Ideologically in between the WSPU and NUWSS were other groups, such as the Women's Freedom League, which embraced nonviolent militarism.

The Suffragettes

Emmeline Pankhurst had been involved in the women's suffrage cause since 1880, but believed that the vote would not be won through conventional channels. The WSPU devised a strategy with tactics that included bombing, arson, and chaining themselves to public property. When the Suffragettes were

▲ **Honouring hunger**
Suffragettes who went on hunger strike in prison were given medals by the WSPU for their bravery. This one belonged to Maud Joachim, the first Scottish hunger striker.

IN BRIEF
SUFFRAGE STRUGGLE

Many women in the West gained the right to vote in the early 20th century, thanks to the efforts of suffrage activists and women's participation in two World Wars.

1800

1866 British MP John Mill presents the first women's suffrage petition to the House of Commons.

1869 Unmarried British women gain voting rights in local elections. Wyoming becomes the first US state to grant full suffrage to women.

1893 New Zealand grants full suffrage to adult European women.

1900

1905 In Britain, the Women's Social and Political Union (WSPU) sanction militant action.

1908 Victoria becomes the last Australian state to give women full voting rights.

1910 A bill to give voting rights to any woman with more than £10 in assets fails in the UK.

1913 Norway gives women full voting rights.

1915 Women in Denmark and Iceland are granted voting rights.

1918 40,000 women march through the streets of St Petersburg, Russia, to demand the right to vote; women over 20 are granted suffrage by the revolutionary regime.

1918 Austria and Germany grant full suffrage to women. Canadian women, excluding indigenous women and those in Quebec, gain voting rights.

1919 The US, Netherlands, Belgium, Ukraine, Luxembourg, Sweden, and Belarus grant women suffrage; white women gain voting rights in the US by the 19th amendment (ratified in 1920).

1921 Women in Armenia, Azerbaijan, and Lithuania gain voting rights; the new suffrage laws in Sweden come into effect

1931 Spain gives women voting rights.

1944 French women are granted suffrage.

1946 Italy gives women full voting rights.

◄ **SUFFRAGISTS MARCH IN NEW YORK** CARRYING PORTABLE SPEAKERS, 1912.

arrested and imprisoned, Suffragettes went on hunger strikes. The government sanctioned the feeding of Suffragette prisoners by force, but public outrage compelled them to stop this brutal practice. In another violent incident that made headlines, in 1913 Emily Wilding Davison ran into the path of the king's horse at Epsom racecourse as a form of protest and was trampled to death.

Until World War I, only four countries – New Zealand, Australia (excluding indigenous women), Finland, and Norway, as well as 11 US states – had given full voting rights to women. However, the war proved a turning point for the movement. Suffragettes supported the British war effort, and were rewarded with a concession in 1918, when property-owning women over 30 (around 40 per cent of the adult female population) were given the vote. It took another decade for all women over 21 (the same as the male voting age) to become eligible.

A worldwide movement

The international connections of its leaders united the global suffrage movement. Australian Jessie Street encountered the Suffragettes while visiting relatives in England and on returning to her homeland became a lifelong champion of equal rights for women. Australia had full voting rights for women by 1908, but activists there campaigned into the 1920s for a woman's right to stand for parliament.

By the beginning of the 20th century, the US suffrage movement was organizing a programme of mass demonstrations and picketing the White House, masterminded by Alice Paul. Inspired by the militancy of the British Suffragettes, Paul became a passionate and articulate advocate for votes for women. She grew dissatisfied with the National American Woman Suffrage Association (NAWSA), whose focus was on individual states, so in 1916 she formed the

Le Petit Journal

QUAND LES ÉLECTRICES ALLEMANDES NE SONT PAS D'ACCORD

L'Almanach du Petit Journal est le complément indispensable du Petit Journal Illustré.

◄ **Disagreements among women**
This illustration from French newspaper *Le Petit Journal* reinforces the idea of the volatility of female voters in its depiction of German women fighting one another at the ballot box during the municipal elections in Warburg in November 1929.

"[PARLIAMENT] CANNOT ... LEGISLATE ON THE HUMAN RACE, ON WOMEN AND ON CHILDREN, WITHOUT US."

CLARA CAMPOAMOR, IN *THE FEMALE VOTE AND ME*, 1936

National Women's Party. Together with other campaigners, such as Doris Stevens, Paul staged a series of protests that eventually wore down governmental opposition and won public support. She initiated nonviolent pickets outside of the White House in 1917, and rallies of women bearing banners demanding the right to vote. Various women (including, in 1917, a group dubbed the "Silent Sentinels") picketed six days a week for two years, until the administration passed the 19th amendment in 1919.

Canadian women (barring those in the province of Quebec) had the right to vote by 1918, but made yet more significant gains in the years that followed. In the so-called "Persons case," a group of women dubbed the "Famous Five" by the media – Nellie McClung, Henrietta Muir Edwards, Irene Parlby, Louise McKinney, and Emily Murphy – petitioned against the vague wording of the British North America Act of 1867. The act implied that women were not "persons" under the law, thereby preventing them from participating fully in politics. Thanks to the work of the "Famous Five," in 1929 the British Privy Council voted that women were indeed "persons" and could become senators.

Women in southern Europe were not granted full voting rights until much later. Clara Campoamor, a young Spanish lawyer who went on

to become her country's first female magistrate, was largely responsible for ensuring that suffrage for women was enshrined in the Spanish constitution of 1931. Across the border in France and Italy, women would have to wait until the end of World War II before receiving the vote, which was finally granted in 1945, decades ahead of Switzerland, where women won the vote in 1971. Suffrage outside of Europe also occurred at a varying rate. Azerbaijan became the first majority Muslim country to grant women the vote in 1921, yet Saudi Arabia did not follow suit until 2015, nearly one hundred years later.

▲ **Suppressing suffragists**
Anti-suffrage labels such as this one were common in France and other parts of Europe. Opponents to female suffrage claimed that women were uninterested in voting. Such opinions persisted in countries that were slow to give women the vote.

◄ **Message on wheels**
This ordinary delivery wagon was used by US suffragette Lucy Stone. She travelled around in it, stopping to make speeches and distribute copies of the *Woman's Journal.* The wagon was later painted with slogans by the suffragists who owned it after Stone.

"Government does not rest upon force ... **it rests upon consent**."

EMMELINE PANKHURST, "FREEDOM OR DEATH" SPEECH, HARTFORD, CONNECTICUT, NOVEMBER 13, 1913

MILITANT PROTEST

Emmeline Pankhurst, leader of the Women's Social and Political Union (WSPU), sold her home in 1907 and travelled around the UK and the US to speak in support of women's suffrage. In her "Freedom or Death" speech, Pankhurst likened herself to a soldier fighting a civil war for women's rights. Viewing the suffrage movement as a revolution, Pankhurst argued for American suffragists to take a more militant approach in their activism. Pankhurst and her fellow WSPU members believed that drastic measures must be taken to make the government listen to them. The actions of WSPU members often led to arrests, but they refused to be cowed even in the face of the brutal response of police and prison wardens. Emmeline Pankhurst was arrested seven times, including being carried away by a constable from a march outside Buckingham Palace in May 1914 (right). The Suffragettes' arrival at the palace had been met with violence from both police and onlookers.

THROUGH THE AGES

Art

Female artists have existed since prehistory, although their achievements were frequently overlooked. Since the 19th century, women have embraced a succession of new art media and practices that do not have the weight of male tradition behind them.

PHOTOGRAPH BY JULIA MARGARET CAMERON OF ELLEN TERRY, 1863

WOMEN'S ART is rooted in a long history of traditional crafts, including pottery, quilting, beadwork, and weaving. Work by female artists has often been dismissed as merely "craft" and denied the status of "fine art" in a male-dominated art world. Consequently, much of the female art throughout history went unrecorded. African women's art has not been fully acknowledged, despite a rich tradition of creativity, such as the geometric paintings on the houses of Ndebele women in South Africa, a custom that dates from the 18th century. Nonetheless, evidence of women's art dates back thousands of years. In the 4th century BCE, Helena of Egypt produced a painting of the Battle of Issus; French needlewomen worked on the Bayeux Tapestry; 12th-century German abbess Hildegard von Bingen painted striking illustrations for religious manuscripts in jewel-like colours; and in Yuan Dynasty China (1271–1368), Guan Daosheng painted paintings of bamboo plants that are considered masterpieces of Chinese art.

> The **fact** that I am a **woman** ... **comes into play** in [how] I structure a **canvas**.

JUDY CHICAGO, ARTIST, 1999

In Renaissance Europe, art production was usually based in family workshops in which women worked alongside fathers and brothers. Although some of these – such as the portrait painter Sofanisba Anguissola and Marietta Robusti, the daughter of Venetian master painter Tintoretto – were renowned painters in their time, none took over the family firms.

▶ **Cubo-Futurism**
Painterly Architectonic is one of a series of works that Lyubov Popova painted from 1916 to 1917. Part of the Russian vanguard that first experimented with geometrical abstraction, she mixed medieval Russian art with new avant-garde techniques.

By the 18th century, the workshop tradition in Europe was being replaced by academies that excluded women from classes and denied them access to the prestigious commissions of the day. Despite this, some female artists achieved success in genres such as portraiture, among them Elizabeth Louise Vigée Le Brun.

In the 19th century, the new medium of photography attracted women as it lacked the restrictions on training and practice that had held women back in painting and sculpture. British portrait photographer Julia Margaret Cameron and influential US photographer Gertrude Käsebier were pioneers of the form.

Women also began to emerge as prominent members of artists' groups which are more commonly associated with men. Mary Cassatt and Berthe Morisot, for example, were leading members of the Impressionist movement in France. In early 20th-century Russia, where the Revolution placed equal emphasis on the training of women and men, artists such as Lyubov Popova and Alexandra Exter were key exponents of Russian Constructivism.

Modernism and beyond

Although growing numbers of female artists achieved success, others continued to be overshadowed by husbands or male colleagues. Lee Krasner, wife of Jackson Pollock, and Joan Mitchell were leading artists of Abstract Expressionism, but never attained the same level of commercial success as Pollock or their friend Willem de Kooning.

In the second half of the 20th century the feminist art movement emerged. North American artists, such as Joyce Wieland and Judy Chicago, incorporated knitting, ceramics, and needlework into their oeuvre. Today, feminist art, which has moved away from the male-dominated genres of painting and sculpture to embrace new media (performance art, installation, and video), has been credited with influencing contemporary art worldwide.

▶ **Female forms**
Elisabeth (Nana) was created in 1965 by Niki de Saint Phalle, who was known for her playful, colourful, rotund sculptures. The French-American artist claimed that her giant works proved women could produce art on a large scale.

NOTABLE CREATORS

Artemisia Gentileschi (1593–1652/3) trained first in her father's workshop in Rome, then with landscape painter Agostino Tassi. He raped her, leading to a trial that came to overshadow her artistic achievements. Gentileschi's dramatic, Baroque-style paintings depicted women in biblical and literary scenes. In 1616, she became the first female member of Florence's Academy of Design.

Berthe Morisot (1841–1895) was a leading member of the French Impressionists. Her output focused on women's domestic lives. In 1867, she met Édouard Manet, becoming his friend and model. In 1874, she had nine works of her own in the first Impressionist exhibition. She showed with the group for the next 12 years.

Georgia O'Keeffe (1887–1986) trained at the Art Institute of Chicago and the Art Students League in New York. In 1916, she met gallerist Alfred Stieglitz, who put on her first solo show in 1917. They married in 1924, and from 1929 she worked in New Mexico. Focusing on flowers and landscapes, O'Keeffe used simplified forms and close-ups as routes to abstraction.

Louise Bourgeois (1911–2010) was born in Paris, but moved to New York in 1938 and attended the Art Students League. From her sculptures of the late 1940s to the giant spider sculptures that marked her final years, her work drew on her past and childhood.

Yayoi Kusama (b.1929) studied traditional Japanese painting in Kyoto. In 1958, she moved to New York, becoming known for her avant-garde *Happenings*, but returned to Japan in 1973. Embracing painting, performance, and fashion, her works include giant pumpkin sculptures and immersive installations.

Cindy Sherman (b.1954) graduated from college in Buffalo and moved to New York City in 1977. She became famous for photographic series such as *Untitled Film Stills* (1977–1980) and *History Portraits* (1989–1990), challenging the images of women presented in popular culture.

IN BRIEF
LOSING THE CHAINS

Communist revolutions during the 20th century saw women's fight for equality as integral to the wider class struggle, and their ideas greatly influenced gender equality.

1800–1900

1848 Marx and Engels publish the *Communist Manifesto*, explaining the class system.

1899 Nadezhda Krupskaya applies Marxist theory to Russian women in *The Woman Worker*.

1907 At the First International Conference of Socialist Women in Stuttgart, Germany, Alexandra Kollontai declares: "The struggle to achieve political equality for proletarian women is part ... of the overall class struggle ..."

1917 Socialist women's journal *Rabotnitsa* calls for an anti-war demonstration. Women start the "bread and peace" strike in Petrograd in March. In July, Russian women win the right to vote and hold public office.

1918 On 30 August, Fanny Kaplan shoots Lenin three times as he is leaving a Moscow factory. She calls him "a traitor to the revolution". Although injured badly, Lenin survives.

1919 Zhenotdel, the women's section of the Russian Communist Party, is established.

1920s Alexandra Kollontai tries to bring more gender diversity into the Communist Party but meets resentment.

1930 Zhenotdel is shut down and women's issues declared "solved" due to nationalization and the abolition of private property.

1934 Zhang Qinqiu heads the Women's Independent Regiment of the Fourth Front Army in China, commanding 2,000 female soldiers.

1949 The Communists seize power in China.

1950 The New Marriage Law of the People's Republic of China sets out civil rights for women.

1959 Women form the front line of struggle during the Cuban Revolution, bringing a communist regime to power.

1961 Cuban women and girls play a leading role in the literacy brigades that teach people to read and write, making Cuba one of the most literate countries in the Western hemisphere.

▶ **1930 PROPAGANDA POSTER** FOR INTERNATIONAL WOMEN WORKER'S DAY

THE RED WAVES OF
revolution

THE RISE OF COMMUNISM

Although Karl Marx and Friedrich Engels did not directly address gender inequalities in their groundbreaking political pamphlet, *The Communist Manifesto* (1848), they did assess women's position in society as part of the class struggle. They demonstrated that women's lives were shaped by their status as an underclass within a class (the proletariat) due to most women's work being unpaid or underpaid. The first Marxist work to solely address the situation of women in Russia was *The Woman Worker* (1899) by Nadezhda Krupskaya, wife of the Soviet revolutionary leader Vladimir Ilyich Ulyanov, better known as Lenin. Krupskaya maintained that women's liberation was only possible through their participation in the class struggle.

> **German Marxist Clara Zetkin declared March 8 International Women's Day in 1910**

It was a women's protest in 1917 that helped spark the Russian Revolution. On 2 March 1917 (18 February, according to the old Russian calendar), workers at a factory in Petrograd (now St Petersburg) announced a strike against the government. On 8 March (23 February, old calendar), female peasants, students, and workers protested over hunger and Russia's participation in World War I (see pp. 200–203).

This "bread and peace" strike had been called for by the socialist women's journal *Rabotnitsa*. Slogans on women's banners demanded "Feed the children of the defenders of the motherland!" In the afternoon, the women were joined by striking female textile workers and their menfolk, swelling the crowd to 100,000. The protest developed into a general strike, in which women clashed with the forces of the Petrograd garrison. Soldiers, unwilling to beat and shoot women, then joined the protest, turning it into an anti-government uprising that started the February Revolution and toppled the czar. In October, Lenin then led the Bolsheviks to overthrow the provisional government.

▶ **Traitor?**
This painting depicts Fanny Kaplan's failed attempt on Lenin's life in 1918. She was executed having refused to name her accomplices, but she is thought to have acted for the SRP.

The woman who shot Lenin

Not everyone accepted the Bolshevik victory. Fanny Kaplan, originally an anarchist and later a member of the Socialist Revolutionary Party (SRP), believed that Lenin had betrayed the revolution when he excluded other left-wing political parties from power. Kaplan attempted to shoot Lenin on 30 August 1918, but Lenin survived and Kaplan was executed.

Although women had actively participated in the revolution, women's issues were not a priority for the Bolsheviks, and none of the revolutionaries' senior leaders were female. Zhenotdel, the "women's section" of the Communist Party, was set up in 1919, but during its short history (it closed in 1930) was never taken seriously by party officials. Activists such as Alexandra Kollontai, the founder of Zhenotdel, tried to inject more gender diversity into the party but its members mostly rejected

the idea of their wives as political activists. Nonetheless, women achieved some advances, including receiving the right to vote in 1917, and obtaining a divorce more easily. At the same time, women began to play an increasing role in public life, and, by the 1930s, many women worked outside the household as teachers,

▼ **The idealist state**
A Chinese propaganda poster entitled "Soldier, People, One Family" places a revolutionary mother at the centre of the message.

◄ **Female rebels**
Victorious female soldiers wave from tanks arriving in Havana after the Cuban Revolution. Women's positions changed markedly for the better as a direct result of their participation in the revolution.

doctors, and even engineers. However, for all the communist rhetoric on gender equality, women still continued to be viewed primarily as mothers and wives.

Inspiring further revolutions

Russia's revolution of 1917 helped to inspire China's Cultural Revolution a decade later. The Communist Party of China also identified women's emancipation as a leading goal of its revolution, and Party commanders made concerted efforts to mobilize women in the 1930s and '40s. Chinese women were attracted by communist ideology, which advocated for the end of patriarchal practices such as arranged marriage and gender inequality in the family. In contrast to the Russian Revolution, after the communists seized power in 1949, the Marriage Law of the People's Republic of China established fundamental civil rights for women, including rights to vote, receive an education, and work outside of their homes.

The Cuban Revolution of 1959 also brought fundamental changes to the status of women. Cuba was arguably more successful than either China or Russia in incorporating women into educated and professional society. Today, Cuban women represent a majority in higher education, and the number of female lawyers, doctors, and scientists is among the highest in the world.

BIOGRAPHY
ZHANG QINQIU

Born in 1904, Zhang Qinqiu went on to become one of the first female members of China's Communist Party. In 1925, she studied at Moscow Sun Yat-sen University, becoming one of the 28 Bolsheviks educated there. In 1932, she became director of the General Political Department of the Fourth Front Army, the highest military position ever held by a woman. Zhang took her own life in 1968, after facing persecution as a scholar in China's Cultural Revolution.

HUSBANDS AND
hysteria

THE INSANE ASYLUM

Culture has had a significant influence on how a society reacts to the mentally ill. Many ancient cultures viewed mental illness as a form of religious punishment or demonic possession and ostracized those who suffered from it. However, as early as the 5th century BCE, Greek physician Hippocrates pioneered the treatment of mental health problems with humane techniques, without reference to religion or superstition.

In most parts of the world, if families could not care for their mentally ill loved ones, these "poor unfortunates" wandered the streets, vulnerable to assault or derision. Asylums initially came into being as a safe refuge for them. In Europe during the Middle Ages, religious orders often provided care – some hospitals run by these orders later

▶ **Hypnotherapy**
Neurologist Jean Martin Charcot uses a "magic lantern" to induce hypnosis in a patient. Women who were diagnosed with "hysteria" were often subjected to public treatments as doctors lectured to groups of students and spectators.

"IN A **SICK SOCIETY**, **WOMEN** WHO HAVE **DIFFICULTY FITTING IN** ARE NOT **ILL**."

CHARLOTTE PERKINS GILMAN, AUTHOR OF *THE YELLOW WALLPAPER*, 1892

formed the basis for private madhouses. The move from charitable care to profit-oriented containment meant that asylums became a useful "dumping ground" for those who did not comply with societal norms, be they radicals, heretics, or women. The madhouse provided the means of controlling such people.

In 18th-century Europe, the prevalent wisdom was that if a husband could not control his deviant wife within the institution of marriage, the madhouse was an option. Until 1774, there was no onus on husbands to prove their wives' so-called madness – they could simply deposit them at the institution indefinitely. Husbands (or fathers) had women committed for reasons such as "deranged masturbation", "political excitement", and "excessive reading" as well as symptoms of mental illnesses such as depression and anxiety. Other times, admitting a woman to an asylum was simply orchestrated as a means to gain control of her estate, as an alternative to divorce, or as a way to make a woman compliant.

Horrors of the asylum

Women were kept in terrible conditions in stinking, overcrowded cells, and suffered brutality and sexual violence. One of the most infamous asylums was Bedlam (Bethlem Royal Hospital) in London. By the end of the 19th century, there were so many stories of wrongful confinement that journalist Nelly Bly spent 10 days in New York's Blackwell Island to expose the abuses. The most chilling aspect of her story was that, once committed, she returned to normal "sane" behaviour, but her warders were incapable of recognizing it as such. For a wrongfully committed woman, even a sane one, there was no escape from the system.

▼ **Portrait of pain**
This female inmate of Surrey County Asylum, UK, was photographed in 1855 by Dr Hugh Welch Diamond, who captured many such portraits of mentally ill women in public asylums. He ceased photography after founding a private institution in 1858.

Beauty

Women have aspired to meet socially constructed notions of beauty and the "ideal" body shape since prehistory. In the last decade or so, however, women have begun to reject such ideas and to embrace bodies of all types and sizes.

THE EARLIEST REPRESENTATIONS of the female body are around 25,000 years old—the so-called "Venus figurines" found in Austria that feature pear-shaped figures with large busts. For most of recorded history, cultures have considered this shape the optimum for childbearing, and therefore a desirable aesthetic, which is seen reproduced in art from ancient Greek statues of Aphrodite, the goddess of love and beauty, and Rubens' 17th-century portraits to the pinups of the 1950s.

A voluptuous body was, and still is, considered preferable on many Polynesian islands. Young women adhere to a practice known as *ha'apori* (to fatten), in which they are encouraged to put on weight to appear more fertile. In Europe and the US during the 19th century, the "fertile" or hourglass look was defined by a large bust and a small waist, which made the hips look curvier. Corsetry for pushing up the bust and minimizing the waist therefore became a key aspect of dress. The 19th-century practice of tight-lacing took this to extremes, with women laced into corsets that pushed in the ribs to create a smaller waist. Other examples of body modification in the name of beauty are the brass neck coils that are worn by the Kayan women in Asia, which compress the clavicle and create the impression of an unnaturally long neck, and the lip plates worn by Mursi women in Africa, which signal that a woman is of marriageable age.

Desire for a white complexion

Pale skin has been a beauty aspiration since at least ancient Egyptian times, because it has been seen to indicate that a woman was privileged enough to spend her time indoors rather than working outside in the fields where her skin would catch the sun. The trend for white skin endures in Southeast Asia, where whitening products dominate cosmetic counters, and skin-bleaching treatments are commonplace. Eyelid surgery with the aim of opening up the eye shape to make it look bigger and more European is also popular among young women in the region.

◀ **For a leggy look**
Unable to procure silk or nylon hosiery during World War II, many women resorted to painting their legs with nude-coloured makeup such as Leg Silque Liquid Stockings.

> " A culture fixated on female **thinness** is … an obsession about female **obedience**. "
>
> **NAOMI WOLF**, *THE BEAUTY MYTH*, 1991

◀ **Queen of pinups**
Iconic images of model Bettie Page made her a sex symbol in the 1950s and helped usher in the sexual revolution of the 1960s. Her style of curves, high heels, and raven bangs still influences ideas about sexual allure today.

Many modern beauty trends can be traced to the past. Beauty pageants have their origins in competitions held in ancient Troy, where a panel of artists, philosophers, poets, and warriors judged the most beautiful woman of the day. The current preoccupation with hair removal is also ages old, with women using such deadly methods as arsenic in medieval times. Eyelash extensions were first explored in the late 1800s and involved stitching a hair into the eyelid with an ordinary needle.

It was only in the 1920s, when women began to compete with men in the workplace, that a thin, boyish figure became fashionable. Undergarments helped to flatten the chest, and diet and exercise regimes became popular to achieve a lean look. In response to criticism in the 1990s that the fashion and beauty industries were promoting unrealistic body types, these businesses now promote more fluid beauty ideals. Dominant images float between two desirable aesthetics: one that promotes big busts and exaggerated buttocks; the other the leaner, more athletic lines of the catwalk model. At the same time, the cosmetic industry has created products for a wider variety of skin tones, as well as an array of injectable substances capable of transforming the face and body.

KAYAN WOMAN FROM THAILAND WITH BRASS NECK RINGS, 2015

PROFILES
BEAUTY QUEENS

Queen Elizabeth I (1533–1603) cultivated her image as England's "Virgin Queen" by wearing low-cut necklines, a style considered only appropriate for virginal women. As she grew older, she wore red wigs to conceal her greying hair, and applied a dangerous lead whitening paste to her skin to mask signs of aging. Women at court copied her, even mimicking her rotten teeth by blackening their own.

Florence Nightingale Graham (1878–1966) built a cosmetics empire under the name Elizabeth Arden. She travelled from rural Canada to the US and opened her first Red Door Salon on New York's Fifth Avenue in 1910. Arden created products that emphasized natural beauty, such as her Eight Hour Cream. Her mantra was: "To be beautiful and natural is the birthright of every woman."

ORLAN (b.1947) is a French artist who explores cultural perceptions of women's bodies by undergoing extreme cosmetic procedures and recording them as performance art. Starting in 1990, ORLAN embarked on a series of plastic surgeries to transform her features into those of iconic beauties in art, including the forehead of Leonardo da Vinci's *Mona Lisa* and the chin of Sandro Botticelli's *Venus*.

Zara Mohamed Abdulmajid (b.1955), known professionally as Iman, is a Somalian model famed for being one of the first nonwhite woman to succeed in high fashion. Discovered in 1975, she went on to become a favorite of designer Yves Saint Lauren, and married British rock star David Bowie in 1992. In 1994 she started a successful cosmetics range for women with darker skin.

Naomi Wolf (b.1962) is a US feminist, journalist, and author. In her landmark book published in 1991, *The Beauty Myth,* she argued that unrealistic social standards of physical beauty are harmful to women and hinder their effectiveness in society. Wolf later became a prominent spokeswoman for third-wave feminism.

Ashley Graham (b.1987) is a trailblazing US fashion model and lingerie designer who became the first plus-size model to be listed among the top-earning models by *Forbes Magazine* in 2017. Graham, who shot to fame after appearing on the cover of a *Sports Illustrated* swimsuit issue, campaigns for the "normalization" of larger women, who, as she points out, are the norm in the US.

FLAPPERS AND
freedom

In the aftermath of World War I, suffrage began to achieve its goals. Some women over 30 gained the vote in the UK in 1918, and in 1920, the 19th Amendment was ratified in the US, granting citizens voting rights regardless of their sex. However, it was increased financial freedom that would most transform women's lives in the 1920s.

The rise of the flapper

The postwar economy of North America experienced a huge boom. The US transformed from a young industrial state to a world superpower with a large consumer economy. Women who had entered the workforce during the war now had access to disposable income of their own, and became a major consumer power able to make active buying choices. Inventions such as the vacuum cleaner and washing machine enabled many women to spend less time on domestic chores – in the 1920s, American women on average spent between 52 and 60 hours a week on housework – and increased leisure time.

Many young men had died during the war or from the 1918 Spanish flu epidemic. Rather than wait at home to be married, some women chose to celebrate their survival and freedom. Barriers that had been broken down during the war led these women to want to be treated as men had previously been – and allowed to do as they pleased. This new, liberated woman was known as a flapper – a woman who smoked, drank, drove a car, wore short skirts, and cut her hair in a bob. The androgynous look of flappers was influenced by French fashion, with such women being called *garçonne* (the feminine form of "boy") in Paris. Tight corsets were abandoned in favor of more practical clothing, such as Coco Chanel's innovative women's suit and little black dress. Her clothes were revolutionary, with designs

▲ **Women about town**
Women in the 1920s gained not only the right to vote, but also more freedom and independence. This British advertisement shows two wealthy women on a shopping spree.

BREAKING THE RULES

The 1920s were a time of social liberation for many women, who began to dress and behave in ways that celebrated their newfound freedom.

1900

1920 The 18th Amendment is ratified in the US, outlawing the manufacture and sale of intoxicating liquors (alcohol); the 19th Amendment is ratified in the US, granting (white) women the vote.

1923 The Matrimonial Causes Act is passed in the UK, making grounds for divorce the same for husband and wife.

1923 Alice Paul, head of the National Women's Party, proposes the Lucretia Mott Amendment calling for equal rights for men and women.

1923 The Charleston dance craze sweeps across the US.

1924 Marie C. Brehm becomes the first female candidate to run legally for the vice-presidency of the US.

1925 Josephine Baker moves to France, where she becomes a sensation following her debut at the Folies Bergère.

1926 Coco Chanel designs the little black dress.

1927 The first talking movie, *The Jazz Singer*, is released, starring Mary Dale as a dancer.

1928 The Olympic Games allow women to contend in athletics and gymnastics.

1928 All women over the age of 21 get the vote in the UK under the Representation of the People Act.

1929 The Flapper Election in the UK – the first general election in which all women can vote – results in a huge turnout.

1929 The *Edwards vs. Canada* lawsuit acknowledges women as "qualified persons" and thus eligible to sit in the Senate in Canada.

1929 The US stock market crashes, signaling the beginning of the Great Depression in the West.

1930 German actress Marlene Dietrich has her big break playing the cabaret singer Lola-Lola in *The Blue Angel*.

◀ **TWO FLAPPERS** DANCE ON THE ROOFTOP OF A CHICAGO HOTEL, 1926.

BIOGRAPHY
JOSEPHINE BAKER

Born in 1906 in the US, Baker began her career as a street performer, but quickly landed a role in *Shuffle Along* on Broadway. Her talent led her to tour Paris in 1925, where she opened *La Revue Negre* at the Theatre des Champs-Elysees. She rose to fame with her Danse Sauvage, performed wearing a girdle of bananas and accompanied by her pet cheetah. Baker was married four times but also had relationships with women. She later aided the French resistance during World War II and supported the US Civil Rights movement.

that borrowed from men's fashions and emphasized women's comfort.

In the United States, women fought on both sides of the Prohibition debate – from 1920, the consumption of alcohol was forbidden by the 18th Amendment. While the Women's Christian Temperance Union supported the law, flappers often flaunted it, enjoying the illicit atmosphere of speakeasies (underground clubs that sold liquor). Flappers had equivalents around the world – from the German *neue Frauen* to the Japanese *moga* and Chinese *modeng xiaojie* – who wore the new fashions, shocked others with their promiscuity, and challenged their society's conventions.

In Paris, the 1920s were known as the *années folles*, or "the crazy years." Café society created spaces where artists and writers of any gender could gather to socialize. This spirit was echoed in British dance halls and American speakeasies, where jazz's improvisational nature encouraged a spirit of release. In Germany, the decade was called the "Golden Twenties" thanks to the nation's economic growth and liberal creative zeitgeist. Berlin was enthralled by stars such as Anita Berber, a bisexual dancer and actress renowned for her brazen nude performances. However, the 1920s were not a time of liberation for all women. In the US, for example, heightened racial tension saw the

◀ **Flapper handbag**
Flapper bags were only able to fit some money and cigarettes – all a woman needed for an unchaperoned night on the town. Bags were often intricately decorated – in this case, in 1920s art deco style – with tassels that swayed as a woman danced.

rebirth of the Ku Klux Klan, a white supremacist organization, race riots, and the institution of restrictive immigration quotas.

From boom to bust

Beneath the surface, economies had been struggling. Participating nations were still paying for World War I, and adapting to the new economic state proved difficult. This struggle culminated in 1929 when the Wall Street stock market crashed, setting the Great Depression in motion. Unemployment levels soared, and working class men were hit hard as many manufacturing industries shut down. In contrast, women's jobs in traditional service industries remained relatively safe; many working-class women became their families' sole breadwinners. Working women were not protected by employment laws; some married women with working husbands did not qualify for jobs, and those who had them could be fired instantly if they became pregnant. While the 1920s were a time of liberation, the decade that followed had an entirely different character.

▶ **Flappers of the Prohibition Era**
Contempt for the rules of Prohibition heavily influenced American flappers. Some chose to be photographed drinking alcohol or defiantly smuggling flasks in their stockings, clothes, and purses.

"THE NEW WOMAN … ASSERTED HER RIGHT TO DANCE, DRINK, SMOKE, AND DATE."

JOSHUA ZEITZ, US HISTORIAN, IN HIS BOOK *FLAPPER*, 2006

◄ Empress of the Blues
Jazz singer Bessie Smith was the highest-paid African American artist of the 1920s. She was a star of the Harlem Renaissance, a black artistic movement that originated in New York.

THE NIGERIAN
Women's War

THE WAR OF 1929

In 1929, women in Igboland, southeastern Nigeria, had had enough of their colonial oppressors. In the provinces of Calabar and Owerri, their unrest ignited a rebellion that came to be known as the Women's War of 1929. Colonial historians took a different view, referring to the event as a riot, but whatever it was called, the uprising was carried out on an unprecedented scale in Africa, and took colonial leaders by surprise. During the riots, 16 native courts were attacked and several European stores were looted. Out of 25,000 Igbo women activists, 55 were killed and over 50 were seriously injured.

Rebel causes

The two-month long rebellion was caused by a chain of circumstances, which started with Britain's policy of indirect rule over its colony through warrant chiefs – mostly Igbo chiefs appointed by the British governor. Over time, these warrant chiefs abused their power, mistreated women, and seized property and livestock for themselves. Traditionally, women were respected members of Igbo society who played a significant role in political life, but warrant chiefs blocked women from holding government positions. Women's dissatisfaction was compounded by economic hardship. Under British rule, the Igbo economy had begun to revolve around palm oil sales, and when prices fell in 1929, taxes stayed the same, putting a huge burden on Igbo women. An increase in school fees was followed by plans to impose direct British taxation on women (Igbo men had been taxed from 1928).

▼ Racist rhetoric
This advertising trade card for a raincoat was made by UK firm Bryson Ltd., who described their product as "one of the best British possessions". Advertising of the imperial period reinforced ideas of racial superiority, depicting native Africans as exotic or "uncivilized".

▼ Wrapped in tradition
This photograph shows Igbo women at the beginning of the 20th century. Their traditional wrappers are made of Akwete cloth, a textile woven by Igbo women throughout history.

"WOMEN WILL NOT PAY TAX UNTIL THE WORLD ENDS."

NWANYEREUWA, 1929

◀ **Fashion victim**
This Igbo woman, photographed in 1922, wears immense brass anklets called *ogba*. These costly and cumbersome fashion accessories were a status symbol, as the wearer could not perform normal domestic duties.

The revolt was sparked by what became a notorious dispute between a woman called Nwanyereuwa, in the village of Oloko, and Mark Emereuwa, a man conducting a detailed census of wives, children, and livestock in each household for tax purposes. Traditionally, Igbo women had not been subject to taxation, so when he asked Nwanyereuwa for information that would be used to tax her, it was the final straw. Nwanyereuwa spread the word by sending out palm leaves as an invitation to women in neighbouring villages to join the rebellion: each woman passed a palm leaf on to another woman. As a result, nearly 10,000 women gathered to protest against the local warrant chief, demanding his removal. Nwanyereuwa advocated nonviolent actions, including "sitting on" or "making war on" men by performing songs and dances to ridicule them. The women also tore down the roofs of buildings owned by European companies.

Other villages in Calabar and Owerri followed the example of Oloko, and the growing rebellion – of not only Igbo but also Ibibio, Andoni, Orgoni, Bonny, and Opobo women – challenged British rule. Colonial troops fired shots at the women, but they stood firm. The British relented, colonial administration was restructured, warrant chiefs were removed, and the plan to tax women ended. Crucially, the protest ensured that Igbo women once more took part in political life, and that the Igbo people regained some of their power to self-govern.

"A woman must have money and a room ... **if she is to write fiction**."

VIRGINIA WOOLF, FROM *A ROOM OF ONE'S OWN,*
PUBLISHED IN 1929

A ROOM OF ONE'S OWN

Virginia Woolf, born in England in 1882, became famous as a writer of both novels and feminist texts – as well as for her relationship with her muse, Vita Sackville-West. In 1929, Woolf published an extended essay entitled *A Room of One's Own* based on two lectures she had recently given on the topic of women; the work went on to be a major feminist text with an enduring legacy. The essay explores many feminist, issues such as women's lack of education and their financial and social dependence on men. The "room" in Woolf's famous proclamation symbolized a space for independence, security, and privacy, all of which women had historically been denied the right to. Woolf is pictured here in her "writing lodge" at her home in Sussex, England.

THROUGH THE AGES

Cinema

Women played major roles in cinema's Golden Age of the 1920s and 1930s, but lost their footing in Hollywood as it became more corporate and male-dominated. In recent decades, women have attempted to bridge the gap of inequality and tell more female-driven stories.

IN MORE THAN A CENTURY of cinema, depictions of women on the silver screen have often reflected the dreams and desires of the male audience. According to pioneering American director D.W. Griffith, audiences in the early 1900s did not want gritty depictions of reality: they wanted "a gun and a girl". Despite this idea, in the 1910s and '20s, women wielded more influence than at any other time. One of Griffith's "girls" was Canadian-born Mary Pickford, who became one of the first true Hollywood stars. After founding her own company in 1916, Pickford produced all of her own films.

In the early 1930s, many films featured self-determined female characters who defied conventional morality, such as Jean Harlow's home-wrecker in *Red-Headed Woman*. From 1934, however, censorship under the puritanical Hays Code forced Hollywood to make less controversial entertainment, with even married couples sleeping in twin beds. Only wholesome heroines triumphed, and women with a past were punished. During the 1950s and '60s, leading actresses such as Doris Day, Debbie Reynolds, Audrey Hepburn, and Grace Kelly achieved success playing good girls.

> "An **actress** is **not a machine**, but they **treat you** like a **machine**."
>
> **MARILYN MONROE**

The shift to a male-dominated Hollywood was reflected behind the scenes too, with the advent of the studio system, starting in 1924 with Metro-Goldwyn-Mayer (MGM). Before 1920, there were more than 30 women directors, but the increasingly corporate nature of Hollywood put men in charge. Among the few exceptions was Dorothy Arzner, who was the only female director working in the 1930s and '40s, until 1949, when actress Ida Lupino began to direct. Lupino was then the only woman to direct a major feature film until Elaine May in 1971.

Bigger roles

One of Hollywood's first female film editors, Verna Fields, won an Oscar for *Jaws* (1975), and around that time, the growing Women's Liberation Movement (see pp. 272–275) helped to bring more interesting female characters to the screen. Breakthroughs came in 1979 with director Gillian Armstrong's *My Brilliant Career*, about an ambitious writer played by

▼ **Girl with the curls**
Mary Pickford won the second ever Academy Award for best actress for her portrayal of a girl whose reputation is ruined, in *Coquette* (1929). It was Pickford's first ever talking role.

Judy Davis, and Ridley Scott's space-age heroine Ripley in *Alien*, played by Sigourney Weaver. Women kept pushing the boundaries: Dawn Steel became one of the first women to run a Hollywood studio (Columbia Pictures) in 1987; and established scriptwriter Nancy Meyers directed *The Parent Trap* (1998), the first of her many box office hits.

Female-driven films have become increasingly successful. In 2010, Kathryn Bigelow became the first female director to win an Oscar, and Patty Jenkins' *Wonder Woman* (2017) became the highest-grossing superhero origin story of all time. In Bollywood, Vidya Balan broke the mold playing a heavily pregnant heroine in the blockbuster *Kahaani* (2012). While women's influence in film continues to grow, exemplified by writer-directors such as Sofia Coppola and Greta Gerwig, campaigning organizations such as Woman and Hollywood recognize there is still some way to go.

▲ **Femme fatale**
German actress Marlene Dietrich's provocative characters defied many traditional gender norms. In this still from *Blue Angel* (1930), she appears donning a tuxedo as the cabaret star Lola Lola.

KATHRYN BIGELOW WINS THE OSCAR FOR BEST DIRECTOR

PROFILES
LEADING LADIES

Alice Guy Blaché (1873–1968) was the first female film director. She began working as a secretary in Paris in 1896, and produced, directed, or supervised some 750 films before moving to New York in 1907. In 1910, she started her own production business, Solax, and went on to direct around 50 of the 325 films it produced. Blaché pioneered techniques such as the split screen and double exposure.

Edith Head (1897–1981) was a costume designer who was nominated for 34 Academy Awards (and won eight). She shaped the style of Hollywood through her work for Paramount and Universal, on films such as *Roman Holiday* (1953), *To Catch a Thief* (1955), and *The Sting* (1973). Her work helped to make style icons of Audrey Hepburn, Grace Kelly, Elizabeth Taylor, and Marlene Dietrich.

Anna May Wong (1905–1961) was Hollywood's first Chinese-American movie star. Her first leading role was in 1922 as a deserted bride in *The Toll of the Sea*, followed by the role of a slave in *The Thief of Bagdad* (1924). In the sound era, her films included *Shanghai Express* (1932). Wong's career later suffered due to the lack of roles written for Asian women.

Jane Campion (b. 1954) is a New Zealand-born screenwriter, producer, and director who became the first woman to win the Palme d'Or at Cannes for her film *The Piano* (1993). The film also won her an Oscar for best original screenplay in 1994, and she became the second woman ever to be nominated for best director for that same movie.

Zoya Akhtar (b. 1972) is one of the few female directors in Bollywood, and one of only three making blockbusters grossing over 100 crore (£11.4 million). She began as an assistant director to her brother Farhan Akhtar and worked with filmmaker Mira Nair, before studying film at New York University. Akhtar's films have been credited with drawing attention to the sexism in Indian society without obscuring the Bollywood narrative.

FASCISM AND FREEDOM
fighters

TOTALITARIAN REGIMES

In 1919, Benito Mussolini created the world's first fascist movement in Italy. His combat group extolled the virtues of masculinity and machismo, appealing to the fighting spirit and fervent patriotism of his fellow World War I veterans. The fascist "revolution" was presented as an entirely male event. Newsreels showed young men marching in formation and singing rousing fascist anthems celebrating nationhood, war, and empire.

Denying women a role in politics and public life, Italian fascism sought to keep women within the confines of the home, to limit their educational and employment opportunities, and to restrict their roles to those of wife and mother. Mussolini's official policies also imposed a state-sponsored system of "compulsory motherhood" upon women, with social incentives and welfare benefits aimed to convince them to become "breeders" to create new soldiers. One of the biggest fascist creations in Italy was the National Organization for the Protection of

◀ **Blackshirts**
Female members of the British Union of Fascists (founded by Oswald Mosley in 1932) wear the fascist uniform – the famous black shirt, alongside a beret and skirt – as they prepare for a rally in Liverpool, England.

Motherhood and Infancy, an institution which gave moral and financial support to pregnant women, mothers, and widows.

Despite the misogynistic ideology, women had a visible presence in fascist movements in some countries and were key to their success. In Britain, a distinct form of feminine fascism emerged, and a woman named Rotha Lintorn-Orman founded the first fascist movement in Britain in 1923.

▶ **Call to arms**
This depiction of a Catalan woman rallying troops was created in 1937 to encourage support for the Basque people, who were besieged by fascist and German forces during the Spanish Civil War.

"**UNDER** CONDITIONS OF **TYRANNY** IT IS FAR **EASIER TO ACT** **THAN** TO **THINK**".

HANNAH ARENDT, *THE HUMAN CONDITION*, 1958

OFENSIVA PARA EUZKADI

German women also played a big part in the triumph of Adolf Hitler as many German women supported Nazism, despite its similar doctrines to Italian fascism. The ideal German woman did not work, but instead built her life around "children, kitchen, and church". In the federal elections of July 1932, 13.7 million Germans voted Nazi, and 6.5 million of those votes came from women.

25%
of the British Union of Fascists in the 1930s were women

Resistance

On the other side, many women bravely opposed fascism. In Spain, fearless women, such as Dolores Ibárruri, General-Secretary of the Spanish Communist Party, called on the nation to defend democracy against fascism. General Francisco Franco, supported by Italy and Germany, led a rebellion and coup attempt against the Second Spanish Republic in 1936, and Ibárruri urged her fellow Spaniards to resist. Her country descended into a prolonged and vicious civil war, which eventually brought Franco to power in 1939. While Franco remained in power (until his death in 1975), Ibárruri, who had fled Spain, lived in exile in the USSR. She finally returned to her homeland as a national hero in 1977. Other women continued to fight while Franco was in charge: in 1939, the 13 Roses – a group of communist and socialist women between the ages of 18 and 29 – were executed by firing squad for working against the new fascist regime.

INTO THE
line of fire

WORLD WAR II

BIOGRAPHY
NOOR INAYAT KHAN

Khan was born in Moscow in 1914 to an Indian father and an American mother. She was raised first in London and then in Paris, returning to England after the Nazi occupation of France. She became a radio operator with the British Special Operations Executive. In 1943, under the codename "Madeline", she became the first female radio operator to be sent to Nazi-occupied France. Later that year, she was betrayed; Khan was arrested by the Gestapo and executed along with three other women at Dachau in September 1944.

Whether as civilians caught up in the maelstrom of violence, members of the armed forces, or working as resistance operatives, women were fully exposed to the horrors of World War II. The war saw an unprecedented scale of attacks on civilian targets, in particular the widespread use of aerial bombardment, which placed millions of women at risk of death and serious injury. As the increasingly brutal conflict engulfed more and more of the world, millions of women were forced from their homes in search of safety. Tragically, thousands of women were raped by enemy soldiers, both opportunistically and as a strategic tactic (one that was later declared a war crime). The Red (Russian) Army estimatedly raped nearly one million German women between 1944 and 1945.

Women in uniform

The massive demands of World War II meant that hundreds of thousands of women entered military service. Germany and Japan were reluctant to consider recruiting women to the armed forces, so the vast majority of women in uniform fought for the Allied powers. Over 800,000 women served in the Soviet (USSR) armed forces, around 640,000 women served in British forces, and some 350,000 in the US armed services. They worked in a wide range of roles including as radio operators, gunners, drivers, and tank commanders. Female snipers were not uncommon; the USSR's Lyudmila Pavlichenko, who was credited with 309 kills, was the most lethal. Another Soviet heroine was Marina Raskova, who persuaded Stalin to allow the

The **conscription** of women into the **British Army** was **legalized** in

1941

IN BRIEF
A GREATER WAR
The sheer scale of World War II was unprecedented; the nature of its warfare meant that more women were in harm's way than in any previous conflict.

1939

December The women's section of the British organization of the Air Transport Auxiliary, is founded.

1941

2 July Canada's Women's Army Corps is created.

October Josef Stalin orders the creation of all-female air force units in Russia.

December British government passes the National Service Act, which allows conscription of some women into war work or armed forces.

1942

14 May Congress approves the creation of the Women's Army Auxiliary Corps, which begins active duty as the Women's Army Corps in July 1943.

21 July Congress approves the creation of the Women Accepted for Volunteer Emergency Service, a female branch of the Naval Reserve.

1943

22 February Sophie Scholl is executed in Munich for her resistance against the Nazis.

5 August The Women Airforce Service Pilots organization is formally founded in the US.

1945

April Princess Elizabeth (later Queen Elizabeth II) trains in the Auxiliary Territorial Service (ATS); as 2nd Lieutenant Elizabeth Windsor, she serves as a mechanic and driver for the ATS.

◀ **ON PARADE** THE US WOMEN'S ARMY CORPS WEAR GAS MASKS AT A DRILL, FLORIDA, 1942.

creation of three all-female regiments in the Soviet Air Forces. The most celebrated were the "Night Witches" – 23 aviators under the command of Yevdokia Bershanskaya – who carried out over 20,000 bombing sorties against the forces of Germany and its allies. Britain and the US also used female pilots but they were not sent into combat. Instead they mainly flew aircraft from factories to military bases. In other countries, women took on auxiliary roles, working as nurses, drivers, and secretaries, to free up male soldiers for combat. Most British women worked on the Home Front, where one of their most vital tasks was operating antiaircraft batteries and searchlights.

Operating undercover

Resistance and partisan groups often recruited women because they were not subject to the same suspicions as men, and could sometimes perform covert operations unnoticed. In the French Resistance women regularly acted as couriers but it was rare for them to assume leadership roles or participate in violent operations. An exception was Marie-Madeleine Fourcade, known as "Herisson" (Hedgehog), who led a group of over 3,000 agents. However, in Poland, which

80,000
British women served in the Land Army during World War II.

had the largest resistance force, women – one-seventh of the Polish Home Army's 40,000 members – did take part in combat operations. The Special Operations Executive (SOE), a British unit founded in 1940 to spy and perform acts of sabotage in occupied Europe, had several female agents. One of the most famous was Virginia Hall, who despite her prosthetic leg, operated behind enemy lines in France. Another was Haviva Reik, one of a group of Jewish agents the SOE parachuted into Slovakia in 1944. She helped to organize resistance groups until the parachutists were discovered and killed by the German Army.

Many leading figures in the anti-Nazi movement were women; student Sophie Scholl was sentenced to death in 1943 for distributing anti-Nazi pamphlets. Women also played roles in smuggling Jews out of the reach of the Nazis. Emilie Schindler helped her husband to save the lives of over 1,200 Jews; she risked her life buying goods on the black market to feed them. But the role of women was not always positive; around 3,500 worked in Nazi concentration camps. The most notorious was Irma Grese, a warden at Bergen-Belsen, who was executed after the war for her inhumane treament of prisoners.

BIOGRAPHY
ANNE FRANK

Born in Frankfurt, Anne and her family fled from Germany to Amsterdam after Hitler's rise to power, but the Nazis soon took control there too. In 1942, the Franks went into hiding in a secret annex above the offices of Anne's father's business, but were betrayed to the authorities in 1944. Anne was deported to a concentration camp where she died of typhus. Her diary, written between 1942 and 1944, was published by her father, and became one of the best-known Jewish accounts of the Holocaust.

◄ **Night witches**
Germans nicknamed the Soviet 588th Night Bomber Regiment the "Night Witches". The regiment was initially banned from combat, but was deployed for active service in 1941.

MOBILIZING THE
workforce

WAR WORK

One of the most enduring images of women's work during World War II (see pp. 234–237) is that of "Rosie the Riveter". Painted by artist Norman Rockwell, she first appeared in May 1943, on the cover of the US magazine *Saturday Evening Post*. Wearing overalls and goggles, she was depicted with a halo while cradling a riveting machine and trampling a copy of Hitler's *Mein Kampf* under her feet. "Rosie" represented a positive image of a strong, capable, working woman. Similar poster girls included Canada's "Ronnie the Bren Gun Girl" (Veronica Foster), who worked on a production line in Toronto, and Ruby Loftus, whose poster was commissioned by the War Artist's Advisory Committee for her work at

◄ **Worn with pride**
Thousands of female workers were given lapel badges such as this one to recognize their contribution to the war effort. This silver badge was worn by members of the British Women's Voluntary Service.

the Royal Ordnance Factory in Newport, England. These valorized images were key to recruiting women into munitions work, which was essential to Allied success, but was tough, dirty, and poorly paid. More than 85,000 US women joined the Women Ordnance Workers, and produced and tested military hardware.

The realities of war work

Millions of women entered the workforce during World War II in Allied nations. More than seven million women in the US were engaged in military production, usually working a 48-hour week with no vacation. On average their salaries were around 50 per cent lower than those paid to men. The war also quadrupled the number of African American women working in industry. Women became essential in agricultural production, too. In Britain, the Women's Land Army was revived in 1939 (having been disbanded after World War I) to increase food production and reduce the country's reliance on imports. Similar organizations were created in North America, as well as in Australia and New Zealand, where women in this field were nicknamed "farmerettes".

Elsewhere, the role of women in war work was more limited. In Germany, women were not recruited as heavily into war industry because female participation in the workforce was at odds with Nazi ideology. However,

▼ **Heavy lifting**
Female forestry workers loading logs in Finland in 1942. In many countries women played a central role on the home front, providing essential manual labour in farming, agriculture, and forestry.

◀ **Building planes**
Women install fixtures and assemblies to the tail fuselage section of a B-17F bomber (a "Flying Fortress") in Long Beach, California, in 1942.

from 1939, it was compulsory for women to serve in the Reich Labour Service (working in agriculture) and in January 1943, worker shortages forced Adolf Hitler to demand all German women aged from 17 to 45 register for employment. Similarly, in Japan, women were initially discouraged from working in industry, but by 1943 so many men had been lost to military service that a women's labour corps was formed. By the next year it had recruited four million Japanese women.

During the war, millions of men and women were coerced into forced labour. Inmates of German concentration camps performed gruelling physical work; some were contracted out to work for private companies. The Nazis deported millions of people from Central and Eastern Europe for use as slave labour; *Ostarbeiter* (workers from the East) toiled in factories and labour camps, often on starvation rations. In addition, Germany and Japan each took thousands of women from occupied territories to use as sex slaves ("comfort women") in military brothels. Japan is now working on an agreement to pay reparations for its capture of South Korean women during wartime.

An estimated **90%** of Japan's **"comfort women"** did not survive the war

> " ... sometimes I **think I shall not be able to endure** it. ... never since I have **worked in the mill** have I been **so very tired** ... "

MARY PAUL, LOWELL MILL GIRL, MASSACHUSETTS, 1845

EXPERIENCES OF WORK

Nine to five

The idea that women in the workforce should earn a salary is a relatively recent one. Women's work was often unpaid, poorly paid, or overlooked altogether. In the 21st century, women are still battling gender inequality in pay and access to various types of jobs.

The daily grind
This figurine of a woman from Egypt's Sixth Dynasty (2325–2175 BCE) shows her working in the home. She crushes grain on a saddle quern (a pair of stones used to grind it into fine pieces).

RESTRICTED ACCESS TO EDUCATION as well as religious and cultural conventions has limited women's working lives. However, that does not mean that women have not worked; their contribution has always played a vital role in how society functions even if that has not always been recognized. Historically, many women worked in the home: cooking, sewing, and making textiles, as well as caring for their children. Outside of the home, they might earn by trading goods in barter economies, or work for nothing as slaves due to their skin colour or social class. In feudal societies, peasants were given land to work by their lord, who would retain part of the crop's yield and some of the profit from its

sale. While women worked the land, they were legally their husbands' property, and therefore did not receive an individual benefit for their own work. In modern economies, the most common form of arrangement is wage work, in which men and women sell their labour in exchange for a salary.

Rural and urban

During the medieval and early modern periods, women in Europe had varying roles and opportunities. Women in rural communities assisted their fathers and husbands in tending livestock, and participated in cottage industries like baking and weaving, while those in urban environments, women assisted male family members in trades and crafts, such as metalwork, producing leather goods and textiles, and running shops and inns. From the 1300s, many women made a living from brewing beer. These "alewives", some of whom were single or widowed, brewed alcohol over large cauldrons and often wore

> " Do not **choose your wife** at a **dance**, but **on the field among** the **harvesters**. "

CZECH PROVERB

TYPISTS AT WORK AT UNILEVER HOUSE, BLACKFRIARS, LONDON, 1955

> ## Our **wages** weren't for **pin money**. They were to **help with** the **cost of living**, to pay your **mortgage** and ... your **bills**.

GWEN DAVIS, PARTICIPANT IN THE 1968 FORD STRIKE, UK

pointed black hats to make them easy to identify when selling their wares. They also put brooms outside of their homes to show that beer was being sold, the combination of these features later became synonymous with witchcraft (see pp. 122–123). Alewives were often the first targets for accusations of witchcraft, perhaps because they were women with some financial autonomy.

In the 19th century, women's work in towns and factories led to the formation of specifically female trade unions. The first such example was that of the Lowell Mill girls in Massachusetts, who went on strike to protest against low wages and dangerous working conditions in 1844; in 1866, African American laundresses in Mississippi followed their example. Bigger unions soon arrived: national Women's Trade Union Leagues were formed at the turn of the 20th century in Britain and the US to advocate for the rights of female workers. Such unions later supported women who went on strike for equal pay (see pp. 272–275).

The professions
Throughout history, many roles were divided along gender lines. While men working in labour-oriented jobs have been called "blue collar" workers (in opposition to "white collar" workers in office and professional positions), the term "pink collar" refers to women in careers that have traditionally been considered women's work. Pink collar jobs include "unskilled" work such as babysitting or retail work, as well as jobs in the beauty industry (as hairdressers or nail technicians) or typing and secretarial work. While many require training, pink collar jobs pay low wages and carry little prestige because of their designation as "women's work".

The 20th century brought more women into traditionally "male" professions, and now women are slowly infiltrating the highest levels of industry. However, women still only make up approximately five per cent of CEOs of Fortune 500 companies.

> ## A **truly equal world** would be one where **women ran half** our countries and **companies** and men **ran half our homes**.

SHERYL SANDBERG, *LEAN IN: WOMEN, WORK, AND THE WILL TO LEAD*, 2013

VIVA LA revolución!

SOUTH AMERICA IN TURMOIL

▲ **Martyred in Bolivia**
In 1930, revolts and revolutions overturned the governments of Argentina, Bolivia, Brazil, Chile, and Uruguay. This French newspaper shows a female revolutionary being shot during the Bolivian revolt.

During the 20th century, South and Central America were rocked by revolutions in which woman played central roles. They fought side by side with men for change in Argentina, Bolivia, Brazil, and Mexico, battling against fascism and totalitarianism, and striving to achieve universal suffrage.

After Getúlio Vargas led a military coup d'état against Brazil's President Washington Luís in 1930, he repealed the constitution and practically established a dictatorship. In 1932, the liberal opposition launched the so-called "Constitutional Revolution" to overthrow Vargas, which led to the deaths of at least 1,000 people. Women such as Dr Carlota Pereira de Queirós were among the revolutionaries. She headed a group of 700 women, who provided medical assistance to the injured. Although Vargas won the war, many of the constitutionalists' demands were met, including women's suffrage. De Queirós was the first woman to vote and she was elected to the Brazilian parliament in 1933.

In Argentina, women's suffrage came after the Pro-Women's Suffrage Commission sent a petition to Juan Perón's populist government formed after the 1943 Revolution, asking it to

"LIKE EVERY WOMAN OF THE **PEOPLE**, I HAVE **MORE STRENGTH** THAN I **APPEAR TO**."

EVA PERÓN, FIRST LADY OF ARGENTINA

grant women the right to vote. However, things deteriorated after the "Liberating Revolution" of 1955 to 1958 that ended the second presidential term of Perón. References to his charismatic late wife Eva, the founder of the Female Peronist Party and champion of women's suffrage, were strictly forbidden.

Argentina's new anti-Peronist government imprisoned hundreds of women it viewed as threats to the regime. State violence increased and culminated in the "Dirty War" of 1976 to 1983 in which government agents kidnapped, tortured, and killed dissidents. Mothers of the so-called "disappeared" established the Mothers of the Plaza de Mayo group to pressure the military government to reveal what had happened to their children. The high-profile campaign led to the discovery of many of the missing children – both alive and dead.

In Bolivia, many women fought in the 19th century for independence from colonial Spain, yet they only earned the right to vote in 1952 after the Bolivian Social Revolution. In 1978 miner's wife and unionist Domitila Barrious de Chúngara led a hunger strike that brought down the dictatorship of General Hugo Bánzer Suárez, leading to the return of democracy.

Fighting for independence

Women took part in Mexico's revolution from 1910 to 1920, particularly indigenous women known as *soldaderas*, who were combatants. Notable among these was Petra Herrera who joined Pancho Villa's army. When her role in taking Torreón went unacknowledged, she left and formed an all-female troop of soldiers. Despite finally gaining the right to vote in national elections in 1953, Mexican women, like many in Latin America, still face discrimination due to a culture of machismo.

▼ **Strong mothers**
Members of the Mothers of the Plaza de Mayo group protest in front of the presidential palace in Buenos Aires during 1982 to find out what happened to their sons and daughters.

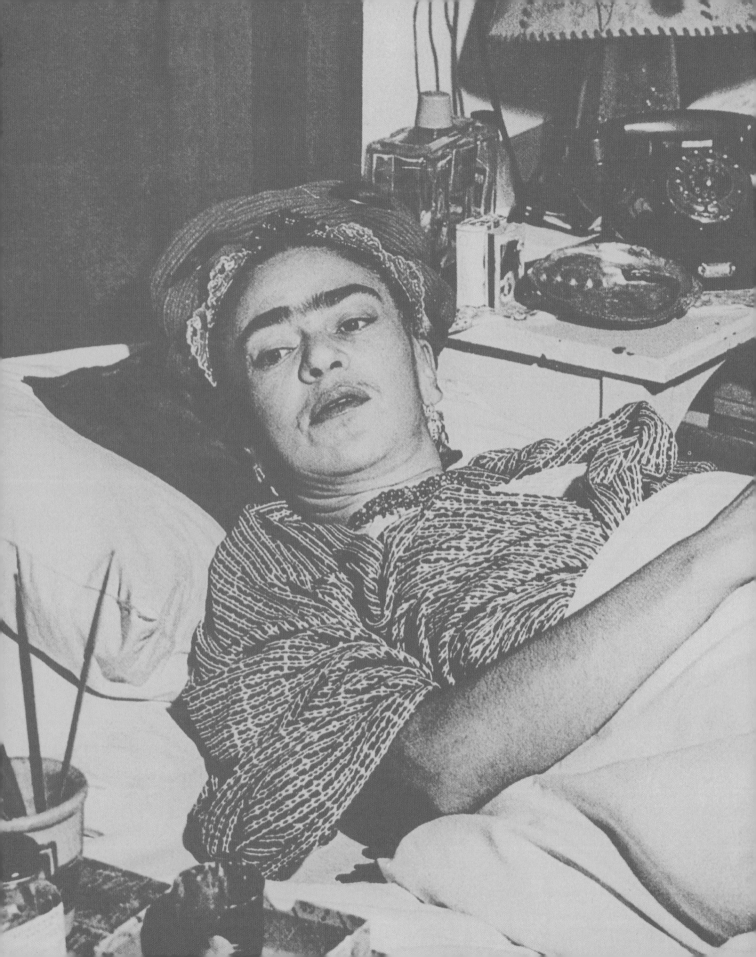

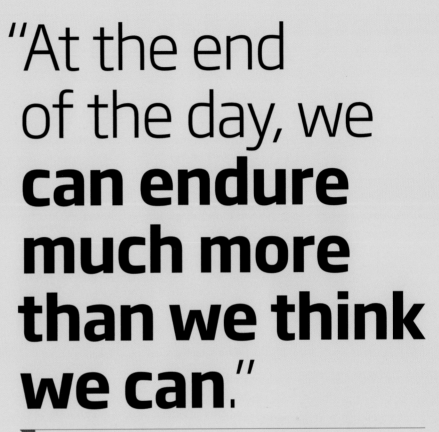

"At the end of the day, we **can endure much more than we think we can.**"

FRIDA KAHLO, FEMINIST ARTIST, ON THE STRENGTH POSSESSED BY WOMEN

ART AND SUFFERING

Frida Kahlo was a Mexican painter who lived from 1907 to 1954. Her bold, iconic style made her popular both during her lifetime and after, and today she is remembered for provocative pieces exploring themes of anticapitalism, feminism, identity, and sexuality (Kahlo herself was bisexual). Kahlo endured much herself; she had polio as a child, a damaged pelvis, and even had a leg amputated before her death. She depicted her own disability and visually represented her pain in pieces such as *The Broken Column* (1944) and *Tree of Hope, Keep Firm* (1946) - painted as she continued to work even while bedridden with spinal pain. Kahlo is depicted here at her home in Mexico City, confined to her bed, but still with an easel on her lap.

SOLDIERS OF
freedom

DECOLONIZATION

Decolonization after World War II resulted in some three dozen countries in Asia and Africa gaining autonomy from their colonial rulers. In many cases, this newfound independence came after a long struggle and a history of resistance against Western rule, including uprisings such as the 1857 rebellion in India (see pp. 156–157) or the 1929 Women's War in Nigeria (see pp. 226–227). The decolonization process was different in each country affected, and its impact on women was not uniform. Although typically led by men, women participated in nationalist movements across Asia and Africa in many capacities, and argued that political and legal gender equality should form part of the postcolonial settlements.

Politics and protest

Women were active as revolutionaries before and after independence, although some colonial regimes restricted women's political mobilization, meaning that such participation was more limited or covert. Anticolonial feeling among women was often given added impetus by the failure of the colonial powers to recognize women's concerns. Existing women's groups took up the nationalist cause and new women's organizations, such as the Sierra Leone Women's Movement in 1951, were formed at national and local levels and within political parties. In this way, women became more active in politics and protest, paving the way for gender equality in future

◀ **Minority report**
Mrs Renner, a barrister from Lagos, Nigeria, attends the fifth Pan-African Congress in Manchester, England, in 1945 to advocate higher standards of education for African women.

STEPS TO FREEDOM

Women's contributions to decolonization were significant, both in destabilizing the hierarchies of power at the heart of colonial rule, and in postcolonial nation building.

1900

1913 Kenyan Mnyazi wa Menza leads the Giriama people against British Colonial Administration.

1920–1922 Women in India participate as organizers of the Non-Cooperation Movement led by Mahatma Gandhi.

1925 Sarojini Naidu is elected president of the Indian National Congress, the first Indian woman to hold the post.

1927 The All India Women's Conference nongovernmental organization is founded to improve women's education and social welfare.

1930 Women are mass participants in Gandhi's Civil Disobedience Movement against the Raj.

1942 Kasturba Gandhi is imprisoned for her involvement with the Quit India Movement. She dies in a detention camp two years later.

1945 World War II ends; decolonization begins.

1947 Indian Independence leads to the Partition of India and the formation of Pakistan.

1951 The Sierra Leone Women's Movement forms, and over the next decade it plays a fundamental role in supporting the nationalist movement and incorporating women into politics.

1952–1960 Women play a significant part in the Mau Mau Uprising in British Kenya, taking on military, civilian, and activist roles.

1954 Bibi Titi Mohamed cofounds the Tanganyika African National Union nationalist party. She forms the women's wing, Umoja wa Wanawake wa Tanzania, which empowers women across the country.

1958 Indian independence activist Aruna Asaf Ali becomes Delhi's first mayor.

1963 Kenya gains independence.

1997 The British Empire officially ends with a ceremony in Hong Kong to mark the handover of sovereignty to the People's Republic of China.

◀ **WOMEN SHOUT SLOGANS** DURING A QUIT INDIA MOVEMENT DEMONSTRATION IN BOMBAY IN 1942.

"... WOMEN HAVE BETTER UNDERSTOOD THE SPIRIT OF THE FIGHT THAN MEN."

KASTURBA GANDHI, ACTIVIST AND WIFE OF MAHATMA GANDHI

independent nations. However, in more male-dominated freedom movements women's issues were often given less priority than economic development, and the role played by women in the struggle was largely determined by the prevailing patriarchal culture of both the colonists and their opponents.

Freedom for India

Mahatma Gandhi, the leader of the Indian independence movement, referred to women as "disciplined soldiers of Indian freedom". From the 1930s, women of different classes and castes became participants in the fight for freedom, often engaged in campaigns on specific issues affecting women, such as the campaign to restrict child marriage. Kamala Nehru, the wife of Jawaharlal Nehru (an activist for Indian independence and India's first prime minister), rallied the public in a campaign of civil disobedience for which she was imprisoned in 1932.

In the Quit India Movement of 1942, which called for an end to British colonial rule, Gandhian Usha Mehta spread a message of rebellion across India via Secret Congress Radio, an underground radio station. She was arrested that year, and imprisoned for four years alongside 250 other female prisoners jailed for their activism.

700 million people outside the UK fell under **British rule** during the British Empire

Following independence, the Partition of India in 1947 led to violence with more than a million killed. Between 75,000 and 100,000 women were abducted and brutally raped.

Many women in the newly formed Pakistan were also forcibly converted to Islam. In response to these traumatic events, women in Pakistan such as Fatima Jinnah and Begum Ra'ana Liaquat Ali Khan founded organizations such as Pakistan Women's Association, which worked to improve the lives of refugees and women migrants.

African experiences

There were a great number of influential women involved in the many, diverse independence movements in African countries, both before and after 1945. In the Mau Mau Uprising of 1952 to 1964, a rebellion against British rule in Kenya, women performed a key

▶ **Liberation at last**
Algerian women cheer the arrival of independence and the end of the Algerian War in 1962. An estimated 11,000 women were involved in the conflict, some served as paramilitaries in urban centres and others joined armed guerrilla bands in rural areas.

role, providing supplies to guerilla fighters as well as fighting themselves. Muthoni wa Kirima even had the rank of field-marshal bestowed on her.

In Tanganyika (now Tanzania), women played a formidable role in the success of the political party Tanganyika African National Union (TANU)

founded in 1954; its women's wing Umoja wa Wanawake wa Tanzania, headed by Bibi Titi Mohamed, united and mobilized women in the independence struggle. Mohamed, who later became minister for women and social affairs, was also involved in the *ngoma* (dance groups) in Tanzania. These women's groups became clandestine vehicles for nationalist mobilization, announcing TANU protests, and raising party funds. Mohamed attributes her political successes to these dance groups, which she sees as providing a chance to practise leadership and make connections within women's networks.

In Ghana, revolutionary leader Kwame Nkrumah relied on women during the fight for independence and afterward. After meeting with him in 1947, Hannah Kudjoe became a major independence activist, single-handedly mobilizing rallies across the country. Following independence, she founded the All-African Women's League, which later became the Ghana Women's League. She is one of many women who played key roles in anti-colonial struggles across the world, who have not been fully credited for the extent and value of their fight.

BIOGRAPHY
ARUNA ASAF ALI

Born in Punjab in 1909, Aruna Asaf Ali was educated at a Catholic school but later married Muslim lawyer and anti-colonialist Asaf Ali. She became involved in the fight for independence, and in 1942 hoisted the Congress flag in Bombay, inaugurating the Quit India Movement. She then went into hiding for four years but still edited the Congress Party's magazine. After independence, she joined the Congress Socialist Party and became secretary of the Delhi Women's League. She died in 1996 and won India's highest civilian award, the Bharat Ratna, a year later.

THROUGH THE AGES

Fashion

What women wear affects how they are perceived and signifies their status. Fashion is constantly evolving and reflects women's changing lives – from trousers in the 1920s to the choice of black in support of the #MeToo campaign at the Golden Globes in 2018.

▶ **If the shoe fits**
Hammam clogs, like the ones worn by this noble lady in 18th-century Constantinople (modern Istanbul), were worn by women at Turkish baths to avoid dirty water on the floor. The shoes' height also indicated their social status.

> **Fashion** is **part of** the **daily air** and **it changes** … **with** all the **events**.
>
> **DIANA VREELAND**, NOTED COLUMNIST AND FASHION EDITOR, 1978

SINCE ANTIQUITY people have expressed their identity through dress. Although historians disagree on the starting point of Western fashion, the desire to dress up was accelerated in the 15th century as Europe grew more prosperous and imported textiles became signifiers of wealth. The urban elite set the styles, which were then adopted by the growing middle class in simpler forms. Fashion also evolved in response to the environments in which women lived. For example, in 16th-century Venice women wore shoes on tall stilts (chopines) to avoid the mud. By the 17th century, the most popular fashions came from France, where women wore lace, silk, and brocade. Dressmakers across the Western world adopted their styles with the help of engravings of the French designs.

Almost all women's clothing before the 19th century was made-to-measure. Wealthy women had garments made for them by couturiers, while working women made their own clothes. Ready-made clothes became available towards the end of the 19th century, and became more prevalent with the advent of mail order catalogues. By the 20th century, most women's clothing was bought ready-made as a result of mass textile production and the creation of department stores.

Fashion statements

In the early 20th century, the campaign for women's rights, particularly suffrage, influenced fashion. To avoid being labelled masculine, suffragettes presented a consciously elegant image, aided by their adoption, in 1908, of three colours – white for purity, green for hope, and purple for dignity (in the US, gold replaced green).

As the demand for women's rights grew louder, fashion reacted against traditional femininity. From the knee-revealing flapper dress and Coco Chanel's trousers for women in the 1920s to Mary Quant's thigh-baring miniskirts in the 1960s, fashion became a form of rebellion for some. From the late 1970s, women dressed in sober, tailored suits as they strove to establish themselves in traditionally male workplaces. By 1983, women were expressing their views on slogan T-shirts, a trend set by UK designer Katharine Hamnett. A host of female fashion designers, among them Diane von Furstenberg and Donna Karan in the US, and Vivienne Westwood in the UK, began to challenge the dominance of male designers.

Although women are integral to today's fashion industry, it does not always favor them. Women in developing nations making cheap, mass-produced clothes (see pp. 296–297) are among the most exploited by the industry. Critics also point to the fashion industry's obsession with thinness, although since the late 20th century some "plus size" models have begun to appear on catwalks and in campaigns.

▲ In vogue
This vintage *Vogue* cover is from 1919. Founded in 1892, the US magazine was originally targeted at New York's upper class but filtered through to the aspirational middle class.

FRENCH COUTURIER COCO CHANEL IN PARIS, 1936

KEY PLAYERS

Rose Bertin (1747-1813) dressed the most fashionable women in 18th-century Europe. Apprenticed to a Parisian milliner, she built up a following among the capital's aristocratic women, and opened a dress store in 1770. Two years later she became Marie-Antoinette's personal dressmaker. Bertin made her a style icon and popularized the *pouf* hairstyle – a precursor of the modern beehive.

Gabrielle "Coco" Chanel (1883-1971) learned to sew at the French orphanage where she was raised. Three years after becoming a licensed milliner, she opened a boutique in the resort of Deauville in 1910, and began to sell deluxe casual wear adapted from men's clothing. She moved her business to Paris, expanded to sell couture, perfume, and ready-to-wear, and became one of the most influential designers of the early 20th century.

Ann Lowe (1898-1981) was one of the first African-American designers to have a successful career in high fashion. She worked in Tampa, Florida, creating dresses for elite women before moving to New York in 1928. There, she became known for designing couture wedding gowns - one of the most famous being that of Jacqueline Bouvier Kennedy, wife of President John F. Kennedy.

Lisa Fonssagrives (1911-1992) was a Swedish model, photographer, designer, and sculptor. She was paid far more than other models, leading some to call her the world's first "supermodel." Fonssagrives - who once described herself as a "good clothes hanger" - had an unusually long modelling career, lasting from the 1930s until the 1950s.

Wilhelmina Cooper (1939-1980) is a Dutch former model who set records by appearing on the cover of *Vogue* 28 times. She was managed by Eileen Ford's pioneering Ford Modeling Agency, but went on to found her own agency, Wilhelmina Models, in 1967. Her own company grew to rival Ford's in success.

Dame Anna Wintour (b. 1949) has been editor-in-chief of *Vogue* magazine since 1988. Known for her signature severe bobbed haircut, Wintour is one of the most powerful tastemakers in the industry. New York's Metropolitan Museum of Art named its Costume Institute after her when it reopened in 2014.

"One is not born, but rather **becomes, a woman**."

SIMONE DE BEAUVOIR, WRITER AND POLITICAL ACTIVIST, *THE SECOND SEX*, 1949

FEMININITY AND SOCIETY

In her book, *The Second Sex*, French feminist Simone de Beauvoir broke new ground: she separated the concept of gender from biological sex. De Beauvoir believed that gender roles are socially constructed, and that rather than having some biological basis, femininity is something that girls learn through socialization. From a young age, girls are conditioned to accept dependence and passivity as integral part of what it means to be feminine. For example, girls are taught that they should strive to be pretty and conform to feminine ideals in order to appeal to men; by doing so, they become passive objects for men to look at. One of society's most glaring objectifications of women (and girls) is the beauty pageant. In this photograph, taken at the Miss Pears pageant in London in 1973, girls compete to be crowned the most beautiful.

REBEL NUNS AND POLITICAL
martyrs

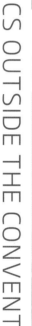

POLITICS OUTSIDE THE CONVENT

Women who decide to be nuns choose to dedicate their lives to an ideology, and such dedication has led some to become political martyrs. Seen as morally pure and nonviolent figures, when a nun makes a political statement it can be both visible and highly effective. One of the world's most famous nuns, Mother Teresa, was not only a religious visionary but a smart political operator, who was able to convince councillors and banks to aid in building homes for the poor.

▶ **Celebrating Tibetan women**
Tibetan Buddhist women in exile wave Tibetan flags and shout slogans to mark the 59th National Tibetan Women's Uprising Day at McLeod Ganj, India, on 12 March 2018.

While nuns are often seen as apolitical women whose lives are dedicated to worship, many moments in history have seen nuns take a political stand, for example in the Tibetan uprising of 1959. Tibet had been an independent nation ruled by a spiritual leader, the Dalai Lama, but in 1950 it fell under control of the Chinese government, who wanted the Dalai Lama removed. In 1959, as Chinese forces gathered in Lhasa where the Dalai Lama lived, tensions came to a peak. On 12 March that year a group of Tibetan women, including many Buddhist nuns, gathered outside Potala Palace, Lhasa – the Dalai Lama's residence – and began a nonviolent protest against the Chinese occupation. At least 5,000 women joined in the uprising. Chinese forces responded violently, seeking out the organizers, and placing them under arrest. Among those arrested was a nun named Ghalingshar Choe-la, who was held and tortured for six years, and later died from her injuries. The women's martyrdom has led to more activism – every year on March 12, activists around the world protest to commemorate the "Women's Uprising".

Nuns in Latin America

Catholic nuns following the tenets of liberation theology – which advocates active participation in changing socioeconomic structures to help the poor – were involved in grassroots organizing for human rights in the 1960s and '70s. In Brazil, many priests guided by this theology were seen as "leftists" and arrested and tortured by the military junta after the coup of 1964. Sister Maurina Borges da Silveira was the only Religious Sister to experience the same fate; she was arrested and tortured in 1969, then banished in 1970. During the Salvadoran Civil War (1980–1992), three US nuns, Maura Clarke, Ita Ford, and Ursuline Dorothy Kazel, and a lay missionary, Jean Donovan, worked with the poor and refugees from the war. The military in El Salvador regarded such activities as subversive and, in 1980, the women were beaten, raped, and murdered by Salvadoran death squads. The commitment of nuns to social justice has often put them at risk of imprisonment, torture, and even death.

▲ **Church versus state**
Greek Orthodox nuns protest against a proposed law to give the Greek government control over the Church's land. Aside from the state, the Church is Greece's biggest landowner.

"THE **MIRACLE** IS NOT THAT **WE DO THIS WORK**, BUT THAT WE ARE **HAPPY** TO **DO IT**."

MOTHER TERESA, ROMAN CATHOLIC NUN AND MISSIONARY

Smashing the Glass Ceiling

1960–present

While women's rights had come a long way by the 1960s, women knew there was still much more to be done. Mass protests such as the Civil Rights Movement in America, and the fight against Apartheid in South Africa, showed that while all women suffer under patriarchal systems and traditions, nonwhite women bear a greater burden. Second-wave feminists in the 1960s and those of the third wave from the 1990s engaged in protests and demonstrations around the world, which called for the liberalization of laws on subjects such as divorce and contraception. As women globally continue to reject old rules and prejudices, barriers keep on being broken down every day.

PROPAGANDA AND POLITICS IN THE
Space Age

THE COLD WAR

From 1947–1991, the Cold War overshadowed global politics. In the aftermath of World War II, two superpowers emerged: the US and the USSR, now called Russia. Together with their allied states, known respectively as the Western and Soviet blocs, they struggled for political, economic, and cultural dominance. The two sides had different ideas about the role women should play in postwar society. In the US, which needed women to return to the home after the war in order to create employment for men, propaganda promoted the idea of the happy housewife and mother. In contrast, in the USSR, which had suffered heavy losses in the war, women were portrayed as key workers in the communist state. The 1936 Soviet Constitution enshrined equal rights for women and both the USSR and the rest of the Soviet bloc

▶ **Space pioneer**
Valentina Tereshkova became the first woman to travel into space in her capsule, Vostok 6. She clocked in more hours than all US astronauts combined to that date, orbiting the earth 48 times over three days.

presented themselves as champions of gender equality. In reality, the idealized expectations of American and Russian women were not completely realized in either country. In the US, women entered the workforce in increasing numbers and campaigned for equality. In the USSR, wage differentials persisted and the workforce was largely segregated by gender, with women given junior roles; women who had performed jobs in heavy industry during the war years were moved to lighter industries such as textiles.

Space women

One field of endeavour where Soviet women appeared to shine, however, was the Space Race, as the US and Russia competed to be the first to explore the new frontier. In 1963, Russian cosmonaut Valentina Tereshkova, a 26-year-old former textile worker, became the first woman to go to space – 20 years before the first female American astronaut. After intensive training with four other women for 18 months, Tereshkova was picked to pilot Vostok 6. She spent three days in space and orbited Earth 48 times. However, ultimately Tereshkova's mission seemed to be mainly for propaganda purposes and the USSR abandoned the training of female cosmonauts in 1969. The Russian government claimed, according to Tereshkova, that the dangers were too great for women. The USSR did not recruit further female cosmonauts until 1980.

Meanwhile, in the US, female scientists helped to forge the country's space programme. Several women were among the team behind the launch of Explorer 1, the first US satellite to orbit the earth, in 1958 (following Russia's Sputnik 1 and Sputnik 2 the previous year), and scientists such as Barbara Paulson, a founding member of the team at NASA, helped develop the first probes to the moon and planets. Yet women were not initially considered suitable astronauts; they were largely perceived as underqualified and physically unfit for space travel. All of the 13 female pilots who trained to become astronauts for the Mercury 13 mission in 1963, who had outperformed some of their male counterparts in tests, were dropped from the mission. It was not until 1983, and NASA's seventh shuttle mission, that the first American woman, Sally Ride, entered space on the space shuttle Challenger. According to the Challenger commander, Robert L. Crippen, she was selected for her expertise in operating the shuttle's arm to deploy and retrieve satellites. Ride spent six days in space, paving the way for other female astronauts. After the mission, she devoted much of her time to encouraging girls to follow in her footsteps.

▲ **American dream**
After World War II, the US promoted the image of the perfect housewife – an attractive woman who kept the home clean, cooked for her family, and raised her children behind a white picket fence.

ВОСТОК-6

СЛАВА ПЕРВОЙ ЖЕНЩИНЕ-КОСМОНАВТУ!

In **1969**, the **USSR** had **775,000** women engineers, almost as many as the **total number** of engineers in the **US**.

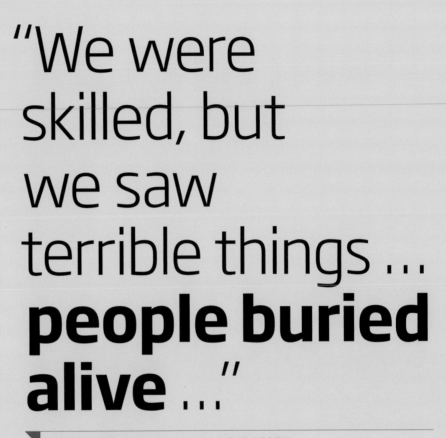

"We were skilled, but we saw terrible things ... **people buried alive ..."**

PHAN NGOC ANH, A WOMAN IN THE NORTH VIETNAMESE ARMY

COMBAT AND COMMUNISM

During the Vietnam War, Ho Chí Minh (the communist leader of North Vietnam) made it clear that women were to play a vital part in war efforts alongside their male counterparts. Women were therefore exposed to the full horrors of war: many joined the North Vietnamese Army and served in support capacities as medics, supply personnel, and bomb disposal teams; others joined the Viet Cong working in rice fields and intelligence services. Whatever their role, all women in North Vietnam were taught to use weapons and fight in hand-to-hand combat, and some – often those who were young, single, and childless – took combat roles. The soldiers depicted here were part of a self-defence detachment in Hanoi that repulsed a US air attack in April 1965.

THROUGH THE AGES

Military service

Despite stories of brave heroines entering combat throughout history, formal enlistment for women into combat roles is a modern phenomenon. Even today, many countries do not allow women to serve as combatants.

▲ Soviet advance
The Woman's Battalion of Death marches during the Russian Revolution of 1917 (see pp. 214–217). The number of women in the Red Army swelled hugely from 1917 to 1920.

> I was **trained** to **do what I did**, and I did it. We all **lived** through that **battle**.

SGT. LEIGH ANN HESTER, 2011

THE AGE OF MODERN WARFARE (dating to the outset of World War I) has drastically changed women's roles within the military. Modern warfare, categorized as warfare which uses modern technology and strategy, has seen a move away from pitched battles to a "total" approach to conflict in which civilian infrastructure is regarded as a legitimate military target.

While women have a long history serving in auxiliary military positions – for example as nurses, drivers, and secretaries – in the 20th and 21st centuries, many barriers preventing women from serving in combat roles have fallen, meaning that instances of female soldiers are no longer exceptional. In Eastern Europe, women have served as combatants since the 19th century. In Hungary, a woman served as an "order guard" in the independence war of 1868 (see pp. 130–133). Increasingly, nations are allowing women into their combat ranks and women are serving within all positions of the military. Today, all of Scandinavia, much of Eastern Europe, France, Germany, the Netherlands, Canada, Australia, and New Zealand allow women to serve in combat positions, as do Israel, Eritrea, and North Korea. The US also lifted their previous combat ban for women in 2013.

Challenges of combat

Women in combat face both physical and psychological challenges. Many soldiers and civilians believe that women should not be given combat roles – citing their supposed physical inferiority and "emotional" state of

DISNEY "FIFINELLA" MASCOT ON A US WOMEN'S AIRFORCE PATCH

mind – meaning that female soldiers fight to prove themselves to their peers. In 2013, when the US ban was lifted, Marine Corps Captain Katie Petronio wrote against the decision, claiming that continuous combat operations took a toll on women's bodies that far outweighed the toll on men. Women in combat also face the same challenges as service members in auxiliary positions did a century before in terms of how they are treated by male colleagues. While military service is rewarding for many who enlist, women have to contend with assault, harassment, and rape. Interviewed in 2017, North Korean soldier Lee So Yeon claimed that rape was a fact of life for women in combat, but that nobody was ever willing to testify against their superiors. A similar culture was evidenced in *The Invisible War* (2012), a documentary on sexual assault within the US military – an issue that is still a problem in gender-integrated military units worldwide. Ironically, the threat of having female prisoners of war raped by the enemy continues to be a reason given against allowing women into combat positions, with critics arguing that male soldiers' morale would suffer from seeing their female comrades assaulted.

▶ **Guns at the ready**
A female Swedish soldier participates in a joint training exercise between Swedish and Russian forces in December 2007. Since 1989, all positions in the Swedish military have been open to women.

PROFILES
SISTERS IN ARMS

Maria Wittek (1899-1997) was the first female general in the history of the Polish military. She served as the leader of *Przysposobienie Wojskowe Kobiet* (Female Military Training), which prepared young girls for military life. In 1919, Wittek fought against Bolshevik forces in Ukraine, and in 1920, served in the defence of Lviv, earning the highest Polish honour: the Virtuti Militari.

Lina Odena (1911-1936) was a *miliciana* (a female combatant) in the Spanish Civil War of 1936 to 1939. From the beginning, Odena served as a leader of the anti-fascist resistance, organizing and commanding militias. She died on a reconnaissance mission on the Granada front; surrounded by the enemy, she shot herself in the head to keep her secrets and avoid becoming a prisoner of war.

Sabiha Gökçen (1913-2001) was the first Turkish woman to serve as a combat pilot, and the first woman in the world to be a fighter pilot. An adopted child of Turkish revolutionary Mustafa Kemal Atatürk, Gökçen was given a military education on his orders, and flew in combat for the first time during the Dersim rebellion of 1937. She earned a medal and a letter of appreciation for damage caused by her bombs during the operation.

Simone Segouin (b. 1925) is a former French resistance fighter who went by the *nom de guerre* Nicole Minet during World War II. She joined *Francs-Tireurs et Partisans Français*, a group of communists and nationalists, at the age of 18, and captured 25 German prisoners of war during the liberation of Chartres. She was awarded the prestigious Croix de Guerre.

Solveig Krey (b. 1963) of the Norwegian Navy became the world's first female captain of a military submarine in 1995, at the helm of the 485-ton KNM *Kobben*. Norway first allowed women to serve on its submarines in 1985; many nations still prohibit this. In 2012, she became commander-in-chief of the Norwegian submarine fleet.

Sergeant Leigh Ann Hester (b. 1982) is a soldier in the National Guard (military police) of the United States Army. She earned a Silver Star for her actions in Iraq in 2005, becoming the first American woman to win one in combat, and was the first to be valorized for close quarters combat, after killing three insurgents with grenades and manoeuvring her troops to safety in a firefight.

SOUTH AFRICA
divided

PROTEST AGAINST APARTHEID

Apartheid in South Africa was an extreme form of racial segregation in which the white government categorized the population into "whites," "coloureds," and "blacks." Apartheid, an Afrikaans word meaning "apartness," designated the minority whites as the ruling class, and held the nonwhite population in poverty and servitude through restrictive laws of racial segregation.

Although black women held the least political power in South Africa, they acted as catalysts in mobilizing the masses, staging some of the most successful protests against apartheid. In 1913, the South African government tried to extend hated pass laws – which already applied to men – to women. Passes provided proof of where a person was allowed to go, restricting black people's movement outside of segregated areas. Activist and public speaker Charlotte Maxeke led a campaign against the extension, which resulted in the government restricting passes to black men in 1920.

Women and the ANC

In 1912, the African National Congress (ANC) united various African groups to fight for black voting rights and, from the 1940s, to end apartheid. Women were not allowed to join the ANC until 1943 when the ANC Women's League (ANCWL) was formed. Then, in 1954, Rachel "Ray" Simons and

Hilda Bernstein, both communist party members, created the Federation of South African Women (FEDSAW), the first broad-based women's group.

In 1952, the ANC and ANCWL initiated the Defiance Campaign Against Unjust Laws – the first large-scale, multiracial mobilization against apartheid, during which over 8,000 were arrested. Women were pivotal to the protest. Trade unionist Bibi "Asa" Dawood recruited about 800 volunteers for the campaign, and Lilian Ngoyi made a name for herself as a powerful speaker and organizer. In 1955, the government once again announced legislation for mandatory passes for women. On 9 August, 1956, 20,000 women responded by marching on the presidential Union Buildings in Pretoria. Although women were eventually made to carry passes, the protest made such an impression that 9 August became South African Women's Day.

The struggle to end apartheid was long and bitter, but in 1994 it was finally abolished – a result that could never have been realized without women's involvement. Women have continued to take part in South African politics since 1994; Winnie Mandela (known as "Mother of the Nation"), who was a leading yet controversial anti-apartheid activist, even went on to serve as a member of parliament.

50%
of **working black women** were employed in **white homes in 1982**

▼ **Congress of colours**
Multiracial members of the ANC Women's League march in protest at Germiston, South Africa, in 1956, during the Defiance Campaign.

▶ **Unity in diversity**
As this 1984 Dutch poster for Women Against Apartheid shows, international women's rights activists of all colours opposed apartheid.

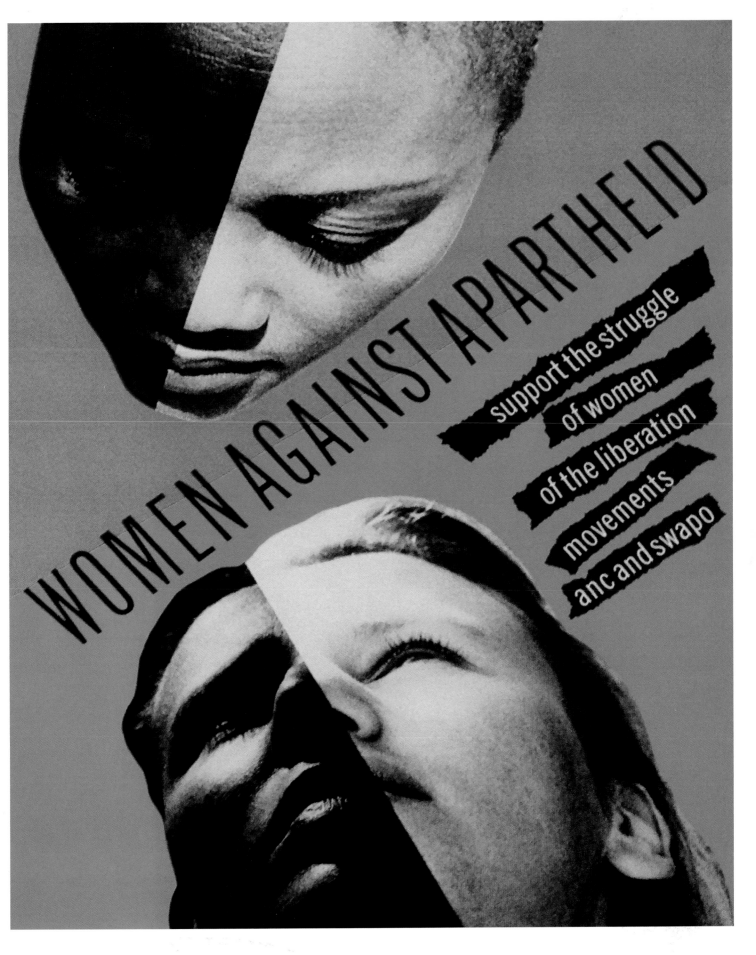

THE MARCH TOWARDS
Civil Rights

THE FIGHT FOR RACIAL EQUALITY

In the US, the Civil Rights Movement of the mid-20th century challenged the Jim Crow system. The system, named after a 19th century minstrel show which portrayed African Americans in a derogatory manner, made nonwhite people second class citizens by segregating them from their white peers. At the same time, the Civil Rights Movement reflected 1950s notions of gender roles, with men assuming leadership positions and negotiating with the white establishment, and women working behind-the-scenes – organizing, printing leaflets, and fundraising. Rosa Parks, the only woman at the first National Association for the Advancement of Colored People (NAACP) meeting in 1943, took the minutes. Thousands of women laid the groundwork of the movement, but many went unrecognized despite their contributions.

Black women had a history of activism. Ida Wells Barnett, Mary McLeod Bethune, and Mary Church Terrell mobilized black women to agitate for political rights and improved social welfare for African Americans, despite a hostile post-slavery environment. Early in the Civil Rights Movement, black women took bold stances. Pauli Murray was arrested in 1940 for refusing to move to the back of a bus, and as a law student led a sit-in that desegregated a restaurant. Her legal writing influenced the case that led to the landmark 1954 Supreme Court decision to desegregate schools, which had previously kept black and white students "separate but equal." Murray crusaded against Jim Crow laws as well as gender discrimination, which she termed Jane Crow. In 1955, lawyer Dovey Johnson Roundtree challenged segregation laws for interstate bus travel and won.

Disobedience and protest

As the movement gathered steam, South Carolina teacher Septima Clark developed voting rights workshops for black citizens. Chicago-born Diane Nash resisted Jim Crow in Tennessee; jailed in 1960 after a sit-in, she became a force for the Student Non-Violent Coordinating Committee (SNCC). Activist Ella Baker guided SNCC, and recruited two white women, Jane Stembridge and Connie Curry, to harness black and white students' passion, creating an army of civil disobedience protesters to encourage black voter registration. With support from SNCC, farmer Fannie Lou Hamer became a politician despite her limited education, and argued for the Mississippi Freedom Democratic Party to have seats at the 1964 Democratic Convention in place of an all-white group of Southern Democrats. Despite their successes in Civil Rights activism, women were excluded from the spotlight at the 1963 March on Washington, one of the movement's biggest protests. Women's pleas to play a prominent, public role in the march were ignored.

▶ **Activist behind bars**
Angela Davis, a communist and associate of the radical Blank Panthers, was arrested in 1970 in connection with a jailbreak and murder case. Her 18-month imprisonment set off a national movement to free both Davis and other political prisoners. Davis was acquitted in 1972.

"I was **not tired physically** … I was **tired** of **giving in**."

ROSA PARKS, CIVIL RIGHTS ACTIVIST, 1956

▲ **Protest line**
Men and women march for Civil Rights in Marion, Alabama, in 1965.

▶ **At the front of the bus**
Seamstress Rosa Parks refused to give her seat to a white passenger on 1 December 1955, sparking a yearlong boycott that ended segregation on buses in Montgomery, Alabama, and elsewhere, and transformed her into an icon of Civil Rights.

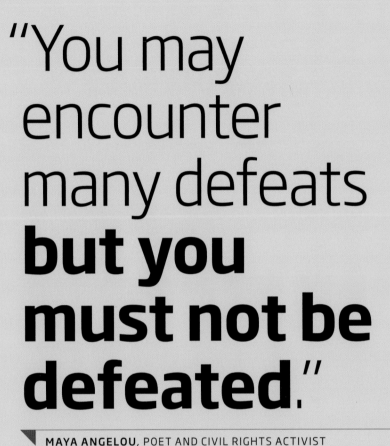

"You may encounter many defeats **but you must not be defeated.**"

MAYA ANGELOU, POET AND CIVIL RIGHTS ACTIVIST

RESISTING RACISM AND OPPRESSION

Known for her artistic achievements, Maya Angelou was also involved as a fund-raiser for the Civil Rights Movement (see pp. 266–267) in the 1960s, and organized mass participation in boycotts and marches. In 1960, she heard one of Martin Luther King, Jr.'s speeches in Harlem, New York, and went on to become a friend of both him and Malcolm X. Heartbroken by King's assassination in 1968, she wrote her autobiography *I Know Why the Caged Bird Sings* (1969). Her writing was a voice of strength and hope that inspired generations of people to resist racism and oppression. Here, Civil Rights activists protest discriminatory hiring practices in Angelou's adopted hometown of New York in 1963.

◄ Geisha notes
This late 19th-century photograph shows geishas playing traditional Japanese music. Known as *jikata*, they learn from a very young age to play instruments such as the *shamisen*, a long-necked guitar.

There was fresh opportunity for women during the Baroque period, beginning in the 17th century, especially in the new genre of opera. Francesca Caccini, from Florence, was likely the first female opera composer, her only extant example being *The Liberation of Ruggiero from the Island of Alcina* (1625). Instrumental Baroque composers included Italian nun Isabella Leonarda and French harpsichordist Elisabeth Jacquet de la Guerre.

Modern musicians

After the dissolution of European courts in the late 18th century, the growing middle classes helped push women forwards by giving young girls music training. By the 19th century, women began to gain recognition for

THROUGH THE AGES

Music

Since medieval times, women have played an important role in music as both composers and performers across many genres. Today, although there are more women musicians than ever before, the majority of the music industry's decision makers are still men.

WOMEN'S ROLES in music were initially very limited. Medival European women were restricted to liturgical chants, sung in convents during worship. Most famed in this scene was 11th-century Benedictine abbess Hildegard von Bingen, one of the first known composers, although she has only recently been credited as such by historians. From a remote monastery in the Rhineland, she composed around 69 pieces, many of which are still performed today.

In contrast, Renaissance noblewomen were expected to have a musical background, and in the late 16th century the *concerto delle donne* was formed in the court of Ferrara, Italy. This small ensemble of female singers was so famed for its virtuosity that others soon emerged. These successes paved the way for women to compete for operatic fame with male *castrati* – well-trained boys who continued to have higher voices as adults.

their skills, with players such as Clara Schumann coming to prominence. In England, Dame Ethel Smyth's composition "March of the Women" became the anthem of the British women's suffrage movement.

In the 20th century, orchestras became mixed gender ensembles and more doors opened for female conductors and

composers. In the world of jazz, African American women such as Billie Holiday and Eartha Kitt had a huge impact on the genre. From the mid-20th century onwards, women wrote and performed in a diverse range of genres. Pop artists, such as Madonna, attained megastar status and became influential role models. Today, many pop stars, including Lady Gaga, speak out about gender discrimination in the business side of the music industry, and use their music to advocate for women's rights.

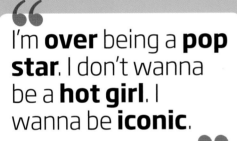

AUSCHWITZ'S ALL-FEMALE ORCHESTRA IN *PLAYING FOR TIME*, 1980

> " I'm **over** being a **pop star**. I don't wanna be a **hot girl**. I wanna be **iconic**. "
>
> BEYONCÉ, SINGER-SONGWRITER

▼ **Girl power**
British girl group the Spice Girls, pictured here at the Brit Awards in 1997, were an iconic pop group who popularized feminism as "girl power," while embracing their sexuality and the power of strong female friendships.

PROFILES
MUSIC MAKERS

Kassia (c. 9th century) came from a noble family and was a potential spouse for Byzantine Emperor Theophilus. Instead, she chose to found her own convent where she composed liturgical music. Many of the works ascribed to her remain questionable; however, she is best known for the Mary Magdalene hymn that retains a position of prominence within the Orthodox Church of Greece.

Hildegard von Bingen (1098–1179) was a German abbess, scientist, theologian, author, and composer. One of the only known medieval women composers, her music consists of melodies with Latin texts used for sacred worship. Her most significant work today remains *Ordo Virtutum* (*Play of the Virtues*, c.1151), the earliest surviving morality play for which she wrote both text and music.

Clara Schumann (1819–1896) was a pianist child prodigy. Her extensive concert touring and flawless technique garnered her respect equal to that earned by her male contemporaries. Her contributions to piano recital were long-lasting: she performed without music and played only solo piano music, a rarity for concerts in her lifetime.

Nadia Boulanger (1887–1979) was the most influential musical pedagogue of the 20th century. Although she stopped composing after the death of her sister, Lili, her renown was such that many flocked to France to study with her. Her students were some of the most prominent composers of the century, including Aaron Copland, Thea Musgrave, Philip Glass, and Leonard Bernstein.

Billie Holiday (1915–1959) is one of the most notable jazz singers of all time. Overcoming a difficult childhood, she rose to great acclaim despite a lack of formal music education. At the height of her career she collaborated with Count Basie, Benny Goodman, and Artie Shaw. Her most significant recording, "Strange Fruit," recounts the racism of the southern United States and remains one of the most important American songs of the 20th century.

Marin Alsop (b. 1956) is the first female conductor of a major American orchestra, the Baltimore Symphony Orchestra, an appointment granted in 2007. She studied conducting under both Leonard Bernstein and Seiji Ozawa, and is known primarily for her devotion to contemporary American music. Alsop has conducted many ensembles including the London Philharmonic Orchestra.

THE PERSONAL GETS
political

SECOND-WAVE FEMINISM

▼ No More Miss America!
Protestors take to the Atlantic City boardwalk in 1968 to protest against the objectification of women and the tyrannical beauty standards enforced by the annual national pageant.

Second-wave feminism burst onto the political and social scene in the 1960s and continued until the late 1980s or early 1990s. Often called the Women's Liberation Movement, it began in Western industrialized nations but eventually spread worldwide. The Women's Liberation Movement (WLM) was rooted in a belief that, despite the achievements of first-wave feminism, most aspects of society were inherently sexist and designed to oppress women or discriminate against them. In 1963, Betty Friedan's *The Feminine Mystique* demonstrated how white middle-class women were oppressed. Other definitive works followed, such as Germaine Greer's *The Female Eunuch* (1970), which argued that the female body had been used to make women be seen as "other", leading to discrimination.

The liberation movement in the US was sparked by a general atmosphere of activism; the 1960s was a decade of protest, from Civil Rights marches to student sit-ins and demonstrations against the Vietnam War. Female activists, hearing their male colleagues dismiss women's concerns, broke away to create what became a crusade for women's liberation. The first US Women's Liberation conference met in Chicago in 1967. A year later, 400 feminists protested against the objectification of women at the Miss America beauty pageant, making women's liberation front page news.

Beginnings

The WLM spread abroad. In Mexico, women protested at the Monument to the Mother against the idea that women should all bear children. Feminists in New Zealand invaded men-only pubs. Meanwhile, British feminists such as Sheila Rowbotham and Juliet Mitchell held the first British Women's Liberation conference in 1970, in Oxford. The WLM

THE SECOND WAVE

The women's liberation movement was broad. North American, European, and Oceanian women shared common ideas while advocating for rights in their own countries.

1900

- **1966** The National Organization for Women (NOW) is founded in the US.

- **1968** Women machinists at the Ford automobile factory in the UK strike for equal pay.

- **1970** Australian feminist Germaine Greer publishes *The Female Eunuch*.

- **1971** Italian feminists launch the International Wages for Housework Campaign; 343 French women sign a manifesto in support of abortion rights, admitting to having had the procedure.

- **1973** The *Roe versus Wade* Supreme Court case decriminalizes abortion in the US; *Our Bodies, Ourselves* is published.

- **1974** Simone Veil facilitates access to contraception in France; a year later, her activism leads to the legalization of abortion.

- **1975** Icelandic women strike to protest pay inequality; the first "Take Back the Night" march occurs in Philadelphia in response to the murder of Susan Alexander Speeth by a stranger.

- **1981** Women set up a women-only camp at Greenham Common, UK, to protest against the use of nuclear weapons; the first Latin American and Caribbean Feminist Conference takes place in Bogotá, Colombia.

▶ **BRAS, SYMBOLS OF WOMEN'S OBJECTIFICATION,** WERE THE FOCUS OF THIS PROTEST OUTSIDE OF A DEPARTMENT STORE IN SAN FRANCISCO IN 1969.

»

was non-hierarchical; there were no leaders. On both sides of the Atlantic women came together to share experiences in "consciousness raising" groups, designed to increase awareness about women's day to day experiences of oppression. Feminists argued that women's personal experiences of health, reproduction, housework, sexuality, marriage, and motherhood were political issues – a powerful statement that made the movement different from other radical causes.

From 1970 – with the publication of *Our Bodies, Ourselves* by the Boston Women's Health Cooperative, which sought to educate women on their own

> ## The Pill was approved by the FDA on
> # 9 May, 1960,
> ## granting American **women more control over their bodies**

healthcare – a movement emerged to challenge the male-dominated medical profession, and insist on a woman's right to have an informed say in her own healthcare and control over her reproduction. Campaigns for a woman's right to abortion led to a major victory in 1973 when the *Roe versus Wade* court case decriminalized abortion in the US.

Equal rights
Feminists actively worked to fight sexism by introducing women's studies courses into universities, studying history to include

women's contributions, and criticizing the objectification of women in media. Feminists such as Andrea Dworkin campaigned against pornography, arguing that it demeaned women and encouraged rape and violence. From the 1970s, "Take Back the Night" or "Reclaim the Night" marches protested and raised awareness about rape, sexual assault, and violence against women. Domestic violence also became a major issue, leading feminists to set up women's shelters and demand both police and courts address the problem.

In the 1960s, women were paid considerably less than men. In 1968, 200 British women workers at the Ford automobile factory in Dagenham went on strike for equal pay and brought production to a halt. In Iceland, 90 per cent of the country's female workforce went on strike in October 1975 to protest wage inequality and unfair working practices; their actions led to new laws the following year. Feminists highlighted the barriers facing women at work, fought for crèches and free childcare, and conceptualized the glass ceiling – an invisible barrier that prevented women from getting the top jobs.

'80s feminism

By the 1980s second-wave feminism was making its mark worldwide, with protests and organizations throughout Europe, in China, South America, and Asia. It was not a unified movement: it included socialist feminists, who linked the fight against oppression to the class struggle; equal rights feminists, who sought equality with men; and radical feminists who saw patriarchal society as the cause of women's oppression and argued for large-scale change. From the 1970s, nonwhite women had criticized feminism for its predominantly white outlook, resulting in the formation of black or Asian feminist groups, such as the Combahee River Collective – a black lesbian group founded in Boston in 1974. In the 1960s in the US and the 1980s in France, lesbian activists challenged the WLM for its emphasis on heterosexuality, and some advocated for women to practise lesbianism as a political identity and means of protest.

As the 1980s gave way to the 1990s, feminism became less popular as a movement, as what some observers called a "backlash" gained traction. The failure in the US of the Equal Rights Amendment, the rise of consumerism, and neo-liberal politics caused the second wave slowly to fade away.

◄ **Marxist feminist poster**
In the 1960s, Italian feminist groups brought attention to the poor treatment of communist women by their male comrades. They argued that there would be "no revolution without women's liberation."

BIOGRAPHY
GLORIA STEINEM

A major voice of the second wave, Gloria Steinem established herself as a journalist in the early 1960s. After attending a talk on abortion, she became an active feminist, publishing *After Black Power, Women's Liberation* in 1969 and cofounding *Ms.* magazine in 1971. That same year, she also cofounded both the Women's Action Alliance and the National Women's Political Caucus. In 1979, she wrote about female genital cutting, bringing it to the attention of the American public for the first time.

"THERE IS NO ... SINGLE-ISSUE **STRUGGLE**. WE DO NOT LIVE SINGLE-ISSUE **LIVES**."

AUDRE LORDE, SPEECH AT HARVARD UNIVERSITY, 1982

"When it begins to get dark, instead of cooking dinner or making love, **we will assemble** ..."

BETTY FRIEDAN, FEMINIST WRITER AND ACTIVIST, CALLS FOR A NATIONWIDE WOMEN'S STRIKE, MARCH 20, 1970

EQUALITY NOW

In 1970, Betty Friedan ended her term as president of the National Organization for Women (NOW) with a speech calling women to action. Friedan's 1963 book *The Feminine Mystique,* which rejected the idealized image of the American housewife, had led many women to join the feminist cause, and Friedan hoped that a march would show the scope and seriousness of feminism's growing second wave. On August 26, 1970, around 50,000 women answered Friedans' call in New York City, where the Women's Strike for Equality blocked off Fifth Avenue as women marched with signs demanding equal opportunities in the workplace, abortion rights, and an end to the war in Vietnam (left).

> "A girl is no ... **better** for believing until her **marriage night** that **children are found** among the **cabbage leaves** in the garden."

THE MARRIED WOMAN'S PRIVATE MEDICAL COMPANION, 1855

EXPERIENCES OF CONTRACEPTION

Family planning

Through history women and their sexual partners have tried to prevent unwanted pregnancies, and most types of contraception used today have long histories. However, the increased availability of reliable contraceptives and sex education proved revolutionary.

THE MOST UNIVERSAL contraceptive method, across times and cultures, is probably *coitus interruptus* (also known as the withdrawal method), which was common in Europe, Africa, Australasia, the Middle East, and popular enough that both Jewish and Roman Catholic leaders spoke out against it. Another similar method, which also required no foreplanning or extra materials, was *coitus obstructus*, which was noted in ancient Sanskrit texts. Hindus, meanwhile, were known to practise *coitus reservatus*. However, both of these methods were less common than *coitus interruptus*, likely because they were less comfortable for men.

As well as methods that put the onus on men, women throughout history have prevented pregnancy through the use of barrier contraceptives. One of the earliest examples was the pessary, which was used to block the cervix or kill off sperm to prevent conception. There were numerous ancient recipes for pessaries – in ancient Egypt, these mixtures consisted of ingredients such as crocodile dung, honey, acacia, and lint, while ancient Greek women used siphium so much that the plant became extinct. Instructions in the Egyptian Ebers Papyrus (1550 BCE) suggests that women mixed concoctions themselves. Other types of pessary were more solid; plugs of chopped grass or cloth were used in Africa; bamboo paper was used in Japan; and some women used textiles such as wool (in Islamic and Greek societies), or linen rags (popular among Slavic women). In modern times, devices have taken the form of Dutch caps and diaphragms.

One of the most common barrier methods to this day has been the condom. French cave paintings from 11,000 BCE show that a form of condom had existed long before they began to be manufactured from rubber in the 19th century. Historical condoms were less pleasant

▲ **Vaginal douche**
Women used a douche to squirt water or spermicide into the vaginal cavity to prevent pregnancy, but it could not wash away sperm that had already reached the uterus.

> "**Self restraint** is the most **desirable** ... and **totally harmless** method."

MAHATMA GANDHI, 1930

than their modern counterparts – they were often made from animal membranes, such as sheep intestines, and people sometimes resorted to animal horns or shells. Condoms were also expensive; at the end of the 19th century in Britain, a dozen could cost up to 10 shillings – an average weekly wage.

Modern methods

Despite the contraceptive methods available, many women still had unwanted pregnancies due to a lack of knowledge about their reproductive system, or lack of access to contraceptives – in 1873, for example, the US Congress passed the Comstock Act to outlaw contraception. British sex educator Marie Stopes was a leading voice at the turn of the 20th century in advocating for contraceptives, and American Margaret Sanger helped to lessen the stigma around them when she coined the term "birth control" in the 1960s.

Contraception's biggest innovation came in the 20th century. Work on developing an oral contraceptive began in the 1930s, and in 1960, the Food and Drug Administration approved Enovid, the first pill, in the US. The pill revolutionized women's lives, giving them the power to enjoy sex without fear of pregnancy. However, among those who first took the pill in 1960, women reported problems such as blood clots, strokes, and depression. In 1969, Barbara Seaman published *The Doctor's Case Against the Pill*, highlighting pill-related health concerns, and her work led to the Nelson Pill Hearings, in which activist Alice Wolfson accused the pharmaceutical industry of using 10 million American women

> " **Women's modern liberation** is inextricably **linked** to their ability to **control reproduction**.

CAMILLE PAGLIA, "NO LAW IN THE ARENA," 1995

as guinea pigs. The ability to choose if and when to become pregnant has had a huge social and economic impact on women – in terms of job opportunities, increased earning power, and admittance to college and university education. Today, most females in the West have access to contraception, and many of them are increasingly turning to long-term medical methods, such as hormone implants and intrauterine devices (IUDs). An estimated 222 million women in developing countries, however, still struggle to access contraceptives due to low funds, a lack of supply chains, and traditional beliefs.

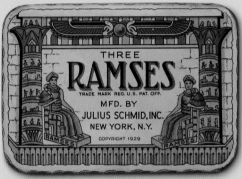

▲ **Modern-day condom**
By the 20th century, condoms were mass-produced, but sold in discreet packaging due to the stigma against birth control - condoms were seen as an incentive for immoral behaviour. This tin condom case was created in New York in 1929.

> " No woman can **call herself free** who does not **own** and **control her body**. No woman can **call herself free** until she can **choose consciously** whether **she will or will not** be a **mother**.

MARGARET SANGER, *WOMAN AND THE NEW RACE*, 1920

THE DIVORCE
revolution

THE MODERN DIVORCE

▼ **Divorce rally**
In 1970, divorce was introduced in Italy, but the country held many subsequent debates over whether the law should be abolished. These 1970s campaigners rally to keep divorce legal.

In the 1960s and 1970s, divorce law in most Western countries was based on the concept of fault. With a few exceptions, if one spouse wished to get a divorce while the other did not, the procedure was difficult. Divorce could only be granted if the petitioner proved that their spouse had broken the marital contract, for example, through adultery, abandonment, or even sexual impotence.

Some scholars argued that the fault system contributed to spousal homicide and suicide by women who felt trapped in bad marriages.

Communist Russia was ahead of its time with no-fault divorces, in which neither party were blamed, which were allowed from 1917.

Vota **NO** all'abolizione del divorzio
PARTITO SOCIALISTA ITALIANO PSI

Nearly 50 years later, the UK and the state of California led a charge to liberalize divorce laws. In 1966, the Archbishop of Canterbury issued a report stating that traditional divorce law in England should be replaced with a law that focused on the state of the marriage rather than the behaviour of the spouses. This led to the Divorce Reform Act of 1969, which kept the old fault system but also allowed divorce on the grounds of irretrievable breakdown. The same year California also introduced new divorce laws.

Transforming divorce law

Between 1969 and 1985, most Western countries radically altered divorce legislation. Some of the most notable changes appeared in Catholic majority countries like Spain and Italy, where civil divorce was introduced; or Portugal, where divorce was allowed for Catholic marriages for the first time. In the Netherlands, West Germany, Sweden, and 19 US states, fault grounds were entirely eliminated. Sweden was the most radical country of all, when, in 1973, it introduced a system that permitted either spouse to end a marriage without proving fault, obtaining the other spouse's consent, or having a long separation period. Legislation varied in non–Western countries and in multireligious states like India, the Judiciary implemented different laws for couples depending on their faith.

From 1960–1990, the divorce rate increased from 1 per cent to 19 per cent in the US. At the same time, the proportion of children who lived with one parent jumped from 9 to 19 per cent, and the percentage of teenage mothers who were not married increased from 15 to 68 per cent. These figures reflected a growing deinstitutionalization of marriage, and a changing zeitgeist in which women felt more free to remain single, or to leave marriages in search of happiness. Some scholars even argued in the *Journal of Divorce* that the divorce revolution promoted "growth potential" for mothers, as they could enjoy more autonomy, feel in control of their lives, and improve their relationships with their children. Others disagreed, claiming that the revolution devastated women, who, once the dust settled, had to face the financial and social burden of raising their children alone with only limited child support.

▲ **Public scandal**
Before the 1980s, obtaining a divorce was difficult for women. This 1906 cartoon shows the circus-like divorce proceedings of American heiress Anna Gould, who held a handful of indictments against her husband, Boni de Castellane.

"I HAVE **LEARNED** THAT NOT **DIAMONDS** BUT DIVORCE **LAWYERS** ARE A **GIRL'S BEST FRIEND**."

ZSA ZSA GABOR, HUNGARIAN-BORN ACTRESS AND SEVEN-TIME DIVORCÉE

WOMEN MEAN
business

THE 1980S

Women smashed the glass ceiling on several fronts in the 1980s, as political leaders, professionals in the workplace, and rebels on the picket line. In politics, Geraldine Ferraro became the first female vice-presidential candidate in the US, and Margaret Thatcher served as the first woman prime minister in the UK. Thatcher's steely resolve on the domestic front and the world stage helped to overturn stereotypes of the "weaker sex".

Entrepreneurs

Women began to enter sectors of the workforce previously occupied by men. In the US from 1972 to 1985, women's share of professional jobs grew from 44 to 49 per cent. During that time, women gained a rising portion of college degrees, including almost one third of degrees in law, business, accounting, and information sciences. Many women took up entrepreneurial activities such as writing, selling real estate, or launching home businesses. This new entrepreneurial status was also linked to domesticity, as women such as Martha Stewart were able to monetize their skills as homemakers. Women across the

world could also earn money as sales representatives through the "home party" business model, in which they invited friends over to sample and purchase products such as Tupperware, makeup, and costume jewellery.

"[IT WAS] A PERIOD OF **ULTRACONSERVATISM**… YOU **NEEDED BRAVE PEOPLE** TO PUSH AHEAD."

CYNDI LAUPER, SINGER, ON ARTISTS OF THE 1980s, 2010

◄ Graceful in defeat
Democratic politician
Geraldine Ferraro
concedes defeat in the US
elections of 1984. She
saw her candidacy as a
sign that discrimination
against women in politics
was coming to an end.

In poorer parts of the
world, particularly Asia,
business-minded women
began to benefit from
microfinance, an idea
kickstarted in 1983 by
economics professor
Muhammad Yunus. He
lent £14.50 ($27) to a group of
rural Bangladeshi women making bamboo
stools who, unable to purchase the raw
materials they needed, were kept in a cycle
of debt by the local traders they borrowed
from. His Grameen Bank has since financed
millions of micro-entrepreneurs.

As the 1980s saw social and economic
conservatism dominate on the political stage,
women joined protest movements against such
policies. In the UK, the Greenham Common
Women's Peace Camp was set up at a Royal
Air Force base in Berkshire in 1981 to protest

◄ Working it out
Jane Fonda's Workout
was released on VHS
tape in 1982 when
most gyms were for
men. It encouraged
women to get fit at
home and sold 17
million copies worldwide.

the British government's decision to store
cruise missiles there. During the British
miner's strike of 1984 to 1985, women also
launched the Women Against Pit Closures
campaign to raise awareness of the hardships
miners' families faced. Women stood alongside
men on the picket lines and promoted their
cause at rallies in London and abroad. After
the strikes ended, many women never returned
to their former domestic lives. Many entered
the world of work, continued to campaign for
causes, or even opted for careers in politics.

BIOGRAPHY
MARGARET THATCHER

Born to a grocer and his wife
in 1925, Margaret Thatcher
went on to become leader of
the UK's Conservative Party
and later prime minister.
During her three terms in
power, she reshaped almost
every aspect of British life,
reforming many institutions,
reducing the role of trade
unions, and privatizing
industries. One of the world's
most influential leaders, her
brand of conservatism
inspired the ideology of many
politicians while alienating
others. She died in 2013.

"As I came to power peacefully, **so shall I keep it.**"

CORAZON AQUINO, SPEECH BEFORE THE JOINT SESSION OF THE UNITED STATES CONGRESS, 1986

THE PEOPLE-POWER REVOLUTION

Corazon Aquino chose to enter politics after her husband, Senator Benigno Aquino Jr., was assassinated in 1983. He had been a major force in opposing the corrupt Philippine president, Ferdinand Marcos. In 1985, Corazon declared her candidacy to run against Marcos for office. An election was held on 7 February and Marcos was declared the victor, but discrepancies between official reports and other sources made it clear that the win was fraudulent. Aquino and her supporters (including high-ranking members of the military) then ousted Marcos in a bloodless revolution, and Aquino was inaugurated on 25 February. Here, Aquino is pictured calling for a national economic boycott and nonviolent action (to protest Marcos's attempts to undermine democracy) at Makati Municipal Hall in Manila, on 8 February, 1986.

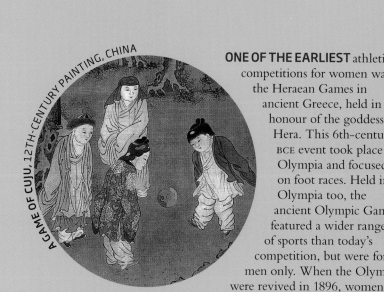

A GAME OF CUJU, 12TH-CENTURY PAINTING, CHINA

ONE OF THE EARLIEST athletic competitions for women was the Heraean Games in ancient Greece, held in honour of the goddess Hera. This 6th-century BCE event took place in Olympia and focused on foot races. Held in Olympia too, the ancient Olympic Games featured a wider range of sports than today's competition, but were for men only. When the Olympics were revived in 1896, women were still not allowed to compete, and even when they began to take part in 1900, their participation was limited to a select few events. Thanks to activists such as Alice Milliat (see right) in France, female involvement increased through the 20th century, but it was only at the 2012 London Olympics that women could compete in every sport at the summer games.

Historically, not all sports were segregated. In 3rd-century BCE China, both men and women played an early form of football called *cuju*, in which the aim was to kick a ball through a goal. A version called *baida*, where points were given for skill in controlling the ball, was also popular among women. Modern soccer emerged in the late 19th century, and women took up the sport in high numbers, but local and international bodies restricted their involvement. From 1921–71, the English Football Association banned member clubs from allowing women's teams to use their stadiums. The first women's World Cup only

THROUGH THE AGES

Sport

Sporting women have had to fight for equal opportunities to participate and compete at both professional and amateur levels. Although today far higher numbers of women take part across a wider range of sporting activities than ever before, the struggle for parity in pay and media coverage continues.

> " Throwing **70 miles per hour** – that's **throwing like a girl**. "
>
> **MO'NE DAVIS**, BASEBALL PLAYER

▶ **Acing the game**
American tennis player Helen Jacobs won nine Grand Slam titles during her career, including the US Championships' singles on four occasions. She was the first woman to break with tradition and wear men's shorts at Wimbledon in 1933.

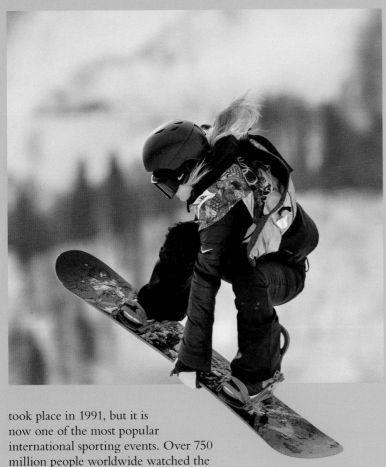

took place in 1991, but it is now one of the most popular international sporting events. Over 750 million people worldwide watched the 2015 tournament on television.

Eyes on the money

One of the greatest gender disparities in sport is financial: male athletes are paid more than women. In the US, the first legal challenge to this was the Women's Educational Equity Act of 1974, better known as Title IX. The law meant that schools and universities had to offer women equal access to athletics scholarships. In 1973, Billie Jean King played a televised tennis match against male former champion Bobby Riggs, dubbed the "Battle of the Sexes". King's victory over Riggs (viewed by 90 million people) was a major milestone for public acceptance of female sporting excellence.

Today, while more sports offer equal prize money, some still lag behind. Male golfers in the US Open take home almost twice as much as the female champion, and in World Cup cricket, the male team can make up to seven times more than the women's side. Such pay gaps are often linked to media rights, with claims that men's sports draw bigger audiences, and therefore generate more profit.

▲ **Snow adventures**
Austrian snowboarding star Anna Gasser competes at the 2014 Olympic Winter Games. Prior to taking up competitive snowboarding, Gasser was a member of the Austrian National Gymnastics Team.

SPORTING HEROINES

Ann Glanville (1796–1880) achieved fame as a British gig rower. Part of a female crew of four rowers who took part in local regattas, Glanville was congratulated by Queen Victoria at Fleetwood when she watched the team beat an all-male crew. In 1842, the team went to an event at Le Havre but the French refused to put up a team against the women. Instead, they raced against an all-male crew from the paddle steamer that transported them – and won.

Alice Milliat (1884–1957) was a teacher, swimmer, rower, and hockey player, who demanded that the Olympic Games open more of their events to women. After they refused, she founded the International Women's Sports Federation in 1921. The body organized four Women's World Games, international competitions modelled on the Olympics, with the first taking place in Paris in 1922.

Babe Zaharias (1911–56) first competed in US women's basketball, before turning to athletics. She qualified for the 1932 Los Angeles Olympics, where she won gold medals in the 80 m hurdles and javelin, and a silver in the high jump. Zaharias excelled at other sports, particularly golf, winning the US Women's Open three times.

Angela James (b. 1964) began competing in the Central Ontario Women's Ice Hockey League, playing for Seneca College from 1982 to 1985. In 1990, she led Canada to victory in the first women's world ice hockey championship, repeating the feat in 1992, 1994, and 1997. She carried on playing until 2000, and in 2010 was one of the first two women elected to the Hockey Hall of Fame.

Steffi Graf (b. 1969) made her professional tennis debut in her native Germany aged 13. In 1986, she won the first of 107 career tournament victories, and the next year she won the first of 22 major singles championships. She dominated women's tennis, and in 1988 became the only person to ever achieve the "Golden Slam" (winning all four major tournaments and Olympic gold in a calendar year).

Caster Semenya (b. 1991) is a leading middle distance runner from South Africa. In 2009, she won gold in the 800m at the Berlin World Championships, but her hyperandrogenism (high testosterone levels) led to controversy; she was made to undergo testing to verify her sex. She temporarily withdrew from competition but returned to win gold at the 2012 and 2016 Olympics.

CRISIS AND
displacement

Since 1945, the global refugee crisis has been at the forefront of contemporary political debate in Europe and the US. Refugees, over the course of the 20th century, have left their homes to escape from war, political disorder, persecution, and natural disasters. The most significant events to trigger refugee crises were World War II and decolonization (see pp. 246-247), the aftermath of the Cold War, and upheaval in the Middle East (especially in Iraq and Syria) towards the end of the 20th century. Today, women and children make up at least 50 per cent of refugees, and in some cases outnumber men: of the refugees fleeing Syria today, more than 70 per cent are women and children – both groups are especially vulnerable to violence and exploitation.

Defining refuge

The refugee agency the United Nations High Commissioner for Refugees was created in 1950 in response to the refugee crisis caused by World War II (see pp. 234-237). In 1951, the United Nations Refugee Convention created a legal framework for dealing with European refugees, and in 1967, responding to the demand from anti-colonial groups and newly independent countries, the Refugee

▼ **Displaced childhood**
Betty Malek, aged three, arrives with her belongings and toys in London from Antwerp in May, 1940, after her city was bombed by German planes.

REFUGEE CRISES

Since 1951, the United Nations has worked to support refugees across the globe, but it is only recently that the struggles of refugee women have received extra attention.

1900

1939-1945 40 million European men, women, and children are displaced by World War II – one example is the real life Maria Von Trapp, who left Austria for the US in 1942.

1951 The United Nations defines refugees and their rights to asylum in the Convention Relating to the Status of Refugees.

1956 The Hungarian Revolution causes around 200,000 people to flee the country.

1975-1990s After the Vietnam War, millions flee by boat to escape persecution by the communist government; some of these refugees are women who had children by American men.

1979 The Soviet invasion of Afghanistan creates 6.3 million new refugees, including Maryam Monsef, who became the Canadian Minister of Status of Women in 2017.

1989 The Women's Refugee Commission is formed as part of the International Rescue Committee; it becomes independent in 2014.

1992 5.7 million people are displaced by the civil war in Mozambique, Africa.

2000

2005 US forces invade Iraq; the war displaces 1.9 million men, women, and children.

2009 US President Obama rules that foreign women may seek asylum from domestic violence.

2011 War in Syria forces 12 million people to flee their homes in search of safety; the majority are women.

2013 Civil war breaks out in Sudan; more than two million people flee their homes.

2015 "Boat people" flee from Myanmar (Burma) in the Rohingya refugee crisis; an estimated 80 per cent of the refugees are women and children.

◄ **A US MARINE** GUARDS VIETNAMESE WOMEN AND CHILDREN IN 1965, WHEN 3 MILLION PEOPLE FLED FROM NORTH TO SOUTH VIETNAM.

▶ **Fleeing conflict**
A mother holds her child as she arrives along with other immigrants and refugees to the Greek island of Lesbos in 2016, after being rescued by Frontex and Greek coast guards.

"NO ONE LEAVES **HOME** UNLESS HOME IS THE **MOUTH OF A SHARK**."

WARSAN SHIRE, POET AND VOICE FOR REFUGEES

Convention expanded its framework to include refugees from all nations. Most member nations within the UN signed the 1967 Convention, which defines the status of refugees and grants them the right to move freely, receive education, and work. However, many signatory nations have since tried to prevent refugees from reaching their own borders.

Historic displacement

After World War II, more than 11 million people were displaced as they fled genocide or the path of combat. Displaced persons camps (DPCs) were created to shelter these refugees – not only in Europe, but also in Egypt, Palestine, and Syria. These camps accommodated refugees from parts of Eastern Europe such as Bulgaria and Yugoslavia, where people had fled from the advances of the Russian Army, as well as Greece and Turkey. Families in these DPCs – some of the biggest of which were Nuseirat, in Gaza, and El Shatt, in Egypt – were kept together, but single men and women were housed separately. Men and women alike were expected to work, and women took on roles such as shopkeeper, cleaner, and seamstress; some even took up vocational training in the camps as nurses. In addition to this, women in the camps also performed the domestic work, such as laundry, cooking, and mending. Many refugees fleeing from the East to the West during the decolonization of Africa, and later Asia and the Americas, did not receive a

warm welcome. In the 1950s, 200,000 refugees fled Algeria for France during the nation's independence uprising against the French. Previously, most Algerians immigrating to France were men, but from

the 1950s, entire families sought new lives in cities such as Paris and Lyon. Many lived, at least at first, in filthy shanty towns around the cities because they could not get social housing. The recent crises in the Middle East have brought renewed attention to the plight of refugee women. After a period of lower global displacement levels, the 2005 invasion of Iraq by US forces marked a return to large waves of refugees. Since the start of the civil war in Syria in 2011, 12 million people have been displaced, while about 8 million have left their homes in Colombia due to civil war. Scrutinized by the modern world, these crises have brought the hardships faced by refugee women out into the open.

Protection and prevention

Refugee women often experience emotional and physical trauma when escaping oppressive conditions and finding themselves in hostile environments. They face many challenges, including dangerous journeys across seas and borders. For example, women and children fleeing from Syria lost their lives crossing the Mediterranean Sea, while recent reports have suggested that Algerian women forced to leave the country at gunpoint have been left to die in the Sahara Desert, some of them pregnant. Due to the lack of security, sexual assault (experienced by one in five refugee women), physical abuse, and pregnancies resulting from rape are all part of life in refugee camps.

Such problems have led to the creation of organizations such as the Women's Refugee Commission, formed in 1989. This has helped to raise awareness of the challenges faced by refugee women, but there is still a long way to go to ensure that they enter a safer place than the one they left behind.

BIOGRAPHY
MADELEINE ALBRIGHT

Born in Prague in 1937, Madeleine Albright and her family were forced into exile in 1938 from her homeland of Czechoslovakia. They moved to Britain and then the US, where Albright studied politics and international relations before eventually working on the White House security council. She served as the first female Secretary of State in 1997–2001, after which she remained involved in politics as a staunch defender of both women's and refugee rights.

◀ **Seeking asylum**
Ethiopian women wait to receive relief from the Red Cross at the makeshift Somare refugee camp in Moyale, Kenya. Nearly 10,000 Ethiopians, over 600 of them expectant mothers, fled after soldiers attacked their villages in 2018.

REVOLUTIONS
and rights

LIFE IN THE MUSLIM WORLD

Throughout the 20th century, there were dramatic transformations in many Muslim-majority nations, particularly in the Middle East and Pakistan. Conflicts between extremist and liberal groups were rife, and political turmoil led to great upheaval, with mixed consequences for Muslim women.

Towards the end of the 20th century, women took part in a number of revolutions in the Middle East. For example, large numbers of women actively participated in the Iranian Revolution in 1979, which overthrew the monarchy to create an Islamic republic. Unfortunately, many of those involved found their rights diminished after the revolution. The new regime sought to stamp out Western influences on women's dress, enforcing full cover in public, and laws were introduced which were designed to drive women out of the workplace. Women also suffered due to the economic consequences of war. The devastation caused by the Gulf War in Iraq (1990–1991) meant that more girls were pulled out of school to support their families, and were later unable to enter the workforce.

Revolutions did not, however, have a universally negative impact for women in the Muslim world. Although in some locations the uprisings of the Arab Spring (2010–2012) resulted in an increase in violence against women, in Tunisia the number of women in government increased and there have been gains in women's rights there, too. In addition, a host of strong female Muslim voices emerged at the end of the 20th century, notably Benazir Bhutto, the first female prime minister of a majority-Muslim country. During her time in office (1988–1990 and 1993–1996), Bhutto advocated for better women's education and employment, and spoke against misogynistic interpretations of Islam. She faced great resistance, and was ultimately assassinated in 2007, likely by the Pakistani Taliban.

Muslim women's rights

More recently, there have been breakthroughs in women's rights in several Muslim countries. For example, in 2015, women in Saudi Arabia were granted the vote (66 years after women in Syria, the first Middle Eastern country to enfranchise women), and in 2018, Saudi women were allowed to drive for the first time. Still, Saudi women, and women in other Muslim countries, continue to face injustices. Weeks before the driving ban was lifted, many high-profile women's rights advocates, who had been campaigning for the end to Saudi Arabia's male guardianship system as well as for the right to drive, were arrested. Under the guardianship system, which applies in several Muslim countries, women cannot travel abroad, marry, or do many other things without the permission of a male relative. In some Muslim nations women are also abused for not covering their bodies sufficiently. In Pakistan, for example, acid attacks have been made on unveiled women by extremists.

▼ **Toppling a tyrant**
Egyptian women and girls gather at Cairo's Tahrir Square on 6 February, 2011, calling for the removal of dictator President Hosni Mubarak.

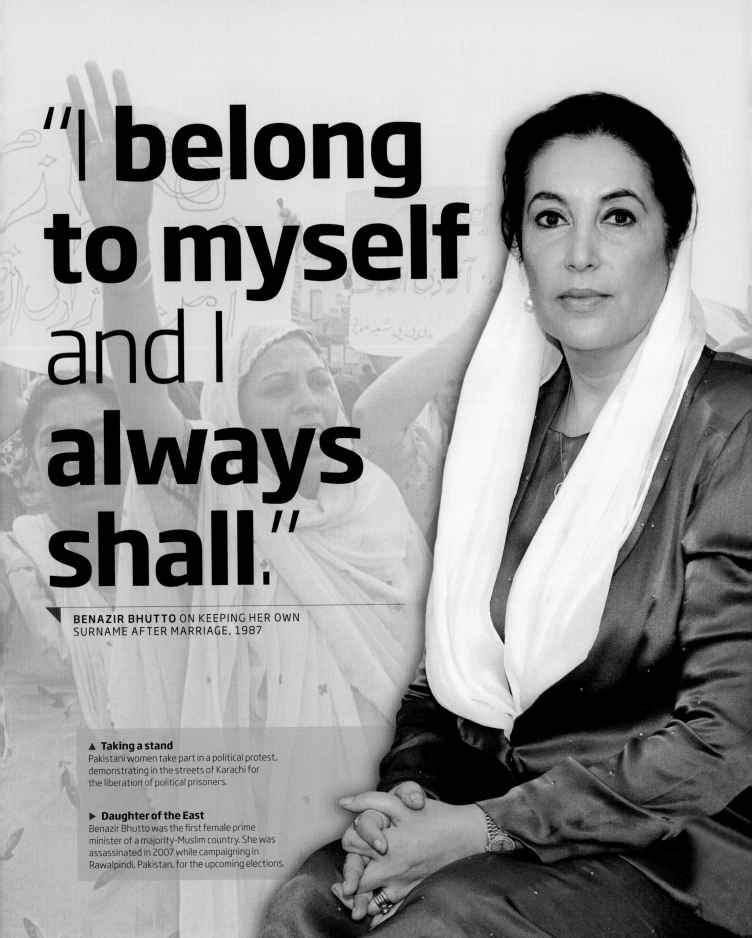

"I belong to myself and I always shall."

BENAZIR BHUTTO ON KEEPING HER OWN
SURNAME AFTER MARRIAGE, 1987

▲ **Taking a stand**
Pakistani women take part in a political protest,
demonstrating in the streets of Karachi for
the liberation of political prisoners.

▶ **Daughter of the East**
Benazir Bhutto was the first female prime
minister of a majority-Muslim country. She was
assassinated in 2007 while campaigning in
Rawalpindi, Pakistan, for the upcoming elections.

"Let us wage a glorious struggle against **illiteracy, poverty, and terrorism".**

MALALA YOUSAFZAI, IN HER SPEECH TO THE UN, 2013

THE FIGHT FOR FEMALE EDUCATION

In October 2012, Pakistani teenager Malala Yousafzai was shot in the head by a Taliban gunman on her way home from school. Under Maulana Fazlullah's leadership, the Taliban had banned girls from education and blown up over 100 girls' schools in Pakistan's Swat Valley. Yousafzai had spoken out against the regime, through contacts in the US and a blog for the BBC, and her shooting was therefore a targeted assassination attempt. Miraculously, she survived and continued to protest; in 2013, Yousafzai made her first public appearance after the shooting, a visit to the United Nations, where she gave a speech to the assembled delegates. She went on to become an human rights activist and in 2014, became the youngest ever winner of the Nobel Peace Prize.

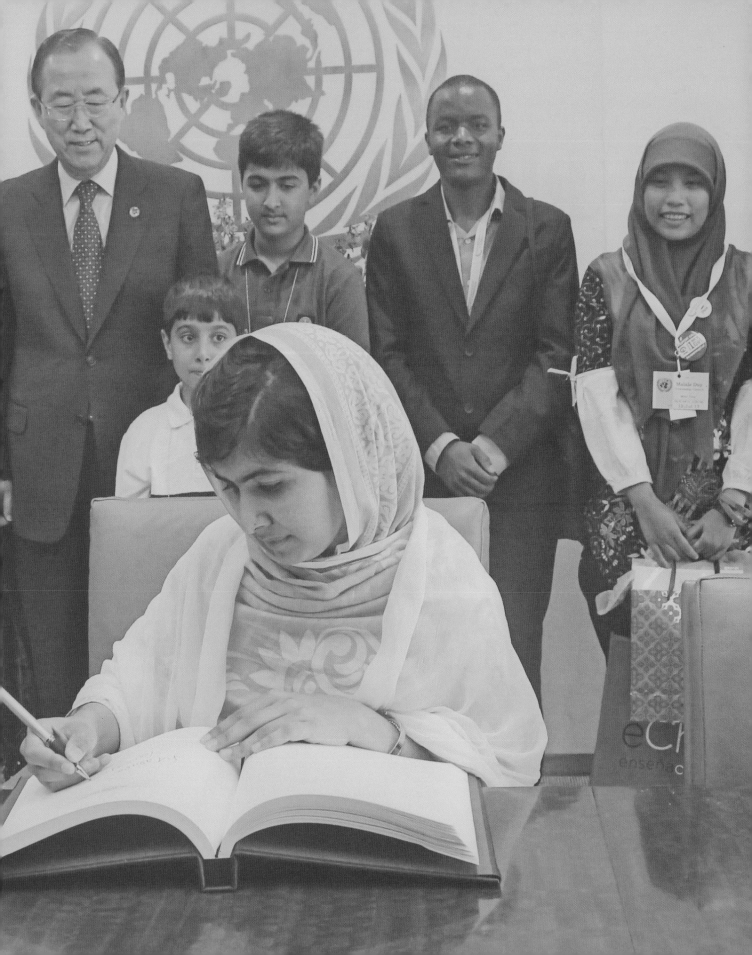

POVERTY AND
exploitation

THE DEVELOPING WORLD

In the 1980s, many people in the West saw great opportunities and benefits in the idea of globalization. They believed that increased global connections between economies, governments, and people would provide opportunities for mutual gain. By purchasing items produced in developing countries, people in the developed world hoped they would boost the economy of poorer countries whilst gaining inexpensive goods for themselves.

In reality, many aspects of globalization exploited workers from developing countries, in particular women, as a source of cheap labour. Major companies began to move their production processes to Africa, Asia, and Latin America to lower their costs and maximize their profits. Some scholars have argued that globalization "feminized poverty", because it took advantage of stereotypes associated with female workers – such as docility and nimble fingers – when employing women in low-cost manufacturing roles. Women working in so-called "sweatshops" (factories that ignore health and safety laws)

25% of young women in **developing countries** never finished primary school education

are often denied benefits such as sick pay, and are forced to work in dangerous conditions. Such factories have also been linked to human trafficking, whereby people are tricked into working without consent, or are forced to work to pay off a debt.

Globalization today

While globalization may have helped to create jobs, in the long term it has failed to get to the root of the problem of poverty. In areas where sweatshops are the primary employers, women often begin working in them from a young age, missing out on education, and becoming trapped in the cycle of poverty. Currently, 767 million people live on less than £1.45 ($1.90) a day.

Furthermore, debt crises in many developing countries in the 1980s, brought about by heavy borrowing in the 1970s, led financial institutions in the West to renegotiate such debts. They insisted on cuts in public spending and a reduction in social programmes, transferring costs to families. As the managers of family budgets, women often bore the brunt of these cuts, which also had negative consequences for women's healthcare. A report from the United Nations Children's Fund (UNICEF) on maternal and newborn health reveals that 500,000 women from developing countries die each year as a result of pregnancy. They often die due to infections, obstructed labour, or the lack of access to a caesarean section. Without stronger local economies, these problems will remain largely unsolved.

◀ **Struggle for medical care**
A mother sits on the floor of an overcrowded hospital in Amuria in the Teso subregion of Uganda. Babies born in developing countries are almost 14 times more likely to die during the first month of life.

▲ Mass production
Textile factory workers in China are often less educated, rural migrants, which translates into them earning lower wages. Women represent 80 per cent of the global workforce in garment manufacturing.

▶ Burden of thirst
Crippling national debt in many developing countries has led to lack of investment in the provision of basic services. Many women still spend hours each day collecting clean water for the household.

"**WOMEN** [ARE] AT A **SEVERE** ECONOMIC DISADVANTAGE COMPARED TO **MEN**."

UN WOMEN AND WORLD BANK DATA REPORT, 2017

THE MODERN FACE OF
feminism

673
Women's Marches were held in the US in 2017, with 4 million people in attendance

THE THIRD WAVE AND BEYOND

In the 1990s, feminists seeking to address the perceived limitations of the second wave (see pp. 272–275) began to refer to their work as the third wave. Activists and theorists of this new wave wanted to make feminism more inclusive and focused less on questions of societal oppression and more on individual agency and empowerment. In reality, however, the third wave and its predecessor were not so distinct, and had plenty of overlap, as many of the same people and issues continued to be a part of feminist discussions.

During the 1990s, popular culture became a means of transformation and activism, with the rise of a feminist punk music scene, zine (self-published, small-circulation magazine) culture, and major feminist interventions in the art world. One example of this new brand of activism was the Riot Grrrl movement, which began on the West Coast of the US in 1991 in response to the male-dominated punk music scene. One of the first bands associated with Riot Grrrl was Bikini Kill, headed by Kathleen Hanna. Riot Grrrl groups started up across the world, with many group publishing their own zines and manifestos to spread the message of a "girl-power" revolution.

Intersectional feminism

During the second wave, black feminists had begun to critique the white-centric focus of the feminist movement. In 1989, feminist legal scholar Kimberlé Crenshaw coined the term "intersectionality", which became central to

◀ **Punk rock feminism**
The 1990s band Bikini Kill and its frontwoman Kathleen Hanna led the Riot Grrrl punk movement with lyrics that addressed issues of sexual abuse, racism, patriarchy, and female empowerment.

SOCIAL JUSTICE

Since the 1990s, feminists have organized in new ways thanks to the growth of the internet, while social media has contributed to the spread of popular feminism.

1900

1989 Kimberlé Crenshaw coins the term "intersectionality."

1990 Naomi Wolf publishes *The Beauty Myth*, highlighting oppressive beauty standards.

1990 Judith Butler publishes *Gender Trouble*, which challenges the idea of binary gender.

1991 Anita Hill testifies against US Supreme Court nominee Clarence Thomas for sexual harassment; the first Riot Grrrl manifesto is published; Camp Trans is held at the Michigan Womyn's Music Festival to protest the expulsion of a transwoman from the event.

1992 Rebecca Walker publishes the piece "Becoming the third wave" in *Ms.* magazine.

1996 *The Vagina Monologues*, a play by Eve Ensler, is first performed in New York City.

2000

2002 Ni Putes Ni Soumises ("Neither Whores Nor Doormats") is formed in France to combat violence against women.

2011 The first "Slutwalk" is held in Toronto after a police officer links a women's appearance to her sexual assault; the feminist punk group Pussy Riot is formed in Moscow.

2012 The Everyday Sexism project is started online by UK feminist Laura Bates to document experiences of sexism across the world.

2014 The "He for She" campaign is launched by the UN to involve men in the feminist cause.

2015 The documentary film *The Hunting Ground* details activism against sexual assault on campuses across the US.

2017 Women's marches are held in response to the inauguration of US President Donald Trump; several actresses accuse Harvey Weinstein of sexual assault; the #MeToo movement begins.

◄ **BRAZILIAN FEMINISTS** PROTEST THE IMPEACHMENT OF FEMALE PRESIDENT DILMA ROUSSEFF IN 2016.

»

discussions of how and why feminists should address the needs of nonwhite women. She focused on a specific legal case, *Degraffenreid versus General Motors*, in 1976, in which black women attempted to sue the company for discrimination after they were fired. The case was unsuccessful because the issue could not be classified as race discrimination – some black men had retained their jobs – nor could it be seen as sex discrimination, because some white women had been hired. Crenshaw used the case to show how some people occupied the "intersections" of discrimination. Today, feminists use the term to describe the specific forms of discrimination that some people face due to combinations of identity factors such as race, sexuality, gender, and class.

Online feminism

The 1990s saw the rapid worldwide expansion of the internet and feminists began to explore the possibilities of this new virtual space. Groups identifying as "cyberfeminist" emerged, proclaiming the internet to be a new arena for feminist activism. While the internet has not quite delivered on the utopian ideals that

▼ **Cry of dissent**
Russian feminist band Pussy Riot protest for women's and LGBT rights opposite the Kremlin in Moscow in January 2012. The band's arrest for staging a performance in Moscow's Cathedral of Christ later that year sparked protests.

► **Pussy power**
Participants at the 2017 Women's Marches wore hand-knitted "pussy hats" in reference to sexist remarks made by President Trump in a video leaked before the 2016 election.

> "WE **COME** HERE TO STAND **SHOULDER TO SHOULDER** TO MAKE CLEAR: **WE ARE HERE**!"
>
> **SENATOR ELIZABETH WARREN**, SPEAKING AT THE WOMEN'S MARCH, 2017

cyberfeminists once imagined, the increased connection has had a big impact on feminist organizing and enabled marginalized people, especially LGBT (lesbian, gay, bisexual and transgender) people, to come together online.

However, the internet has also provided a platform for antifeminist agendas. In 2013, the hashtag #NotAllMen trended on social media to argue that "not all men" are responsible for sexism and the oppression of women. It is symptomatic of a movement known as "Men's Rights Activism" or "meninism"; members of such movements have been implicated in the organized trolling and harassment of women online.

Today, at a time in which popular feminism is at the forefront of public consciousness, the importance of social media in activism has led some to state that feminism is now in a fourth wave. In October 2017, after Hollywood producer Harvey Weinstein was accused of multiple sexual assaults – charges that he denied – women were encouraged by actress Alyssa Milano to share stories of their own experiences on Twitter, accompanied by the hashtag #MeToo, a phrase originally used by activist Tarana Burke in 2006. The staggering response from women, across social media platforms and around the world, showed the wide reach of rape culture, in which sexual assault is normalized and excused. Following the inauguration of Donald Trump as US president in 2017, millions of women also participated in marches around the world. LGBT, black, disabled, working class, and otherwise, women mobilized on a global scale to demand that their voices be heard.

► **Protest in Peru**
Women demonstrate outside the office of the public prosecutor in Lima, Peru, in 2016. They hoped to gain recognition and compensation for those who were forcibly sterilized during the 1990s.

▶ **Bohemian icon**
The Seated Clowness
by French painter Henri
de Toulouse-Lautrec
depicts dancing clown
Cha-u-kao, who
performed at the
Moulin Rouge in the
1890s. She dressed in
men's clothes and was
openly lesbian.

WOMEN WHO ARE ATTRACTED to women;
who were assigned male at birth; or who
otherwise fall under the modern term "LGBT"
(lesbian, gay, bisexual, and transgender) have
always existed, yet their lives and experiences
have rarely found their way into history
books. It is only in the 20th century that LGBT
women's histories have begun to be told, but
in many cases, they rely on hearsay due to the
lack of concrete evidence.

Hidden histories

Accounts of female homosexuality date back
to the ancient world, in societies on every
continent. Greek poet Sappho (see pp. 24–27)
wrote about her desire for another woman,
and in the 11th century, the rabbi Maimonides
ordered men to keep their wives away from
women who wished to sleep with them.
Many cultures did not outlaw homosexual
sex until the medieval period (in Europe) or
later, and even then, in most societies male
homosexuals bore the brunt of punishments.

In Europe and the US in the 18th and 19th
centuries, it was not unusual for women to
form close friendships in which they lived

THROUGH THE AGES

LGBT women

Stories of LGBT women in history are relatively few and far between. Many cultures have
punished or ignored women who pushed against sexual and gender norms, meaning that
before the 20th century, such women's lives frequently remained hidden under the radar.

> " If you **forget me**, think of **our
> gifts to Aphrodite** and all the
> **loveliness** that **we shared** …
> violet tiaras, braided **rosebuds** … "
>
> SAPPHO, LYRIC POET, "I HAVE NOT HAD ONE
> WORD FROM HER," 6TH CENTURY BCE

together, travelled together, and wrote letters
expressing their love for each other. Such
"romantic friendships" were fashionable, but
in some cases, girls were separated by their
parents when their relationships became seen
to be too intimate. In 18th-century Ireland,
Lady Eleanor Butler and Sarah Ponsonby ran
away to Wales together after their parents
tried to keep them apart, becoming known as
the Ladies of Llangollen. Their diaries attest
to the fact that they shared a bed and dressed

as men. In the US at the turn of the 20th century, such living arrangements (between two women, whether romantically involved or not) became known as a "Boston Marriage" due to Henry James's novel *The Bostonians* (1886), which tells the story of two unmarried, wealthy women living together in the city and having an intimate friendship.

The 20th century brought LGBT women out into the open. The 1920s in particular saw many "new women" (see pp. 222–225) have high-profile affairs with men and women alike, and the end of the century saw increasing numbers of female celebrities coming out of the closet. A major factor in these women choosing to live openly was the ongoing struggle for LGBT rights, which has been the focus of the gay liberation movement of the 1960s and subsequent gay rights movement from 1972. While these LGBT movements have been criticized for marginalizing women's voices, they have nonetheless won major rights and protections for all LGBT people, including (in many nations) the right to same-sex marriage.

LESBIAN LOVERS IN GERMAN FILM MÄDCHEN IN UNIFORM, 1931

▼ **Raising the flag**
Women carry rainbow flags (designed by Gilbert Baker in 1978) at the 2015 Pride Parade in Montreal, Canada. Formerly a protest, Pride is now also a celebration of LGBT people.

PROFILES
RAINBOW GIRLS

Christina of Sweden (1626–1689) ruled from 1644–1654. Known for wearing men's clothes and disdaining feminine activities, the queen had a number of male suitors (and female favourites) but refused to marry or produce an heir. When she converted to Catholicism, her councillors took the opportunity to convince her to abdicate her throne. Some historians have since speculated that Christina, confused for a boy at birth, may have been intersex.

Radclyffe Hall (1880–1943) was a British writer known for writing *The Well of Loneliness* (1928), which was banned in Britain until 1949 for its lesbian content. Hall, whose friends called her John, dressed as a man and lived with her partner, Lady Una Troubridge, from the time she was 26 until her death. She identified as a "congenital invert," inspired by the work of contemporary sexologists.

Lili Elbe (1882–1931) was one of the first transgender women to undergo sexual reassignment surgery. Elbe first dressed as a woman, "Lili," in 1904 for a portrait for her wife, but soon took up the mantle permanently. She moved from Denmark to Paris to Dresden, where she had pioneering surgeries that allowed her to change her legal sex. After her marriage was voided by the Danish king, Elbe accepted a proposal from a man, but died from an attempted uterus transplant before they could marry.

Marsha P. Johnson (1945–1992) was an African American gay rights activist and leader of the 1969 Stonewall Uprising in Greenwich Village, New York. Later, she and Sylvia Rivera formed the Street Transvestite Action Revolutionaries, a charity for homeless transgender youth. Although Johnson used the term "transvestite," historians today consider her a transgender woman. She was murdered in 1992.

Ellen DeGeneres (b. 1958) is a comedian, talk show host, and actress, known for being the first openly lesbian woman on prime time television. She came out in 1997 along with her titular character on the sitcom *Ellen*, inspiring generations of women. DeGeneres married actress Portia de Rossi in 2008.

▼ **Not One Less**
Women protest as part of the Ni Una Menos ("Not One Less," inspired by the same quote as #NiUnaMas) movement in Buenos Aires, Argentina, June 2017. Each woman carries a sign with the name and age of a victim of femicide to show the scale of the problem.

VICTIMS OF
violence

FIGHTING FEMICIDE

Male-perpetrated violence against women is a global and age-old crime. In ancient Rome a man could beat, divorce, or murder his wife if she threatened his honour or property rights, while English common law in the 18th century allowed a husband to beat his wife to maintain "family discipline", as long as he used a stick no thicker than his thumb. In the 19th century early feminists sought marriage law reform, but it was not until 1871 that Alabama became the first US state to rescind the legal right of men to beat their families.

Seeking refuge

During the 1960s, and second-wave feminism (see pp. 272–275), women began to view their problems as the result of gender-based discrimination. These realizations spurred on the founding of women's shelters, abuse hotlines, and rape crisis centres. In 1971, Erin Pizzey opened the first women's refuge in the UK, and Anne Summers set up the first feminist women's refuge in Australia in 1974.

A major development in taking violence against women seriously was the popularization of the term "femicide" in the 1970s. Although first coined in 1801, femicide has been going on for centuries – from the burning of witches (see pp. 122–123) to female infanticide and "honour" killings. Femicide links the killing of girls or women to the violence they experience within patriarchal societies.

Typically, the most marginalized women are most vulnerable to violence. In the US and Brazil, for example, low-income transgender nonwhite women are at a higher risk of femicide. Black and Latina women in the US and indigenous women in North America are disproportionately subjected to physical and sexual violence. For decades, activists in Canada have been protesting against the disappearance and murder of indigenous women, including along a stretch of British Columbia highway nicknamed the "Highway of Tears". In 2010, Jaime Black, a Métis Canadian artist, created the REDress Project, an ongoing public art installation that hangs up red dresses in cities across Canada to mark the absence of missing and murdered women.

According to the United Nations, 14 of the 25 countries with the highest rates of femicide are in Latin America and the Caribbean. Feminists are now fighting back. The #NiUnaMas ("Not One More") movement that began in Mexico has spread to Argentina, Uruguay, Ecuador, Peru, Bolivia, Colombia, Chile, Venezuela, and Paraguay. More than a dozen Latin American countries have now passed laws against femicide, but there is still a long way to go to end violence against women worldwide.

"WE **WANTED** TO **DO SOMETHING** ABOUT **DOMESTIC VIOLENCE**."

ANNE SUMMERS ON THE CREATION OF HER FIRST WOMEN'S REFUGE, 2014

"Anger has a long history of bringing about **positive change**."

CHIMAMANDA NGOZI ADICHIE, FROM THE TEDx TALK
"WE SHOULD ALL BE FEMINISTS," 2012

MODERN FEMINISM

Nigerian novelist Chimamanda Ngozi Adichie became a feminist icon after her 2012 TEDx Talk went viral, was sampled by pop superstar Beyoncé in 2013, and was adapted into a book-length essay in 2014. "We Should All Be Feminists" both explains the need for feminism and attempts to define what feminism means in the 21st century. The essay also criticizes how society defines masculinity in a narrow way and teaches boys to be "hard men". Adichie writes that women should embrace the anger they experience at the state of gender relations, and channel it into protest. The female activists pictured (left) are members of the group Women In Black, who channelled their anger when they protested against gender-based violence in Madrid in 2015 by lying down in the streets and playing dead. Men also joined in the protest, which aimed to educate men to stop male chauvinism.

▶ **Women of state**
Prime Minister Sirimavo Bandaranaike of Sri Lanka (left) meets with Indian Prime Minister Indira Gandhi, (right) in 1976. Gandhi's close relationship with Bandaranaike moved the latter's politics to the left.

Australia but could not yet stand for election. Since then, over 70 countries – including the UK, France, Canada, New Zealand, Thailand, the Philippines, Brazil, Poland, Mozambique, Argentina, Australia, and Ukraine – have had female heads of government or state. Several women have served as political leaders on the Indian subcontinent too. In 1960, Sirimavo Bandaranaike became the world's first elected

> " In times of **crisis**, **women** eventually are **called upon** to sort out the **mess**. "
>
> **CHRISTINE LAGARDE**, 2014

THROUGH THE AGES

Politics

Historically, relatively few females have held powerful positions in politics, but since the 1960s the numbers have steadily increased. Although women are yet to approach parity with men as influential global figures, they have made notable progress in the last 50 years.

HILLARY CLINTON RAN FOR THE US PRESIDENCY IN 2016

HILLARY CLINTON
2016

ALTHOUGH WOMEN WON the right to vote in most democratic nations by the mid-20th century, today they still lack equal representation in political office. The average proportion of female members in national-level parliaments (that admit women) is 23.3 per cent. Rwanda is a key exception; in 2008, it became the first nation with a female parliamentary majority.

The 1907 elections in Finland were the first in which women could run for national office. By then, women had the vote in New Zealand and

female head of government as Prime Minister of Sri Lanka; six years later Indira Gandhi was elected Prime Minister of India, the world's largest democracy. Gandhi served until 1977 and was reelected in 1980. She was assassinated in 1984. No woman has spent longer as head of government. Bangladesh has had a female prime minister for nearly three decades, with Khaleda Zia holding power for two five-year terms, and Sheikh Hasina Wazed leading the nation from 1996–2001, and 2009 to the present day.

The Nordic states have led the way for gender equality in politics. Although Sweden is yet to elect a female head of government, Swedish women have some of the highest levels of representation in parliament and cabinet position. From 2009 to 2013 Iceland's prime minister was Jóhanna Sigurðardóttir – the world's first openly LGBT head of state.

To date, the most senior position in the US government held by a woman is Secretary of State, held by Madeleine Albright (see pp. 288–291) from 1997–2001, Condoleezza Rice from 2005–2009, and Hillary Clinton from 2009–2013. In addition, Sandra Day O'Connor was appointed to the Supreme Court in 1981; since then, there have been three female justices in the highest US court.

Money and industry

The growing power of women is not limited to politics; women now hold positions as CEOs, entrepreneurs, and business leaders. Women – such as Mary Barra of General Motors, IBM's Ginni Rometty, and YouTube's Susan Wojcicki – have led some of the world's major international corporations. However, women are still underrepresented in the highest echelons of industry, particularly in the energy, financial, and technology sectors. For example, a 2017 study found that among the 500 largest US corporations, just 6.4 per cent of them had female CEOs. Disparity also remains on the Forbes "Rich List" – most of the names are male – but some of the richest people alive are women, including self-made billionaire and media mogul Oprah Winfrey.

▼ **Setting an example**
Licia Ronzulli, an Italian Member of the European Parliament between 2009 and 2014, took her daughter, Vittoria, to plenary sessions for two years. Vittoria is shown here "voting" alongside her mother at a session in Strasbourg, France, on November 19, 2013.

PROFILES
POWER PLAYERS

Golda Meir (1898-1978) was born in Kiev, but migrated to the US with her family in 1906. She became involved in the Socialist Zionist movement and, in 1921, moved to Palestine, where, in 1948, she was a signatory of Israel's declaration of independence. She was elected to the Israeli parliament in 1949, serving as Minister of Labour, then Foreign Minister. Following the death of the Prime Minister in 1969, Meir took the office, leading her country through the Yom Kippur War before resigning in 1974.

Ruth Bader Ginsberg (b. 1933) was initially a law professor, and was cofounder of the Women's Rights Project at the American Civil Liberties Union, which took six landmark gender discrimination cases to the Supreme Court. In 1993, she was nominated to the Court herself, and has served as a Supreme Court Justice for more than 25 years, writing many liberal decisions and dissents.

Angela Merkel (b. 1954) started her career as a research scientist in East Germany, gaining a doctorate in quantum chemistry in 1986. After the fall of the Berlin Wall in 1989, she became involved in politics, and was elected to parliament during the first elections after German reunification. She became leader of her party in 2000, and in 2005 became the first female chancellor in German history.

Indra Nooyi (b. 1955) grew up in Chennai in southern India and moved to the US in 1978 to attend business school at Yale. In 1994, she joined PepsiCo, a multinational food and beverage corporation. Nooyi rose to become PepsiCo's Chief Financial Officer in 2001, CEO in 2006, and in 2007 took up the position of the company's chair. Nooyi oversaw huge increases in PepsiCo's profits before her resignation in 2018.

Sheryl Sandberg (b. 1969) began her career working for the US Secretary of the Treasury in 1996 but left to work in Silicon Valley in 2001. Her first job there was at the technological giant Google, where she stayed until 2008 before becoming the Chief Operating Officer of Facebook. In 2013, Sandberg published her book *Lean In: Women, Work, and the Will to Lead,* which discusses how women can take a more active role in the business world.